OTHER FLOORS,
OTHER VOICES

A Textography of a Small University Building

Rhetoric, Knowledge, and Society

A Series of Monographs Edited by
Charles Bazerman

OTHER FLOORS, OTHER VOICES

A Textography of a Small University Building

JOHN M. SWALES
The University of Michigan

IEA LAWRENCE ERLBAUM ASSOCIATES, PUBLISHERS
1998   Mahwah, New Jersey   London

Lawrence Erlbaum Associates, Inc., Publishers
10 Industrial Avenue
Mahwah, New Jersey 07430

Cover design by Kathryn Houghtaling Lacy

Library of Congress Cataloging-in-Publication Data

Swales, John.
   Other floors, other voices : a textography of a small university
building / John M. Swales.
      p.   cm.
   Includes bibliographical references and indexes.
   ISBN 0-8058-2087-6 (alk. paper). — ISBN 0-8058-2088-4 (pbk. : alk.
paper).
   1. English language—Discourse analysis. 2. English language—
Study and teaching—Foreign speakers. 3. Universities and
colleges—Buildings. 4. English language—Technical English.
5. English language—Written English. 6. College teachers—
Language. 7. College students—Language. 8. Academic writing.
I. Title.
PE1422.S93 1998
420'.1'41—dc21   98-12631
                                                                CIP

Books published by Lawrence Erlbaum Associates are printed on acid-free paper,
and their bindings are chosen for strength and durability.

Printed in the United States of America
10 9 8 7 6 5 4 3 2 1

Contents

Contributors

Principal Research Assistant	Margaret Luebs (Linguistics)
Other Research Assistants	Yu-Ying Chang (Linguistics) Theresa Rohlck (English Language Institute)

Principal Informants

Computing Resource Site	Michael Alexander Timothy Donnelly Darcy Niven Tung B. Ngo Elizabeth Salley Deborah Zarem
English Language Institute	Carolyn Madden H. Joan Morley Mary Spaan Tony Dudley-Evans (Interlinear Commentator)
The Herbarium	William R. Anderson Linda Bowden Robert D. Fogel Richard K. Rabeler Anton A. Reznicek Edward G. Voss

Photography	Saburu Matsomoto
	Joseph A. Welch
Library Assistance	Christiane Anderson (Herbarium)
	Patricia Aldridge (ELI)
	Nancy Bartlett
	(The Bentley Library)
Indexer	Margaret Luebs
Readers	Charles Bazerman
	A. L. Becker
	Vi Benner
	Anna Mauranen
	Charles Tamason

Editor's Introduction

Charles Bazerman, Series Editor
University of California, Santa Barbara

John Swales identifies *Other Floors, Other Voices* as an example of a new genre: textography. Through analysis of text, of textual forms, and of systems of texts, we are shown the lives, life commitments, and life projects of people deeply embedded in the literate culture of the university. The people Swales examines all work today in a single building (a building materially evoked through description, history, and photographs), but their textual lives are maintained in different times and spaces, measured by the dimensions of text production and text circulation in their fields of work. These domains of text time and space are to some degree differentiated by the three specialties that mark the three floors of the North University Building (NUBS), the ethnographic site of this journey into textual lives: computing, taxonomic botany, and English as a Second Language. But within the general space of each floor and discipline, each individual establishes a distinctive kind of work, reaching out to different communities, mediated by different patterns of publication— so that each individual also lives in a distinctive time and space of a distinctive textual universe. Those individual and disciplinary networks are brought home in what happens each day on each floor and at each desk in NUBS, organizing that local space and time in highly articulated ways, so as textographer Swales walks through the building looking for pieces of paper he finds many cultures and ways of life. The material here and now and the evanescent distant intertexts merge to bring complex worlds together under one roof.

In pursuing the elusive concept of discourse community, Swales uncovers something far more concrete, novel, and revealing: the discursive lives of individuals made within complexes of organized communications and social relations, mediated through writing. Imagine a movie of a life lived in a small town, where the main character's life is built in relation to family, school, church, local merchants and professionals, and a workplace. These relations, in turn, get played out in forums of family dinner, shop counter, and town meeting, through discursive forms like intimate whispers and school valedictory addresses. So a life is made. Swales finds in the North University Building lives are made through providing help online to students whose disks have crashed; through collecting and circulating botanical samples, writing taxonomies, and writing for amateur conservationist newsletters; and through preparing and administering international exams, publishing textbooks, and writing research articles on language acquisition. Through their work we come to know each of the selected inhabitants of NUBS and we come to feel the daily texture of their lives, so we move from ethnography to multiple biographies. We come to see people producing themselves, making unique lives, in literate worlds.

John Swales, as many of us have come to know him, is a distinctive member of both the applied linguistics and composition communities—an original, but an original stamped by the global village of language education he has lived his life in, revealed in his own textographic account embedded within this book. The innovations in his earlier books—from *Writing Scientific English* in 1971 through *Genre Analysis* in 1990 and *Academic Writing for Graduate Students* (with Christine Feak) in 1994—have led the way for the field of English for Specific Purposes. In *Other Floors, Other Voices* he turns from applied concerns to an appreciation of the richness and variety of academic discourse for its own sake. Here he explores how the people are embedded in making their textual lives, within the discursive landscapes their communities afford. In so doing he shows not only his own love of language as a way of life, but his appreciation of how all his subjects find their labors of love in the language they create. He provides a fresh way of viewing universities and disciplines, revealing the complex intersections among research, institutional, community, and public discourses that each individual negotiates. And he provides an empirically grounded, fine-grained analysis of those communicative networks people identify as discourse communities. In all these ways John Swales again points to new directions all of us concerned with the written language would be wise to explore.

Scenarios

OVERVIEW: THE STUDY

For the most part, this book offers an account of selected text-makers and their texts in a small university building. Seven individuals have been singled out for detailed study in an attempt to increase our understanding of what it means to say that academic writing is "situated." On the one hand, I examine how that writing is located within and along the evolution of a particular career; on the other, I try to place these various bodies of text both within a particular set of disciplinary norms and expectations, and within the local, institutional context of their production. For this last, I have also studied certain kinds of "routine writing business" that take place on each floor of the building, and have in turn situated those everyday activities within their historical and spatial settings. This, then, is a site study of particularity and communality as seen through the lens of written discourse.

The label given to the volume is *textography*, by which I mean something more than a disembodied textual or discoursal analysis, but something less than a full ethnographic account. Although anthropologist John Van Maanen can observe "that a text is axiomatically an ethnography if it is put forth by its author as a nonfiction work intended to represent, interpret, or (perhaps best) translate a culture or selected aspects of a culture" (1995, pp. 13–14), *ethnography* is not a label I am comfortable with. For one thing, I am a discourse analyst and an applied linguist, not a cultural anthropologist or a sociologist with an orientation toward fieldwork. For another, the term itself has become a conflicted and controversial one.

Here is Van Maanan again: "Ethnography is no longer pictured as a relatively simple look, listen and learn procedure but, rather, as something akin to an intense epistemological trial by fire" (1995, p. 2). Thirdly, *Other Floors, Other Voices* is a deliberately circumscribed investigation, as it focuses more on particular individuals within the building than on its entire collectivities, and builds its arguments through a close analysis of individual *textual* extracts. "Textography" would thus seem a suitable term for the enterprise.

There are, of course, many ways of approaching academic, scholarly, or professional writing, some of which are reviewed in greater detail in the closing chapter. There have been studies of a particular *discipline*, such as Economics; investigations into a particular type of text or *genre*, such as the research article; inquiries into the ways *experts* read and write texts in their chosen specialties; other studies of how graduate student *apprentices* become acculturated and socialized into their disciplinary communities; explorations of the writing of famous *individuals*, such as Charles Darwin; approaches that are variously historical, rhetorical, sociological, literary, or linguistic; and the list goes on. A site-based textographic study is a simple addition to this long list, not a substitution for some part of it. In effect, textography's distinctive type of context offers some additional, alternative perspective. For example, I hope to be able to show that a textographic account can indeed provide new insight into the relationships between particularity and communality, between "service" and "scholarly" activities, and between prior and present texts. The nature of the enterprise has also produced a number of "discoveries" about genres that suggest some redrawing of the traditional and conventional rhetorical maps we have for the academy. Further, the quiddities of textual life on each of the site's three floors point to wildly different temporal horizons of expectation, ranging from "just in time" trouble-shooting texts in one location to a 17-volume project in another that began almost five decades ago and will likely continue for a further three. Finally, the study has elicited some empirical, if complex, evidence for the validation (or otherwise) of the powerful but troubled concept of *discourse community* (discussed further in the fourth section of this opening chapter).

OVERVIEW: THE SITE

The building itself is undistinguished and sits surrounded on three sides by a parking lot, which in turn is flanked by the busy business loop of I-94 as it makes its way through the small city of Ann Arbor in the American Midwest. As many readers may already have guessed, the building belongs to the University of Michigan, a large and well-known educational institution and one where I happen to work as a teacher of linguistics and of English as a second language.

The name commonly given to the edifice is as plain as its appearance: *The North University Building*. Indeed, if there is anything distinctive about NUBS (as it is usually abbreviated), it must apparently be sought in the unusual mixture of its occupants. There is, to all intents and purposes, one small unit (with not more than 20 regular members) on each of the three floors of the main block—the principal focus for this study. On the first floor is the Computing Resource Site (CRS), one of several computing and computing-assistance sites run by the university's centralized Information Technology Division. The second floor houses the University Herbarium, an independent unit of Literature, Science, and Arts (LS&A), the university's liberal arts college, which looks after and fosters the university's extensive collections of dried vascular plants, fungi, mosses, lichens, and algae, and carries out research in Systematic Botany. Its curators also identify specimens, usually for professionals, but also for the general public, as in: "Is this a native plant, and what is its name?" or "Can I eat this mushroom?" or even "Is my neighbor growing marijuana?" Above the Herbarium is the English Language Institute (ELI), which is also an independent unit in LS&A. The institute is the university unit responsible for helping those international students (and staff) on the Ann Arbor campus who need or want assistance with their English. In addition, it runs a world-wide English language testing operation (colloquially known as "The Michigan Tests") and conducts research into academic discourse and other areas of applied linguistics relevant to its mission. I have an office in the ELI.

None of the building's three units is a typical academic unit, such as a Department or Program. None, for example, offers a degree of any kind—and, as we have seen, all three are involved with services. Further, the three floors all seem to represent "settled" communities, at least in the sense that each brings professional expertise to the circumscribed tasks it undertakes, and does so within a local consensus of what those tasks should be and how they should be implemented in an efficient and timely manner.

But, as we might expect, despite their proximity and their common service roles, the three units in this study are markedly different. Obviously, they offer very different kinds of expertise, but they differ in important other ways too. Today computer technology is the world's major growth industry. In comparison to this giant, English as a second language (ESL) is small, but it still has a sizeable international commercial role developed in recent decades to meet increasing worldwide demand by non-native speakers of English for help with improving their English proficiency. In part response to this upsurge in demand, ESL has relatively strong research and development traditions, certainly in comparison to the teaching of other foreign languages. The U.S. national association, the Teachers of English to Speakers of Other Languages (or TESOL) has currently close to 25,000 subscribing members. Even when compared to ESL, Systematic Botany is small-scale (with only about 1,200 members in its U.S. national association) and, especially in the New World below the U.S–Mexican border, engaged in a desperate struggle to inventory species before they disappear.

On the other side of the ledger, Botany is one of the most ancient of sciences and has very long time-lines, as attested by the fact that the curators in the Herbarium can often be found consulting texts published several decades previously. In contrast, the viability and currency of texts in ESL rarely extend beyond 10 years, and in Computer Technology active shelf-life may be 10 months (if that). A final twist to these disparities derives from the particular demographics of the North University Building during the period of the study (1994–1996). The nonclerical staff in the Herbarium were mostly men in their 50s, 60s, and 70s; in the ELI mostly women in their 40s; and in the CRS mostly men in their 20s or early 30s. Given all these differences, the scene seems set for an engaging comparative study.

That study begins with a brief look at the history and geography of the building, followed—later in this chapter—by informal accounts of why I believe the site can make a distinctive contribution to contemporary rhetorical theory, and how I went about the task of investigating the building's discoursal practices. Chapter 2 then focuses on certain types of routine business that take place on each floor. In some contrast, the following two chapters delve into the scholarly heart of the building, first by examining the textual biographies of four curators (three of whom are also professors) in the Herbarium, and then of a lecturer and two professors in the ELI. In the final chapter, I return to review the more general theoretical and methodological issues briefly mentioned at the outset, and I briefly discuss pedagogical and other implications.

THEN AND NOW:
A SHORT HISTORY OF THE BUILDING

The attempts by my research assistant, Margaret Luebs, to trace the history of the building had its own surprises in store for us. What we did not know at the outset was that the many and diverse publications about the University of Michigan had very little to say about the building, in marked contrast to the descriptions and analyses of many of the grander edifices on campus. Historical information about the building was largely hidden away in manuscripts and administrative files contained in the archives of the university's Bentley Historical Library. One likely reason for this "benign neglect" was that NUBS was originally designed and built for—and by—the lowly Building and Grounds Department in 1922, which occupied it until the present units began moving into the now-vacated space during the late 1950s.

Moreover, the university's Campus News and Information Services unit has many thousands of university photographs and slides in its archives, all from after 1974 (earlier ones are in the Bentley). However, a search did not reveal any of the North University Building, and Robert Kalmbach, in a 40-year career as the unit's main photographer, did not recollect ever having taken one. The North University Building was never a jewel in any architect's crown, nor the kind of building that the university would ever be likely to use in its publicity and informational materials.

We did quickly discover *why* it was called the North University Build-ing—because it was originally on North University Street. Today, how-ever, *North University* has been diverted to make way for a footbridge over Business I-94, and goes not within 100 yards of the building. Even more curiously, the building still retains its original but now phantom street address of *1205 North University*, because Federal Express requires a street location for delivery. Even so, this address is known only to a few old hands and long-serving secretaries. And if you are beginning to think this is turning into a gothic tale, there is more. Confusion exists about the very name of the building itself. If one cares to look at the addresses of the three units in the university phone book, one will note that the ELI describes its location as "NUB" (North University Building), the Herbarium as "NU" (North University), and the Computing Resource Site as "NUBS" (North University Building Station), although the original reading of "NUBS" from its Buildings and Grounds days was "North University Building Services," and one in fact that can still be heard. With regard to the CRS name, here is an extract from an undated memo (but undoubtedly from the 1970s) by the first director of the university's Computing Center, R.C.F. Bartels, a professor of Mathematics:

> At first, the Computing Center was housed in the North University Building, a location now known as NUBS, *the North University Building Station*. After the Computing Center moved to its present location on North Campus in 1971, NUBS was the first of several branch stations to be established. The others are at the Flint and Dearborn campuses, the School of Business Ad-ministration, and a small station at the Undergraduate Library. [emphasis added]

In general, all this terminological confusion suggests that we are indeed looking at, from this minor perspective, "other floors, other voices." More specifically, it points to a certain arrogance on the Computing Center's part—as the big brother—to attempt to redesignate the whole building in terms of its *own* functions. And, as we have seen, this has been a move tacitly resisted by the Herbarium and the ELI as reflected by their alternative readings of their university addresses.

One of the few published accounts of the building complex with which we are concerned is the following brief note in *A Guide to the Campus of the University of Michigan*:

> In 1914 the Department of Building and Grounds served as architect and contractor for the construction of a storehouse and shop building to provide offices for the superintendent, maintenance and construction materials, and space for janitor and hospital supplies. Railroad tracks fed into the building and it is said that at one time part of the building was used as a stable for the horses that pulled snowplows. (MacInnes & Stevens, 1978, p. 44)

This two-story 1914 structure is not, in fact, the part of NUBS that is the focus of this study, although part of its second floor does house the specimen cabinets of the Herbarium's collections. Even so, Margaret was able to confirm the rumor in the extract's last line by tracking down a photocopy of a grainy 1924 newspaper photograph (photo 1) of the workhorses. In the background, we can see the three-story building that *is* the site of this study and, as a 1994 shot shows (photo 2), it has remained virtually unchanged except for the addition of air-conditioning ductwork.

According to Donnelly, Shaw, and Gjelsness' *The University of Michigan—An Encyclopedic Survey* (1958), this building was constructed in 1922. This "addition," constructed yet again by the Buildings and Grounds Department at a cost of $120,000 and again for its own use, was designed

MICHIGAN YESTERDAY   April, 1924   Horsepower in front of Buildings and Grounds

Photo 1. The building in 1924.

Photo 2. The building in 1994.

as a Storehouse and as a location for the university's "Shops": carpentry, metal-working, plumbing, electrical, and so on. One consequence is that the building is very massively built, doubtless to carry the weight of heavy materials such as building supplies and heavy machinery. Given NUBS' utilitarian purpose and journeyman architecture, it is not altogether surprising that the building has failed to attract the attention of the university's historians and archivists. It is, however, a little surprising that the building is not mentioned by George Lutz in his 1935 manuscript entitled *Data on Campus Development and Reminiscences*, inasmuch as Mr. Lutz, who worked at the university from 1888 until the late 1930s, was for many years foreman of the painting shop and, in consequence, almost certainly had an office in NUBS. Margaret, in fact, was able to find only one rather dark and gloomy—and undated—photograph of the building in the Bentley library (photo 3); the rather sunnier one (photo 4) taken in 1994, and from a different angle, confirms that the front of the building has also changed very little in its exterior appearance throughout the 75 years or so of its existence.

Apart from occasional small items in *The B and G News* (1925–1927), we have only been able to trace one published account of activities in the building conducted by its original occupiers. Following is an extract from *The Alumnus* headed "Activities at the Storehouse":

> In the course of a year this organization handles packages from every corner of the known world, and materials of all characters. Snakes intended for the Museum may arrive one day—the Storehouse people still remember

Photo 3. Undated photo of the main building.

Photo 4. 1994 photo of the main entrance.

chasing one shipment; another day it may be botanical specimens from Sumatra. Between 135 and 150 different accounts with various departments have to be kept, not to speak of about 500 maintenance and construction accounts. For the six months ending January 1, 1930, the Storehouse purchased $333,000 worth of material and sold $350,000. In its heaviest year, when the building program was at its height, the record was $1,135,000 of purchases and $1,152,000 sales. This was in 1924.

To handle this large income and outgo the University in 1922 built a modern fire proof three-story building, which also houses the Buildings and Grounds Department, its offices and shops. There are 23 employees to look after the stores. (*Alumnus*, 2/22/30, p. 364)

The Buildings and Grounds Department (after 1946 the Plant Department) occupied the building until the mid-1950s, when the department's increasing size finally forced it to relocate to a new, much larger building complex, farther from the central campus area. Soon after the move, Plant Department employees returned to their former workplace to remodel the building for its new tenants. The new tenants were, as we know, the Computing Center, the Herbarium, and the ELI. Of these, only the Computing Center began at NUBS, having been created by Regental Decree in 1959. As Bruce W. Arden reported in 1963 in *The Michigan Technic*, "In 1959 the IBM 704 computer was installed in the North University Building as part of the IBM educational program, and the facility was established as a separate unit of the Graduate School" (p. 46). The other two units had been in existence elsewhere on campus for some time. Indeed, the university is believed to have begun assembling collections of plant specimens as far back as 1838, a year after its move from Detroit to its present Ann Arbor main campus. The English Language Institute was in comparison a relative newcomer, having been founded in 1941, but even then it was the first institute of its type in North America.

By the end of the 1950s, the Herbarium had outgrown its allotted space in the restricted areas of the Natural History Museum. The ELI also needed to expand and consolidate its operations as the first large wave of international students began to invade U.S. campuses (see chapter 2). Up until that time, its activities had been split between two locations: the Graduate School building and one of the humanities buildings. Particularly extensive renovation was required before the newly created Computer Center could move into the first floor of NUBS, including, according to old-timers, the removal of horse manure from the sub-basement (Mike Alexander, in a 1995 interview). Further, the breakneck speed of computer advance required continual remodeling work over the subsequent decade. Consider, for instance, this extract from a rather frenetic Plant Department Work Order dated September 12, 1966:

Work to be done

Install a [*sic*] temporary floor to ceiling (rough) plywood or composition walls in order to partition Room 1101 of North University Building as shown on the attached sketch. This will involve the installation of two doors.

. . . .

This work is intended to provide temporary quarters for the Computing Center. It will be torn down again in about four months.

Eventually, additional modifications became virtually impossible, and in 1971 many of the technical/research staff and the big computer moved out to a specially constructed building on the new Engineering campus, leaving behind a smaller mainframe computer and a few operators to run it. This was the beginning of the current NUBS Computing Resource Site.

Internally, the three floors today look rather different. As might be expected, the CRS is definitely modern with its recessed lighting, gleaming computers, and beige carpeting (photo 5), and with its blond shelving for completed large printing jobs (photo 6). In contrast, much of the Herbarium seems rather old-fashioned (aside from Bob's lab space and the office area that belongs to Linda, the Administrative Assistant). The workroom (photo 7), where the assistants mount, remount, or repair specimens, probably today most closely recalls the appearance of the building as it must have been in its Plant Department days. The main Herbarium

Photo 5. The main area of the CRS.

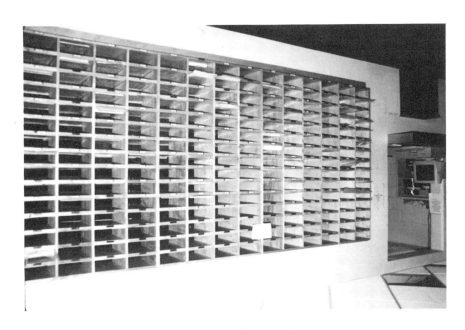

Photo 6. Shelving for print jobs.

Photo 7. Part of the Herbarium workroom.

corridor appears rather narrow and dimly lit. The office off that corridor shown in photo 8 is the one belonging to Ed, one of the curators discussed in chapter 3. As the reader can see, this is a tidy but super-jammed office of a long-serving scientist. Upstairs in the ELI, the atmosphere is lighter and perhaps more congenial, but parts of the floor also look rather higgledy-piggledy and slightly disorganized. Unique to the building, there is a display case containing "mug shots" of the staff (photo 9), and at least some of the offices show a considerable aesthetic sense. In the case of Joan's office (photo 10), for example, the standard office paraphernalia are embellished by lamps, vases, and pictures.

The three floors are, physically, oddly disjunct. Although there is a major stairway leading from the main door on the second floor to the ELI, the only physical links among all the three floors are the back staircase and the freight elevator. The former is cramped and rather dark (photo 11) and, in its lower sections, screened off in a manner perhaps most reminiscent of a penitentiary (photo 12). The freight elevator, widely believed to be the oldest working elevator of this type on campus, is a clanking monster of uncertain temperament (photo 13). Thankfully, it is not open to the public since a building key is required to operate it, and such is its sinister reputation that an employee of NUBS needing to move boxes or equipment from one floor to another may well insist on being accompanied by a colleague.

Photo 8. Ed's office in the Herbarium.

Photo 9. "Mug shots" in the ELI main corridor.

Photo 10. Joan's office in the ELI.

Photo 11. A view of the backstairs.

Perhaps the most telling indication of the contrasting ambience on each floor is to be found in the unit libraries. The ELI library is the spatial and symbolic heart of the institute and is a rather untidy and busy place, especially because it is also the home of the Institute's heavily used main photocopier. This library is an "independent" library and thus not part of the official university system; it houses the collections of both the ELI and the Program in Linguistics and is managed by a half-time professional librarian. Access is easy for the Institute's international students, and for students and staff from other departments and neighboring institutions. The substantial specialized holdings of books, theses, journals, videos, and filed offprints/typescripts have typically a careworn and battered aspect, so that the overall impression is very much that of a practitioner *working* library in a field where much material appears in paperback or duplicated form (photo 14).

Photo 12. Another view of the backstairs.

Photo 13. The freight elevator (and Margaret).

Photo 14. The ELI library.

In contrast, the Herbarium library is closed to all but key-holders and is always immaculate (indeed, its tidiness is a point of pride with the honorary librarian); again, in contrast, this library *is* an official part of the university system, being a Museums sublibrary. Here the predominating impression is of large leather-bound volumes (folios), often of considerable age, value, and rarity (photo 15), and other impressive-looking books (photo 16). This then is a classic *reference* library for classic scholars. In even greater contrast, the CRS has no public library as such (at least in book form), but merely a file cabinet of pristine xeroxed sheets of information entitled "Quicknotes" (photo 17). In effect, "historical" reference material is housed in software such as *MacArchives*, while other "contemporary" reference assistance is housed in the team leaders' and consultants' heads, or is increasingly available on the Web.

In this section I have attempted a brief illustrated account of the unsung North University Building. As might be expected from the activities that take place on them, the three floors do indeed look rather different: homely and colorful on the top, gray-and-dark-green austere in the middle, modishly neutral-toned and high-tech on the bottom. They also operate rather differently: the CRS, for example, and not without a well-deserved sense of pride, announces that it is "open 24 hours a day, seven days a

Photo 15. Part of the Herbarium library.

week" (photo 18); the Herbarium is a strict 8 am–5 pm operation (even though some curators are often in the building over the weekends); and the ELI runs many of its classes in the early evenings (4 pm–6 pm). Students of all types surge in and out of the CRS, and international students rattle up and down the main stairs to the ELI throughout much of the first four working days of the week. On the other hand, the second-floor Herbarium is an island of tranquility, largely isolated from these flows. This floor-by-floor distinctiveness in appearance and atmosphere is probably reinforced by two further things. One, as we have already seen, is the somewhat limited access from floor to floor. The other is the relatively small amount of business that needs to be conducted up and down the building. The CRS reports to the Informational Technology Division in the Provost's office. Although the Herbarium and the ELI

Photo 16. Another view of the Herbarium library.

Photo 17. "Quicknotes" in the CRS.

Photo 18. Notice outside the CRS.

both report to LS&A, the Herbarium falls under the Science Division and the ELI under the Humanities. One of the small bits of business that *does* concern the building as a whole is establishing a roster for which unit is going to sort the incoming mail for which month. Apart from that, there are precious few contacts—except for the fact that at the moment of this writing the Herbarium continues to use the ELI's fax machine for its occasional faxes. So far, then, the material culture of the building does lend its own specific kind of support to the idea that the North University Building likely represents an intriguing three-way juxtaposition of academic and professional activities and attitudes on its three floors.

ADDING SOME THEORETICAL PERSPECTIVE

To some, this rather odd three-way juxtaposition might seem to be only a minor administrative anomaly, or perhaps a passing curiosity or historical accident. However, to those (like myself) who are interested in academic discourse and scholarly and professional rhetoric, the NUBS situation provides a splendid opportunity to explore, among other things, an important but troubled theoretical construct central to a series entitled *Rhetoric, Knowledge, and Society*. Although a more extensive discussion, with a fuller panoply of citation, is given in chapter 5, a brief account may be helpful at this juncture, if only to round out the rationale for this study.

The troubled concept referred to is usually known today by the expression *"discourse community,"* although variants such as "disciplinary community," "communicative community," "rhetorical community," and, more recently, "community of practice" are preferred by some scholars. In 1990 I attempted to characterize this concept as follows:

> Discourse communities are sociorhetorical networks that form in order to work towards sets of common goals. One of the characteristics that established members of these discourse communities possess is familiarity with the particular genres that are used in the communicative furtherance of those sets of goals. In consequence, genres are the properties of discourse communities; that is to say, genres belong to discourse communities, not to individuals, other kinds of grouping or to wider speech communities. (Swales, 1990a, p. 9)

In essence, then, discourse communities are occupational or recreational groups that are somewhat different from the traditional *geographic* speech communities of sociolinguistics, as discussed, for example, in William Labov's classic 1963 study of the speech of the local inhabitants of Martha's Vineyard. In effect, in discourse communities, communalities reside in what people do, rather than in who they are. They could be making widgets in a factory, teaching physics in a department, playing in an orchestra, or being active members of a local bicycle club, and in doing these things they would be acquiring, using, and modifying the language that goes along with these jobs or hobbies. In-group abbreviations, acronyms, argots, and other special terms flourish and multiply; beyond that, these discourse communities evolve their own conventions and traditions for such diverse verbal activities as running meetings, producing reports, and publicizing their activities. These recurrent classes of communicative events are the *genres* that orchestrate verbal life. These genres link the past and the present, and so balance forces for tradition and innovation. They structure the roles of individuals within wider frameworks, and further assist those individuals with the actualization of their communicative plans and purposes.

The notion of discourse community thus seems to have considerable explanatory potential. It offers, especially for a linguist like myself, an appealing way of seeing how neophytes or apprentices become discoursally established as full members of academic groups. It offers a way of studying how language plays a key role in the "situated learning" theories of contemporary educational researchers and theorists influenced by the Russian psychologist, Vygotsky, and his intellectual successors. It provides a discoursal perspective on the attempts of those, like Tony Becher (1989) and many others, who are interested in disciplinary differences and the boundaries between them. It even seems to indicate an interesting way of thinking about individual university classes, as the coming together of an initially rather heterogenous group of students into a classroom discourse community can be seen as a powerful indicator of a successful class, and, conversely, its not coming together as a sign of a more troubled one.

My commitment to the concept of discourse community as a theoretical construct has waxed and waned. As early as 1989, Joseph Harris had correctly pointed out the utopian substrate to the concept, arguing that its advocates failed to recognize the self-evident conflicts in many communities. My doctoral students complained that my examples of discourse communities were unusual and arcane collectivities (such as a multinational and highly specialized group of philatelists) not much like the mixed speech and discourse communities they knew of. These were communities that could merge office and bar, factory and public park, town and gown. In consequence, they persuaded me, we have "contaminated" phenomena like university towns (Heidelberg, Cambridge, Princeton), religious towns (Lourdes, Mecca), sporting towns (Saratoga, Daytona), factory towns (Dearborn, Dagenham), and political towns (Ottawa, Canberra).

Worse, two definitional problems continued to plague the concept. One involves coverage or latitude: Is a university a discourse community, or rather a college, or only a department, or even a specialization within a department? Answers to at least the larger groupings inevitably seemed to be an unhelpful mix of "yes" and "no." Second, in order to avoid circularity, a number of us proffered criteria for circumscribing uses of the concept, so that some communities would not be discourse communities, and some discourse would fall outside discourse-community-owned genres. This led to a conundrum familiar to historical linguistics: A linguistic change cannot be detected until *after* it has happened. So Dwight Atkinson, in his dissertation, suggested the characteristics that I had described "appear to be mostly the public *results or consequences* of the strong communal motivations which lead, in the first place, to the constitution and maintenance of discourse communities" (1993, p. 19). Further, recent studies of E-mail user groups by Yu-Ying Chang and others demonstrate that in emerging, embryonic, or transitional communities, text-types and genres cannot be used for identification purposes because their linguistic characteristics are so unstable (e.g., Chang, 1996). The discourse community concept was thus more useful for *validating* the existence of groupings that already shared a complex of ideas and sentiments, and less useful for seeing how such groupings were initiated and nurtured, or for assessing the precise characteristics of any purported collectivity.

By 1993, I published a paper that in effect was a valedictory for the demise of discourse community. Therein I concluded that discourse communities did not exist via membership or collectivity, but persisted in some more ghostly way by instantiation and engagement. In other words, we are not what we are (tinker, tailor, soldier, sailor), but we are what we are doing at any particular moment. However, this was a strongly reductionist position and so ducked the issue of "significative worlds." Certainly, there are minor roles that we all play: now I am trying to send a registered packet; now I am ordering a book by credit card; now I am completing my 1040 tax form; now I am trying to align my field notes with one of the butterflies in a field guide. These literacy events, however, are neither things that I am paid to do, nor skills that appear on my c.v. On the other hand, when I engage in those things I am paid to do—and which do appear on my c.v.—this is, in Clifford Geertz's magic prose, "not just to take up a technical task but to take up a cultural frame that defines a great part of one's life" (1983, p. 155). For all its defensibility, this mosaic of little discoursal acts somehow misses the big picture of how we professionally come to be the people we are.

Despite all these perplexities, for a decade now, the expression *discourse community* (or its variants) has continued to be widely used, and is widely used today, especially in fields such as rhetoric, education, cultural, women's and writing studies, and linguistics. However, its use appears to have largely reverted to where it began—as a convenient but ill-defined "term of art." It seems to have lost its authority as a delineated theoretical construct of some descriptive power and, a little less certainly, of some predictive value.

I therefore decided to have another look at discourse community in the world that I know best, that of academic institutions. As a first step in having another look, I wanted as far as possible to start afresh, detached—at least initially—from rhetorical or discoursal theories or from previous genre studies themselves. I wanted for this starting point neither a standard "corpus," such as 50 research papers in Psychology, nor a well-established disciplinary field such as Physics, Economics, or Biology, all three of which coincidentally the targets of important discoursal studies (Bazerman, 1988; McCloskey, 1994; and Myers, 1990, respectively). Rather, it seemed that a more congenial point of departure would be something like Dan Douglas and Larry Selinker's *discourse domain* (1994); that is, a fairly specialized branch of textually encoded knowledge and/or expertise. I could then see how that body of knowledge/expertise gets acquired, transmitted, and transformed among its participant members and how and why that knowledge/expertise becomes textually distributed among different genres. In other words, the approach promises a way of seeing how some body of "content" gets variously shaped by convention, communicative purpose, and audience design.

A further reason for starting with *discourse domain* was that it might allow me to avoid making prior assumptions about what counted as "scholarly," as opposed to "pedagogic," "technical," or "administrative," a mistake I had in fact made in the 1990a book. Finally, in addition to these theoretical issues, the *discourse-domain* approach also offered hopes of uncovering genres and types of writing that were thus far unknown to or had been ignored by scholars with professional interests in university writing. As I hope to show, these aspirations have been at least adequately realized. All these factors, then, pointed to a site study of textual practices and products within one or more smallish and more-or-less self-contained university units. Hence the North University Building.

It seems, then, that the NUBS study can be viewed as a kind of test case. In effect, if the concept of discourse community (or, for that matter, community of practice) does not, in some sense, survive its encounter with NUBS, then it probably is—as its critics have recently argued—of diminished utility and of somewhat exceptional occurrence. If the three floors do not have their own distinctive voices, adequately defined and attuned within their own premises and yet curiously different from those above or below, then we would do well to back away from believing that discourse communities are somehow real, rather than merely convenient fictions or abstractions constructed to provide simplified maps of academic, professional, or occupational territories and their occupying tribes.

ASSEMBLING AND HANDLING THE EVIDENCE

In essence, then, this book offers itself as a site study of three text-community associations. As the study is (or so I fondly imagine) somewhat unusual, it might be helpful to further distinguish it from other possible approaches—beyond what I have already said at the chapter's outset. For example, a sociolinguist with an interest in spoken discourse might well have centered on the social networks within the building and seen how those play out differently among the mature women on the top floor, the older men on the middle floor, and the young men on the bottom. Alternatively, an analyst with an interest in information science could have examined each unit's textual productivity, reputation, and citation, and could have contrasted the international focus in the ELI and the Herbarium, with the more local environment of the CRS. Another scholar with a history-technology bent might have studied the very different evolutions of the three units and how technology has impacted them differently. A specialist in the history of rhetoric might have focused on the "founding texts" in each field, such as Linnaeus' writings in Systematic Botany, and traced their various influences. Or, even closer to home, a text-linguistic colleague might have studied, for instance, differences in the levels of formality in the writings emanating from each floor.

In my own case, if the primary intent of re-exploring the concept of discourse community was clear enough, the types of verbal evidence (written and/or spoken) that would most usefully count—either for or against the reality of discourse community—were somewhat less clear. What should my occasional research assistants and I be looking at? Official documents, publicity material, publications, correspondence, manuscripts, pictures on the wall, books on shelves? What should we be hearing, or overhearing? Life histories, staff meetings, collaborative editing sessions and other text–talk interactions, unit-specific jokes, gossip? And who should we be looking at? The professors, the lecturers, the professional and administrative staff, the secretaries, the janitors, the student-users? For a mid-level administrator with a modest research grant, "All of the above" were not possible answers to these questions. And what to do—especially these days—about John Swales, me, *l'auteur*? Is he to be part of this story, or somehow placed outside it, or even above it?

Because my linguistics specialty is written discourse analysis, an examination of texts would be central. And indeed, there is a fair amount of this, although I have tended to rely as much on descriptive commentary as on technical analysis. In fact, I have largely avoided the apparatus of linguistic science, and mostly used the categories of traditional grammar known to the educated general public. I have also, on occasion, taken an interest in how some of the core texts came to be written and in how and where they have been picked up on by other writers (i.e., what is more technically known as their *reception histories*).

As the "Then and Now" section shows, two aspects of the framing context already put to use have been the historical and pictorial. These were originally thought of as providing preliminary contextual background—a kind of "lest we overlook something important" insurance policy. They also functioned as a way of convincing my principal research assistant, Margaret Luebs, and myself that we were indeed embarked upon a site-study. Further, when we began to plan this aspect of the project, Margaret had recently returned from a science and society conference and had been impressed there with what some speakers had been able to achieve via rhetorical analyses of museums and their exhibits. A methodology à la mode, we supposed.

However, the central and most time-consuming activity involved the construction of individual textual life histories (seven in all). The basic procedure (in all cases but one) was to obtain a *curriculum vitae* and collect a number of sample publications, study the latter for quite substantial periods of time and from a number of angles, and then conduct one or more major text-based interviews with the chosen author. The resulting transcripts and draft sections then went back and forth with the authors, and then back and forth with the outside readers, in the hopes that misunderstandings and obscurities could be ironed out, or at least negotiated. These iterative processes of becoming intimately involved with another's writing and its evolution have, in my case at least, meant that the early image-capture of the outsider-observer has become steadily replaced by the selective interpretation of the confidante. These processes then are exactly as the famous French cultural theorist Michel Foucault described them: "practices that systematically form the objects of which they speak" (1972, p. 49).

With only a few thousand words for each textual biography, I have also come to focus on particularities that might be insightful in terms of both understanding an individual's working rhetoric and placing that rhetoric in a wider disciplinary context. These are personally chosen textual stretches, but ones that reflect intuitions accumulated over many years about what might count as "good evidence" for the claims being made. In support of this orientation, here is a second quotation from Clifford Geertz, that master of particularity: "The problem with . . . a no-nonsense approach to things, one which extracts the general from the particular and then sets the particular aside as detail, illustration, background, or qualification, is that it leaves us helpless in the face of the very difference we need to explore" (1995, p. 40). It was the particulate epiphanies that I was principally after.

Although the NUBS site has considerable advantages for my purposes, it has one apparent drawback. Today, the Computing Resource Site in NUBS is no longer the main location for this activity on campus. As a result, most of the textual production associated with computer research actually takes place elsewhere. In terms of extensive writing, the three-way comparison is not complete, but this fact too can be made into an interesting part of the story. In consequence, the six individuals approached in the standard way consisted of four men from the Herbarium, Bill, Bob, Ed, and Tony (see chapter 3), and two women from the ELI, Carolyn and Joan (see chapter 4). The seventh individual turned out to be myself (also see chapter 4). Although I had firmly intended to exclude my own textual history from the study, I eventually had a change of heart. One reason, as discussed earlier, was the way in which my involvement with the participants began to take on a greater biographical and more intimate character than I had anticipated. The insider–outsider distinction had already become blurred. A second reason lay in my growing awareness of trends in the wider scholarly ethos of this end-of-millenium decade, such as its renewed interest in and appreciation of narrative, as well as its greater openness to reflections on personal circumstance. However, I did not see how I could interview myself, and I neither wanted to put a local colleague to the trouble of all that preparation, nor impose such a potentially awkward task on one of my own research assistants. So I went to Tony Dudley-Evans, now of the University of Birmingham in England, as the person who has certainly known my academic work the longest and probably knows it as well as anyone. I asked him to provide a series of interlinear commentaries on my drafts, so that we could achieve something of that back-and-forth refinement that had proved so successful in the other cases.

There is a final point to make about the methodologies that underlie chapter 3 (The Herbarium) and chapter 4 (The ELI). The selection of the units themselves, as opposed to, say, larger and probably more fissiparous departments or even disciplines, might be seen as predisposing the argument in favor of the viability of the discourse community concept. In order to counter any such tendencies, I have, in these two of the three central chapters, deliberately tried to find a way of accounting for discoursal lives that has stressed from the outset the particularity of the individual stories. I could doubtless have done otherwise; I might, for instance, have focused on the agreed similarities in the advanced training of systematic botanists, or on the strong and constraining gate-keeping roles of major journals like *TESOL Quarterly* on applied linguistics/ESL scholarly texts. Overall, I therefore believe that my way of proceeding has been set up not to predispose or prejudge the existence of discourse communities, but if anything to presume the opposite.

The final component of the picture, at least chronologically, involved moving away from the more individualistic and scholarly activities toward a selective study of the "routine business" that occurs on each floor, even though the accounts of these are now placed in chapter 2 because they provide some useful background information for the seven individual case studies. Margaret did the initial study of the Computing Resource Site, which both of us then followed up; Yu-Ying and I shared the work for the Herbarium workroom; and I was primarily responsible for the ELI "testing co-operative." Our approach was broadly similar to that adopted for the individual text-histories, although fewer of the interviews were text-based. For the ELI, I also asked Theresa to keep a diary of activities in Room 3025 during a period of particularly intense test- and text-making activity.

Finally, there are a few more mundane matters to be dealt with. Mention has already been made of the text-based interviews. On numerous occasions I have worked verbatim extracts from these into the various accounts. In so doing, I have removed certain hesitations and false starts, and done several other kinds of cleaning up, insofar as the original *form* of the spoken text is usually of less interest to me than its content. (This is in sharp contrast to the written texts, where I do have a consuming interest in the particularities of their rhetorical structure, syntax, and style.) Despite this modest "house-cleaning," I believe I have still managed to retain the spoken flavor of the transcipted pieces, while at the same time improving their readability. I have, also to this end, kept transcription conventions to a minimum. Ellipsis points (. . .) indicate that certain spoken words and phrases have been omitted. Square brackets, for instance, "the [classification] system does not . . . ," indicate that a word or phrase has been added for clarification. Parentheses are used as a punctuation device to indicate asides, parentheses, and the like.

In a previous publication dealing with aspects of the NUBS project (Swales & Luebs, 1995), we changed the names of all the participants to maintain confidentiality. In this work, I have reverted to their real names. These are real people whose reality—and whose cooperation—I would like to recognize and acknowledge. Moreover, this new die was pretty well cast once I decided to include a section on my own texts; it would have been decidedly odd, to say the least, to have had to invent and carry forward a pseudonym for myself. A more difficult decision involved endnotes. Despite Anthony Grafton's elegant and colorful defense of notes in history (Grafton, 1994), I have decided to let the main text stand or fall on its own without their support. I confess that there have been occasions when I have rued that decision, but it does have the advantage of making a writer focus on the reader's imagined state of mind at any juncture in the text. As to how well I have succeeded in imagining those imaginings, the reader will judge.

2

Communities of Practice?

RHYTHMS OF WORK AND UNIVERSITY CLOCKS

In chapters 3 and 4 I will explore the published textual biographies of selected members of the Herbarium and the ELI. (As the reader will recollect, by the middle 1990s no people with such scholarly careers remained in the Computing Resource Site, the active researchers having migrated to other computer science units elsewhere on campus.) However, in this chapter the focus is on the quotidian discourse-related activities that occur and recur on the three floors of the building. As previously mentioned, I have been selective here, choosing certain more or less regular processes that seem emblematic of the way things generally get done on each floor. These are "the defined rhythms of work" (Charles Tamason, personal communication, 1996) that orchestrate the roles of text and task and are, in turn, orchestrated by them. I take the CRS first, where attention focuses on a climate of change, and on the roles of the consultants as purveyors of technical advice and customer help. Then comes the Herbarium and its storage, its maintenance and, particularly, its loans of vascular plant specimens to other institutions. Finally, there is the ELI, where the regular activity chosen for study is situated in the institute's Testing and Certification Division, and concerns the co-operative scrambles of the research associates and assistants therein to prepare new forms of two or three international ESL tests every year.

A recurrent theme that has emerged from this investigation of three communities of practice is that of time; more specifically, how the clocks move at different speeds in the three communities. However, this phenomenon is somewhat disguised by two others. One is simply that everybody is busy. In terms of E. P. Thompson's celebrated 1967 essay

"Time, Work-discipline and Industrial Capitalism," NUB represents the modern era:

> Puritanism, in its marriage of convenience with industrial capitalism, was the agent which converted men to new valuations of time; which taught children even in their infancy to improve each shining hour; and which saturated men's minds with the equation, time is money. (p. 95)

So too, these three groups carry with them this sense of using time purposefully, just as they carry watches on their wrists.

The second phenomenon which, at first sight, obfuscates that of "different floors, different clocks" is the prominent and visible overlay of the academic calendar. Here, for example, is that controlling cycle in my institution for Winter Term, 1996:

Ann Arbor Campus
Registration (for students not pre-registered) . . . . Jan 8–9
Classes begin . . . . Jan 10
Martin Luther King, Jr. Birthday . . . . Jan 15
    University Symposia—No Regular Classes
Vacation begins 12:00 noon . . . . March 2
Classes resume 8:00 a.m. . . . . March 11
University Honors Convocation . . . . March 24
Classes end . . . . April 24
Study day . . . . April 25
Examinations . . . . April 25–26, April 29–May 2
Commencement Activities . . . . May 3–5

Needless to say, this calendar is in many ways the *main* clock which partitions, runs, and assembles the primary educational processes and their supporting administration activities. However, in all three of the NUB cases this main clock has only limited influence on the community clocks, and in one case practically none. In the Computing Resource Site, peak demand for services does, of course, tend to coincide with due dates for mid-term and final papers, but this effect is more quantitative than qualitative because many of its regular customers are graduate students writing dissertations and other major texts. In the ELI, external testing activities are largely suspended at the beginning of each semester in order to re-evaluate the English of many of the entering international students, while at other periods in the year, certain members of the Testing Division may be busy for part of a week running screening tests for potential international graduate student instructors, or updating the U-M tests. Although these testing activities certainly show some influence from the academic calendar clock, in practical terms the synergies between the internal and external testing operations mitigate that impingement. Finally, in the Herbarium Workroom, the only influence that I have been able to trace of the academic year is the very minor one of being more easily able to hire work-studies during the months when the university is in regular session. It is true that internal demand for Workroom assistance from Curators in the Herbarium itself may be reduced in the Spring/Summer semester, because some of them are out of town, perhaps on field trips or teaching up north at the Biological Research Station. On the other hand, outside demand for services increases as botanists elsewhere get down to their summer tasks of writing up *treatments* (see chapter 3). According to the collections' Manager, these minor shifts pretty well cancel each other out.

Nor is it the case, of course, that community clocks are the only alternate arrangements to the academic year cycle. Scholarly and research clocks also run somewhat apart from the main university calendar clock. The only one of these broadly recognized by horological name is the somewhat notorious institutional practice of running "a tenure clock" (typically from 5 to 7 years) for assistant professors to make it to the tenured ranks, with much current discussion about criteria for "stopping the clock" for childbearing and parenting activities and the like. Beyond that, the professoriate, as a body, has its scholarly round impacted by the temporal structurations created through deadlines for grant applications and annual research reports, and by the regular rhythms of congresses, conventions and conferences. And beyond that, we can detect disciplinary rhythms that vary, in their extremes, from a decades-long *Flora* project to the rush-to-print of *Letters* in major science journals. And finally, as the following two chapters will illustrate, there are the temporal contingencies, the *making, finding,* or even *buying* of time, which variably influence when and with what expedition individual scholars get their academic work brought to written completion and distribution.

All that said, the "communities of practice" (Eckert & McConnell-Ginet, 1992; Lave & Wenger, 1991) in the North University Building also have their separate and highly temporal rhythms. This tempo is *allegro assai* in the CRS, for the consultants often function like text-recovery paramedics in some discoursal Emergency Room. There are pressing urgencies here, as in the prototypical "My computer just ate my disk, and I have to turn in my paper by five o'clock—please help me!" Upstairs in the Herbarium, the tempo is *lentissimo*, because the tangible return on the loaning or gifting of specimens in the form of either expert "determinations" or published treatments may be, as we shall see, a matter of many years. Although the physical rhythms are expeditious enough, with a fair amount of walking about, and with a palpable sense of deft movement in the assembling and disassembling of sets of specimens, the horizons of expectation in terms of outcome can be immensely long. Finally, on the top floor, the observer will experience a steadier *adagio* pace in which the set examination "seasons" have the regular repetitive quality of traditional agricultural practice. These are annual cycles of work, even if a particular test may have its yearly fallow period after the sending out of certificates to successful candidates and before the machinery for preparing next year's examination needs to be set in motion. In effect, the ground is prepared, the seed is sown, unsatisfactory test items are weeded out of the crop, the harvest is gathered, and the results disseminated in a time-honored kind of way. These seasons though are not those of the official academic year.

THE CHANGING SCENE
IN THE COMPUTING RESOURCE SITE

> . . . we've actually talked about combing through our documentation and getting rid of that word "resource." (Liz, in interview)

The Scene in 1994

In 1994, Margaret and I could describe the CRS in the following terms. The Computing Resource Site, a constant hub of activity, is open 24 hours a day and 7 days a week, closing only a few times a year for major national holidays. Students who walk through the main door to the CRS find themselves in a large, softly lit, oddly shaped room carved out of the original basement, with row upon row of personal computers (some 80 in all, 50 of them Macs). At one end of the room is the office of the CRS support staff, or "monitors" as they are called, separated from the computer area by a half-door. Students, known as "users" in this environment, come to this window to ask for help of all kinds (ignoring the stern red sign which reads "Refer all software questions to the consultants"). Sometimes the monitors open the half-door and come out onto the main floor to deal with equipment problems or do some policing (in the CRS, users are not allowed to eat, talk loudly, or play computer games when others are waiting for computers), but users are never allowed on the other side of the half-door.

Users are, however, permitted to walk right into the office of the computer consultants, next door to the monitor's office, to ask software questions. There are usually two or three computer consultants in the office at any time, each sitting at a computer, waiting for users to show up. Almost all (around 90%) are male, and are either current or former students. Although not necessarily computer science majors, they are typically very interested in computers and spend their "waiting" time at the CRS trying out new software or writing programs. This is a computer culture described by Meriel Bloor (1996) as one in which individuals have particularly extensive *and* intensive relations with their terminals, which in turn are linked up to ever-expanding networks within "the system." Thus, the consultants differ somewhat from the "monitors," who usually have less background or interest in computers and who, partly in response to a hiring freeze, tend to be older and to have worked at the CRS for a larger number of years.

In many ways the CRS can be a stressful place to work, particularly because both the monitors and the consultants are often the target of users' anger. As Tim, the supervisor, observed, "people get really freaked out when things go wrong." Computers are fragile, floppy disks even more so, and users with damaged disks and term papers due yesterday are likely to take their frustration out on the CRS staff. Another potential source of stress is that the CRS is now one of several branch "sites" of the large and highly ramified Information Technology Division headed by no less a person than a Vice-Provost for Information Technology. Occasional remarks can be heard about how the "the high levels of administration" do not always understand what really goes on in the site. These tensions are doubtless compounded by the size and speed of current technological expansion in the computer field.

Tim is the most senior person with his office in the CRS, but he is more of an administrator than a computer expert (he does not have a background in computer science). He hires temporary workers and does all their paperwork and scheduling, and is continually E-mailing or calling students trying to find replacements for people who call in sick—often at the last minute. He is also responsible for ordering all the supplies; as might be expected, the CRS operation uses a massive amount of paper, and each printer gets through, on average, a $100 cartridge each day. If we add to these concerns the temperamental nature of the hardware and the software, we can see that the CRS symbolizes late 20th-century modernity. Despite its apparent aura of quietness, the low hum of the machines, the soft clicking of innumerable computer keys, the occasional murmurs from the consultants' room, this is a world that, in reality, is both frenetic and fragile.

Indeed the CRS continues to change constantly, as has the entire university computing establishment during the 35 years of its existence. In fact, in the short period between the first and second drafts of this subsection, the CRS reorganized the monitors' and consultants' offices, moving the consultants out of their little room and into the front of the monitors' office. This move puts the consultants behind the half-door, making it harder for users to talk to them. To address this new problem, the half-door was briefly removed, but then users tended to walk beyond the consultants' desks and into the forbidden area of the monitors. So now the half-door is back on, at least for the time being.

Two Years Later

In late 1996 some aspects of the CRS were very much as they were two years earlier. The main "oddly shaped" computer room looks largely the same, apart from some rather garish new signs saying "Consultants," "Print Jobs," "Queueing," and "Printers." The half-door to the consultants' room remains in place, but it is usually left ajar as a half-hearted and muted invitation to proceed within. The back quarters are largely the same, although it turns out that there is a special reason for this. According to Liz, the Operations Manager for Campus Computing Sites, in late 1994, they did once again examine the physical layout of the site because some staff were in an area behind a wall separating them from the rest of the site. She commented,

> It's a little bit of a barrier, not a particularly habitable space . . . because that space was intended to be used for mainframe computers and large printers like the 9700 . . . it wasn't meant to be used for office space.

However, ITD was hesitant "to spend any significant amount of money on improvements in that area" because of persistent rumors about plans to demolish the building and eventually replace it by some kind of under-graduate center. The Herbarium and the ELI have heard those rumors too, and, for various reasons, don't like them one bit.

However, the computers had—inevitably—been upgraded, probably several times. Indeed, when Margaret talked to Tung, who had taken over from Tim as the (retitled) "team leader" for the NUBS site, in September 1996, he noted that the Unix machines had been upgraded "just 2 to 3 weeks ago." At the time of writing, according to the ITD web page for the CRS:

> NUBS has numerous specialty computing facilities available for use. The site contains 62 Power Macintosh, 21 Dell, and 10 Unix Workstation computers. It is a self-serve site, meaning that users do not have to be assigned to a station by a staff member. NUBS is open 24 hours [a day] throughout the year.

The CRS has also retained its traditional customer base. Liz offered these interesting observations:

> Each site does tend to have its own unique flavor, and some of that is, you know, historical, and some of it has to do with the particular technology that's available at the site. NUBS has been there for quite a long time . . .

Students who were taking programming classes with punch cards used to go to that site, and it has always tended to [have] . . . more of the high-end users. Some of the sites that have been built more recently, like Angell Hall, tend to be more for undergraduate use. Angell Hall in particular is known not only as a computing site, but [also] a place to meet and mix with your fellow students (laughs) . . . You know, it's a more social atmosphere.

For another view, broadly similar in conclusion but showing an "inhabitant of NUBS" perspective, we turn to Darcy, a female consultant in NUBS, where she has worked for nearly a year part-time, first as a student, and now 24 hours a week as an ex-student. Darcy is a recent graduate in psychology, and when I talked to her in December 1996, she had just finished work as a "teaching assistant" for Computer Science 184, and was contemplating going to the School of Education for a teaching certificate, with a minor in multimedia and computer-aided learning. Here is her perspective:

I like NUBS because it is smaller. Angell hall is probably the major computing site, and it's huge. I like that it is open and the fact that it's got windows in it, and it's nice and bright sometimes, but it's dirtier . . . NUBS doesn't have very many windows and it's depressing and dark in that way [see photo 5], but there are more graduate students there, more PhD students, and I like that because they are more regular, and I have become conscious of some, and talked to some, and get along pretty well—in contrast to the smaller ones [sites] where it's just random students. It's nicer in NUBS.

Another continuing element in NUBS is user personal crises, and Darcy says she feels particularly awful when a senior graduate student comes in upset, and perhaps even crying, because his or her disk has crashed. As she vividly expressed it:

You see a lot of them panic. You see a lot of them come in and say "I've lost my dissertation" and, Oh God, we have people that come in and say "my disk is damaged and it's the only copy I have and it's my *life*," and so here I am and "it's your life." So there are bigger problems sometimes.

Darcy and her fellow consultants are not exactly helped in these difficult situations by the fact that changes in ITD run ahead of public knowledge of them. As it turns out, disk-recovery is no longer a specialty of NUBS, but has been recently transferred to another site in the Michigan Union. Although Liz's team leaders know this and, presumably through them, it is known to the 80–90 temporary site consultants scattered across the campus, the "received wisdom" among the many thousands of computer users at the university is that the Computing *Resource* Site is the place to scurry to when a crisis occurs. As Darcy says: "All the hand-by-mouth word is to send them to NUBS . . . People come to NUBS for just about everything and we have to send them out to different buildings."

As might be expected, the Information Technology Division has a rapidly developing web site. Among the many pages on this site, there are currently (December 1996) three that deal with "Frequently Asked Computing Questions." As again might be expected, the first of these is:

> *I think I damaged my floppy disk. What can I do?*
> You can have an ITD consultant try to recover the files on the disk for you. The charge is $10/hour ($5 non-refundable minimum deposit). Bring the damaged floppy disk, a blank disk of the same type, and the $5 deposit to the Michigan Union Computing Site. The deposit must be cash (exact change only), a check made payable to U-M, or a University account number. Macintosh disk recoveries are generally completed within two business days. DOS disk recoveries usually take from two to five business days.

The *ITDweb* will doubtless play an increasing role as a source of the latest information about ITD services and their locations. However, the fact that this prioritized FAQ neither bolds the new location for disk recovery nor adds a reminder like "(*no longer at NUBS*)" does not assist Tung, Darcy, and their colleagues as much as it might in reducing the number of people who visit the NUBS consultants for the wrong reasons.

A major change that has affected all the computing sites involves the nonpermanent personnel. In the earlier part of 1994, there were—as we described—two separate groups of people: *monitors* and *consultants*. By the end of that year the monitors had disappeared, or more accurately, had been (largely) retrained as consultants. When I asked Liz whether this change had come from above, from the team leaders ("her eyes and ears" for software problems or virus outbreaks and the like), or from user comments and suggestions, she reconstructed this small piece of recent ITD history as being an innovation set in motion by her immediate predecessor. Until the microprocessor revolution, one of the monitors' main tasks had been looking after heavy-duty and specialized equipment such as card punches, magnetic tapes, and the 9700 printers attached to the MTS mainframe. These all rapidly began to disappear. Meanwhile, in the early 1990s, the consultants, at that time a student coterie of Young Turks distinct from the more regularly employed monitors, were not available 24 hours a day. So when students found the consultants' office locked up for the evening, they would naturally gravitate to the monitors to find out why, for example, their footnotes were not printing out correctly. As Liz said in interview: "And, you know, by and large the monitors stepped up to answering these questions; they just looked it up in a manual, or figured it out, and tried to help people as best they could."

So the advent of a different type of computing environment and the need at the 24-hour sites to have technical assistance around the clock have together led to the collapsing of the old two categories into a single amalgamation. Although odd comments and remarks suggest that the translation of monitors into consultants was not without its transitional problems, from his supervisory perspective Tung now seems pretty satisfied with the current situation at his NUBS site and certainly considers the resulting mix of older and younger consultants a definite advantage.

During the 1994–1996 period, another shift in ethos seems to have occurred: a reconsideration of the relative importance of technical help versus customer service, at least with the sites consultants. (The situation is different with the 4-HELP telephone lines, because callers to 4-HELP may be calling in from anywhere on campus with any and every kind of computer problem imaginable, and so in this operation there remains a premium on technical expertise.) Darcy, for example, recollects that the test she took to gain a consultant position had customer service as well as technical questions, and during her training sessions "they were pushing customer service." Liz, from her managerial perspective, would probably concur; she also stressed, over and above technical interest and competence, the need for "people with good communication skills and trouble-shooting problem-solving skills" (interview).

A final take on this issue comes from Darcy's tape-recorded reflections on gender issues in the computing sites. She explained that she wanted to become a consultant because, as a female student, she had found it more difficult to approach men for assistance than women. The direct language in the following extract captures well her concerns—and recollect that Darcy was a psychology major (a very strong department at Michigan) with long-standing interests in computer technology:

> Especially because I had been bummed out by them [the men] on different occasions. They can be rather rude. Well, I shouldn't say it but *some* are. I think they have gotten rid of most of those people, but it was awful to go through that.

So Darcy became a consultant. By the end of 1996, women consultants had increased their representation from the 10% 1994 level, but they are still a decided minority. This increase has its own perils, though. Here is Darcy again:

> I find I get ignored because I am female. I'll be sitting up in front and I'll say "How can I help you?" and they will look right past me and interrupt someone who is busy and ask *them* instead. So I get offended at that. But some [of us] understand that they are worried about their paper and they

need someone to blame and it turns out to be us. They are anxious to project their frustration on us. And that happens a lot, for sure, at finals.

I later asked her, on E-mail, how the NUBS group reacted to such incidents. She replied,

It all depends on who's working, the atmosphere at the time, whether or not I feel like letting it slide, etc. Most of the time it's situational, although it shouldn't be.

As is well known, the computer world, and its emergent "discourse communities," evolved in a very masculine—and masculinized—environment. Darcy's experiences suggest that the behavorial legacies of these origins can linger on and that her observation "it's nicer in NUBS" may have, to use her own word, a *situational* aspect to it.

Texts in the CRS

True to its ethos, The Information Technology Division relies heavily on its own technology and technological skills to manage its business. There are, for instance, proportionally fewer meetings, memos, faxes, and minutes in the ITD than in the Herbarium and the ELI, and a much greater reliance on E-mail *user groups*. Tung's entry on the university's on-line address system lists 17 such groups to which he belongs, including "NUBS Site Suggestions" and "Sites Team Leaders." Although Liz says she does see Tung and the other team leaders on a regular basis, as they are her "communication channel to the rest of the consultants that work there," most of her communications with staff at various levels are via E-mail.

Mention was made in chapter 1 of the CRS's collection of "Quicknotes," by late 1996 flagged with a new sign announcing the location of the oddly plural "Documentations." These handy briefing sheets are not in fact produced by the Sites operation, but by a separate ITD documentation group. When changes or additions are needed, the documentation group uses a small number of volunteer consultants to review the new draft texts. Darcy has done this a couple of times, mostly focusing on the technical aspects, such as whether there could be a standard set of instructions for accessing E-mail for "pop" clients with Pegasus, Versaterm, and so on. (It turned out that there couldn't be.) As we might anticipate, this advisory work was all "remote," that is, done via E-mail by a user group.

Like his predecessor, Tim, Tung produces a small number of mostly instructional texts, some internal to his own staff, such as how to change the toner cartridges on the printer, and some in response to recurrent problems or difficulties that users experience at the NUBS site. Here is an example:

OH NO, MY STATION FROZE UP

If your Unix station freezes up, try hitting the **esc** key. Often this will unfreeze the station. If this method doesn't work, you can try the following steps:

1. Telnet and log into the same Unix station from another computer using the same uniqname that you used when the Unix station froze up.
2. At the Unix prompt, type in
   ps -elf l grep uniqname
   This will display all current processes being run by uniqname.
3. Find the process ID that corresponds to whatever application that was running when the station froze UP and type
   kill -9 PID (where PID is the process ID number)
   The station should no longer be frozen.

Here, then, is Tung trying to rectify yet another of those user crises. His engaging title captures well that moment of panic that afflicts most computer users on such occasions. Thereafter, the instructions, for all their technical complexity, move quietly, calmly, and sanely forward toward the desired solution. The direct address to the reader ("If this method doesn't work, you can try . . .") further assists in projecting a sympathetic, almost avuncular, tone to the instructions. (Later in this book, we look at other instructional texts based on rather different assumptions and composed in rather different styles.)

Yesterday, Today, and Tomorrow

As a matter of convenience in this section, I have consistently referred to the computer operation as the NUBS *Computer Resource Site* because this is the name painted on the blue-and-white metal panel on the outside of the building and on the two public-access doors into the site. In reality, however, terminology is unstable in the "change as a way of life" environment of the ITD. Several years ago, the NUBS operation was known as the *Computer Center*, as may be just detected in the relict sign above the door shown in photo 19. At the onset of the period of this study, it was called *The Computing Resource Center*. The 1994 picture of the door (photo 19) also shows another label, *ITD Full-service Computing Site*, but this has since been removed. Finally, the most recent notices, such as those announcing closures over the 1996 Christmas vacation, refer to the unit as the *NUBS Computing Site*—in other words, *Resource* has disappeared. All this terminological activity is in marked contrast to the

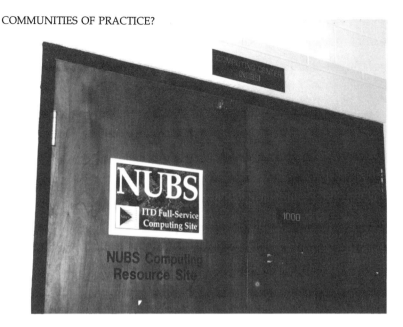

Photo 19. The south entrance to the CRS in 1994.

rest of the building: *The University Herbarium* has kept its name ever since the various herbaria were consolidated in 1921; and the *English Language Institute* has remained as is since its founding in 1941, despite a half-hearted attempt by the Dean's office in the late 1980s to deprive it of its prestigious-sounding third element.

As the following interview extract shows, Liz has a highly informed perspective on terminological change and its causes:

> Many of the services of the CRC [formerly in the Ed School], including the 4-HELP staff, moved to NUBS a couple of years ago, and for that reason we thought we would change the name slightly to indicate that there was something different about the site—that there was more to it than just a computer lab.
>
> To be honest, many of those things have since moved out. 4-HELP is no longer there, the disk recoveries are no longer there . . . and we've actually talked about combing through our documentation and getting rid of that word "resource." Because, to be honest, NUBS no longer has those additional—it was mostly additional—consulting services.

In fact, Liz now expects this change to be in place for September 1997, because September is the month when ITD introduces changes in its "documentations," services, prices, and so forth.

As NUBS becomes just a site, albeit one with high-end equipment for high-end users, its long-term future becomes less assured. Liz, with her involvements in continual change, notes a number of contemporary trends. As more and more students arrive on campus with computers, or purchase them from the ITD soon after arrival, the actual need for simple student computer terminals on campus may finally start to decline after its long and phenomenal rise. Her *sites* may become more like places where students can use equipment that they cannot be expected to own such as Unix machines, scanners, color printers, multimedia, or digital video, or use software like Adobe Photoshop and Pagemaker. Secondly, there is the new trend to combine computer and library services, both in the dormitories and in new academic buildings. The North University Building, because of its location, its limited physical first-floor possibilities and its uncertain future, may not figure much longer in ITD's continuously evolving plans to balance supply and demand in an era of dramatic technological change.

In this section, I have tried, with Margaret's help, to capture a sense of the activities within the *Computing Resource Site* and how those activities are seen by a part-time consultant, its team leader, and the off-site manager. Overall, the ITD provides the key electronic infrastructure for a major research university, and does so as a managerial and increasingly business-like operation. The December 17, 1996 issue of *The University Record*, the official weekly, carried a news item from ITD:

> On Jan. 6, all faculty, staff and students will need sufficient funds in their U-M Computing Environment (UMCE) accounts in order to continue to use computing services. If there are insufficient funds at the beginning of each month, access to all services subscribed to will be temporarily suspended until additional funding is arranged.

Of the sites that Liz manages, NUBS is, as the foregoing has intimated, the most awkward in physical terms for user-consultant relationships. Compare, for example, NUBS with Genevieve Patthey-Chavez's (1994) description of a computer lab at the University of Southern California:

> In the lab, a consultant area consisting of four desks arranged into a rectangle against a central partitioning wall occupied center stage: it was in one's path the moment one walked in the door . . . Their area had the attributes of a "lab square" (akin to a town square) at the center of the lab's continuous swirl of activity, a "square" from which user access to the lab and to the lab's material and intellectual wealth was controlled and dispensed. (pp. 82–83)

Although such arrangements characterize the recent custom-built sites such as Angell Hall, no such luck at NUBS. Even so, Tung and his team do their best to cope with user problems, even as special services move out apparently unbeknownst to many users. Darcy seems something of a "new breed" consultant, partly because she is female, and partly because—as the extracts from her interview reveal—she is communicatively gifted. Tung also, as we have seen, can on occasion produce a virtuoso set of instructions. Such skills are surely needed in the first-floor pressure cooker of the North University Building.

FOR THE LONG HAUL:
COLLECTIONS AND LOANS IN THE HERBARIUM

> They sit at their tables doing their work, not paying attention to the fact that the world outside their windows is moving at a faster pace. (Yu-Ying, in conversation)

The northeast corner of the Herbarium floor in the main building contains a large number of worktables, mostly facing the extensive windows for better light, a collection of tall filing cabinets largely containing specimens, some areas of open shelving, either for housing packing materials or for holding specimens for the attention of the curators, plus sundry other pieces of old-fashioned furniture. The general impression is somewhat spartan, utilitarian, and factory-like. Along with the other relics of the past like the freight elevator, this open "workroom" area is surely reminiscent of what the building must have been like before the transformations that have been regularly taking place over the last 30 years. That is not to say that all signs of modernity are missing; for example, the area also contains two computers, one on the Collection Manager's desk, and the other near a card index close to the doorway to the annex. This second computer is the machine that now documents most of the inflows and outflows of the Herbarium collections of vascular plants, the most visible and active component of its holdings. (Other smaller groups such as fungi are handled somewhat differently and will not be discussed.)

At the time of our visits in January–February 1996, there were five people working in the vascular plant workroom area on a regular basis. There was Rich, the Collections Manager and a professional botanist (photo 20); Bev, a vascular plant technician with a degree in Botany and Herbarium experience from Michigan State University; and three *mounters*, Betty, Jan, and Linda (see photo 7). Some temporary assistance is also provided via work-study students or the occasional employment of a graduate research assistant. Curators seem to pass through the workroom on a regular basis. For example, during the tape-recorded part of our first interview with Rich (lasting about 30 minutes), Yu-Ying and I noted that Ed came and went once and Tony did so twice. These passages provide a very noticeable punctuation on the audio-tape because the door to the "out back" bangs very loudly whenever anybody has gone through it. "Out back" is the place where the specimens are stored; it occupies much

Photo 20. Rich (and assistant) packing a loan.

of the second floor of the annex extension to the main building, and at this juncture in an earlier draft Rich wrote the marginal comment "That's exactly what I call it!", although both he and I also have heard it referred to as "the range."

In 1995, a long-cherished dream of the Herbarium was realized when a major renovation of their "specimen library" was completed at a cost of close to $1 million. The centerpiece of this renovation is *The Compactor*, a massive electrically driven system of 29 rows of filing cabinets (each row consisting of 32–34 tall cabinets). These lines of cabinets run back and forth on rails, opening and closing spaces between the rows as and when they are needed. Rich says that *The Compactor* system has resulted in a space saving of 75% over the previous non-mobile setup in the same floor space.

The Compactor now houses the Herbarium collection of approximately 1.1 million specimens of vascular plants, plus its smaller collections of bryophytes (mosses), lichens, and algae (photo 21). The more three-dimensional specimens such as fruits and fungi are stored elsewhere, typically in boxes (photo 22). Each cabinet opens up to reveal a double column of deep pigeonholes containing a number of folders, except that the two uppermost ones may be left empty to facilitate the incorporation of future accessions. Each folder contains one or more specimen sheets of the same species. The specimen sheets, and hence the accompanying folders, are slightly unusual in size, being 11½ × 16½ inches. This size is apparently standard for all U.S. herbaria, except for the New York State Museum.

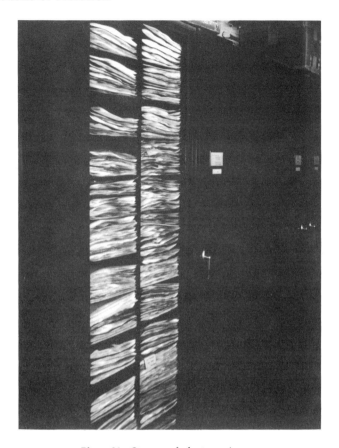

Photo 21. Storage of plant specimens.

(Some European herbaria use "oversize" sheets and special arrangements have to be made for their storage.) At Michigan, sheets are ordered in batches of 30,000 (enough for a few years) and then the sheets are locally printed with the university seal at the center-top. In this context, the proud prominence in the seal of the university's founding in 1817 seems more than usually appropriate, inasmuch as plant-collection has been going on at the university pretty well ever since it moved from Detroit to Ann Arbor in 1837.

The plant specimens are arranged by plant family. Within each family, genera are arranged alphabetically, and sorted geographically. By way of illustration, we can take the case of the complex genus *Solidago*, or goldenrods. Michigan specimens come first in alphabetical species order, followed by the rest of the US and Canada; all these are placed within manila folders. Then come the red folders for Latin America, and finally the blue folders for the rest of the world (in biological parlance "The Old World").

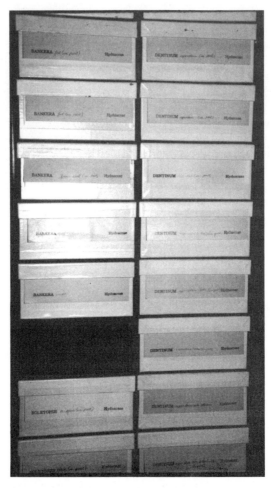

Photo 22. Storage of fungi.

Although there are, according to Rich and Tony, a few specimens from the late 1700s, the first major assemblage occurred in the years between 1837 and 1840 as a result of pioneering work in Michigan by Douglass Houghton and others. According to Voss (1972), "When Michigan became a state in 1837, the first act of the legislature was to establish a geological survey, which was to include botanical and zoological studies" (p. 12). Another period of major accessions occurred in the 1930s and 1940s, following important expeditions to places like Sumatra (recall the reference to plants from Sumatra in the extract from *The Michigan Alumnus* in chapter 1), Borneo, and Mexico. Aside from these exceptional periods, addition of material continues to be an ongoing process, and Rich estimates that currently accessions of specimens are running at about 10,000 a year. When I asked him how long it would be before the Compactor ran out of space for new specimens, he replied that the system was designed for a 15–20 year window of expansion, but he now thought that the lower limit was "more realistic."

According to Rich, Michigan has a reputation for being "very carefully curated for many years," and Bill, who (as we will see) takes the curating side of his work "very seriously," is clearly determined to maintain the tradition associated with Rogers McVaugh, now an octogenarian professor emeritus, but still Bill's primary collaborator on the *Flora Novo-Galiciana* and who still comes to work in the Herbarium for two periods a year from his present home in North Carolina. Rich also sees himself very much as an upholder and defender of this tradition, and hence strives to balance the traditional curatorial roles of specimen care and assistance to researchers with the newer ones of introducing computerized tracking systems and the like. Indeed, Rich's desire not to "skew the resources" unnecessarily both largely coincides with and reinforces Bill's thinking on these matters. Here, for instance, is Bill in interview on computerized management systems:

> . . . in some cases, not here, but in some herbaria, excessive concern with things like that has led people to paying too much attention to the management system and not enough to things that are important like how well the specimens are cared for. But anywhere of course computers can become an excuse for filling your day.

Given its size and its specialized holdings, the Herbarium, like any "library," receives a number of visitors who wish to review and study certain specimens. Rich estimates this traffic as running at 80–100 visitors a year, mostly day trips from botanists within driving distance, but some for longer periods and from farther away. At the time of our first visit to the Workroom, for example, there was a visitor from Australia who was spending several days in the Herbarium. All visits are carefully recorded in a "guest book," because being able to demonstrate and document that the herbarium is being used by outsiders is of value when applying for grants. Only occasionally, Rich says, will a visitor come across material that he or she will then ask to be loaned "for further study." Thus, "browsing" is not a particularly common or standard method of initiating a loan request.

Although these visitors have their place in the daily and weekly activities of the workroom and "out back," a couple of visitors per week does not add up to a time-consuming service, especially as most, after a quick introduction, can be left to their own devices. (In fact, the ELI Library probably has more visitors per year from off-campus, especially if graduate students from Eastern Michigan University are included.) Rather, the *raison d'être* for the collections staff lies elsewhere—dealing

with exchanges of specimens, and with accessions, but, as much as anything else, with loans of material. On January 22, 1996, the second or
"curatorial" computer, as it is known, recorded that there were 538 loans
outstanding, adding up to a grand total of some 42,679 sheets, or about
4% of the total stock. It is this loan processing that constitutes a major
activity and so deserves closer attention. Needless to say, there are other
important activities that include the accessions that I have already mentioned, the processing of Michigan's duplicate specimens for exchange
with other collections, and the handling of material requested from elsewhere by the Michigan Herbarium, but these will not be explored in
detail. In fact, this last activity can be broadly conceived of as a mirror
image of the process to be described next.

Although E-mail is starting to be used more, typical requests come in
the form of formal letters addressed to "Dr. Anderson," "The Director,"
or "The (Head) Curator." Bill reviews these for a couple of reasons; he
may know of an ongoing research project within the Herbarium that
might make a particular loan awkward at the particular moment of
request; or there may be questions about a particular institution. For
instance, in summer 1995, attempts were made to find out more about a
Korean university that had requested material but was not listed in the
latest 1990 edition of the *Index Herbariorum* or in its supplements and
updates published in the journal *Taxon*. The Index, in this latest edition,
is essentially a 700-page annotated listing of all the world's herbaria (the
University of Michigan entry is discussed later). Correspondence and
discussion with the current editor at the New York Botanical Garden
eventually established the *bona fides* of the requesting institution, and the
loan was duly sent.

Bill, in the letters I have seen, approves each loan by writing a neat
"OK WRA" in the left margin of the letter and then passes it along to
Rich. On January 22, 1996, Rich was looking at two such letters he had
received from Bill, and he was also in the process of putting together a
major loan request of some 2,100 sheets for the University of Alabama
that had already occupied several days.

The first letter, dated January 9th, was from the "Keeper of the Herbarium" at the Royal Botanical Gardens at Kew in England, the "body"
of which ran as follows:

> My colleague Dr T＿＿ is working on a revision of the genus *Inga* . . . , and
> I should like to request a loan of type specimens of this group, which are
> located in your herbarium. The relevant specimens are listed on the attached
> sheet.
>
> Thanking you for your collaboration.
>
> (attached sheet)

MICH.
1) Inga andersonii McVaugh, Fl. Novo-Galiciana 5: 178 (1987). Type. Mexico, El Tuito, E of Cabo Corrientes, *Anderson & Anderson 6058* (holotype MICH).

The compressed and—to outsiders—probably enigmatic nature of texts like those in this attachment is discussed in the next chapter. Here I focus more on the hierarchical system apparently in place whereby it is "the keeper" who writes to "the head curator" on behalf of a colleague for the loan of a single specimen. Although part of the explanation may lie in the widespread perception that large science (and engineering) departments are more hierachically structured than other academic units, the main reason for inter-institutional rather than inter-individual arrangements is once again due to the glacial time-scales of systematic botany. Individuals may move, retire, or die, but institutions only rarely do any of these things.

Michigan's general policy is to grant loans initially for two years, and also to grant extensions upon request. Given this unwonted *generosity* in length of loan, at least when set against standard library practice, the need for institutional responsibility makes further sense. A useful illustration of this also occurred in January 1996, when the following letter, dated the 17th, reached Rich (via Bill) from a research unit in the USDA:

> Dear Director,
>
> The loan number 2770 of grasses sent for the research program of Dr R____ is being returned to you. We thank you very much for the loan of this material.
>
> Dr R____ is no longer affiliated with this Laboratory. His new address is:
> ____
>
> If you have any questions regarding the specimens, please contact him. Thank you.

In fact, 2770 was a loan originally dispatched on March 3, 1992, with a partial return of 75 of the 194 sheets on January 27, 1995 (those dealing with Mexico and the U.S., the former being called back for a revision of one of the early volumes of the *Flora Novo-Galiciana* and to cater for a number of anticipated Mexican visitors). The remaining sheets were dispatched on January 11, 1996, having been "out" for just under four years. However, it transpires that the keeping of a loan for this length of time is in no way perceived of as being excessively dilatory or inconsiderate. Rich showed us the computer listing for "Outgoing loans sent during or before 1995—not returned." The oldest three entries were for loans numbered 326, 437, and 478 with "sent" dates of December 4, 1953, July 17, 1958, and September 28, 1959. In the first case, only two out of 85 sheets were retained after the main return on November 7, 1990—even so, the bulk of the material had been on loan for 37 years! In the second case, the loan was a small and local one to a professor who is still active on campus. However, the 1959 loan consisted of 290 sheets sent to central Europe, of which as many as 80 are still being "retained" as of this writing (early 1996). Rich explained that a now-elderly scholar there had been working on a flora of a Middle East region for many years but without any secretarial help. No wonder, then, that institutions have to assume responsibility for loans to their human members because these loans can apparently extend, if only in exceptional cases, over a person's working lifetime, and doubtless occasionally even beyond that lifetime. When Rich, Yu-Ying, and I reached this point in a discussion on an earlier draft, Rich volunteered the instance of a botanist at Oxford who had had a long-standing loan of neo-tropical pine material; when the botanist passed away, a renewal request came, through the usual official channels, from *somebody else* at Oxford who wished to retain the material because he planned to "continue the work" of his now-deceased colleague.

The second letter Rich was pondering that cold January day had come from the Herbarium Curator at a small university in the Texas State University System. The body reads as follows:

A____ is pursuing an M.S. degree in Biology here at ____ State University, and doing research on the genus *Hexalectris* (Orchidaceae). To aid in this study, we would like to borrow the following specimens:

Hexalectris grandiflora (A. Rich & Gal.) L.O. Wms.
Corallorhiza grandiflora A. Rich & Gal.
Hexalectris mexicana Greenm.

(4 more species listed with synonyms, as above)

All specimens sent on loan will be treated with great care, stored in insect-proof cases, and returned promptly with the annotations at the conclusion of the study. Thank you very much for your valuable assistance.

Rich observed that the final paragraph was "standard language," going on to mention that the greatest threat to herbarium specimens comes from insects, particularly from the small cigarette beetle, rather than from humidity, light, temperature, or handling. Presumably the Herbarium Keeper at the world-famous Kew Gardens did not feel such assurances would be necessary; equally presumably, the curator at a small Texas institution writing on behalf of a masters student felt otherwise.

Rich thinks the requests in these two letters will be "easy." In the Kew case, "it turns out they want only one type; we go to the one spot for one specimen, then we are done." In the Texas case, "they're asking for material within one genus, but since they gave us synonyms, we wind up looking for all possible specimens to make sure we have all the materials they really want to have." At this juncture, Rich stresses the fact that they send *everything* they have, and contrasts this policy with some other herbaria which "might keep back one or two sheets for so-called reference purposes." He further notes that "they may not even tell *the researchers* that they've done that, or even what the sheets are." Rich's unwontedly caustic criticism of such practices as well as his contrastive stress on *researchers* confirmed my sense that this particular Collections Manager wanted as full a circulation of material as possible, even though such a policy might temporarily inconvenience on-site users, whether regular members or visitors.

The specimens are retrieved from "out back" by either Rich or Bev, although at the time of this writing they had hopes of being able to recruit a third member of the team. When retrieved, the collections are *processed*, by which Rich means that they are carefully examined for defects in mounting, physical damage, or other faults. This "processing" epitomizes the *esprit de corps* of the Workroom. Rich's use of what linguists call a "Cleft Construction" (italicized in the following quote) underscores the significance of the following statement for himself and those he works with: "*There's one thing we want to do*; we want the materials sent out in good condition." He went on to add that they also wanted the materials to arrive in equally good condition, thus implying that skill and care in packaging also had an important role to play. The preparation of sheets for loan starts with Bev who sits at her own bench a little inward and at right angles to the trio of *mounters* who sit together at their worktables by the east window. Bev looks through the pulled sheets; if they are fine, she puts them to one side, and if they need only minor repairs, she deals with them herself. If they need remounting and/or other major work, she puts them in a different place. When a pile is made up, "off to the mounters they go." Major problems can arise from the plant material itself, its loose or broken attachment, or from the mounting sheet, especially as older sheets may have deteriorated because of their higher acid content.

To me personally, many of the (older) specimen sheets have immediate aesthetic appeal, although I suspect some influence in this regard from my long-standing hobbyist interest in 19th-century postal history envelopes from British post offices in Hong Kong and China, with their subtly hued Victorian stamps, old handwriting, and many postal markings often in a range of colors. So, at least for me, these sheets are similarly impressive artifacts from an earlier time. The faded yellows, greens, and browns of the actual dried plant material are as soft on the eye as the vegetable dyes of antique oriental carpets or the first postage stamps. The arrangement on the page of the various specimen parts often achieves a fine illustrator-like balance and harmony, while the looping swirls of longer elements such as fronds can create a sense of quite unsuspected artistic liveliness. The sheet itself may have other seals beyond that of Michigan, as a consequence of donation or exchange, and one or more *annotations* pointing to identification or re-identification, location, date, collector, and so forth, in older specimens written in India ink by a medley of crabbed, spidery, and copperplate hands.

Alas time, perhaps accelerated by the cigarette beetle, has often taken its toll, especially for specimens that are now about to go on journeys as envoys of the Herbarium's curatorial care. Some, as we have seen, may need remounting altogether; many others will require reglueing, new linen "straps," or new thread to hold down the thicker elements like twigs, while packets may need to be attached to the sheets to collect bits of material that fall off during handling; as Linda noted in interview, "we never throw anything away. . . ." Observing the mounters de-assembling and re-assembling specimens is to observe deftness, speed, and surety of touch. But as the products get finished, one can observe something else. When I commented—in recorded interview—on the attractiveness of the remounted specimens, Rich observed:

> Yes. And that's one of the things that the mounters have as part of their charge, if you may call it that. You do want to add some aesthetics to it. You want to make sure that you have the material that the researcher is likely to want to examine visible. The flowers and fruits have to be, so to say, right side up. And you want to make sure both leaf surfaces, if at all possible, are visible. So you want to make sure the researcher has what they [sic] need available. But if you can add some aesthetics to the situation then that's perfectly appropriate.

The mounters have their own distinctive perspectives on these processes and on their roles within them. First, there is satisfaction in the materials they use. Here are Linda and Betty in interview:

Linda: The glue we use now—I guess it is one of the things we are noted for because it maintains itself . . . it doesn't depreciate. However it is, when we put it on, it stays stuck.

Betty: We also use the best materials, the paper is the best we can buy, and the thread; all of the materials that we use are the best that they can find . . . and not all universities use that.

Later, Betty attested to the value of this when, on pointing to a specimen, she remarked, "We make it last a hundred years; they are supposed to last a hundred years." Linda also saw the benefits of the improved materials:

Now we have the ability to make the sedges look as well as, say, the plants of Brazil or Dr Anderson's specimens, and that's very important to me.

When Yu-Ying interviewed the mounters the conversation returned again and again to what Rich referred to as "the bit of aesthetics" as part of their charge. Here is a typical extract from Linda on this limited but important room for maneuver:

> There are some procedures that are standard, but once you get those you can more or less do it your way. You can have your own style and your own personality, but there are some standard things you do and don't do. You try not to let the specimen hang over the sides. Another rule of thumb is always . . . to put the packet opening on the inside. We never cover up the label. We always try to show both sides of the specimen. We try not to cover the stamp; that is important so that they can see it's the University of Michigan . . . You always like to leave something in the packet so they can study it.

Beyond that, though:

> You just develop your own style. Here [points to specimen] it's optional. I could have put a strap across there, but personally I would stitch it right there and put straps up here, while someone else may put a stitch here and no straps and just glue it down. So it varies . . . we have room to play with.

If a problem or doubt arises, there is also room for consultation. Linda, one more time on a problem:

> Usually we pass it among each other, but if there is something we don't know we go and ask Tony. That's one thing I like—we all tend to aid each other. If Betty sees something on the sheet she would have done differently, she might say "Well, Lin, I would have done such-and-such" . . . and that's acceptable.

A question arises as to how this craft-knowledge, this felt sense of how to proceed, is acquired, and the answer would seem to be a prototypical instance of Lave and Wenger's (1991) depiction of "legitimate peripheral participation":

> . . . a way to speak about the relations between newcomers and old-timers, and about activities, identities, artifacts, and communities of practice. It concerns the process by which newcomers become part of a community of practice. A person's intentions to learn are engaged and the meaning of learning is configured through the process of becoming a full participant in a sociocultural practice. (p. 29)

Thus, Linda sees herself as in the middle position of this process: "She [referring to Betty] was here before I was, and they have passed it down, and I am passing it down [referring to Jan], as rules of thumb." And a little later, she added:

> The professors don't know too much about mounting (laughter); I think we know quite a bit more than they do, and they have even said that. . . .

Finally, there are also some particular sensitivities that have to be taken into account and that also have to be incorporated into the folklore of the Workroom. Here is a nice example:

> Dr. Anderson, if I may use his name, well I have done it (laughs), doesn't particularly care for a lot of glue under your flowers and that's something we all know and try to adjust to . . . and there are particulars like that. . . .

As I hope the preceding paragraphs have shown, there is a distinctive *esprit de corps* among the mounters, who are typically high-school graduates, which gives meaning and satisfaction to their occupational roles. They have, as it were, their rightful and responsible place within the complex web of the Herbarium's transactional activities, and within the textwork that both manages those activities and provides the ultimate justification for their efforts. Perhaps Betty, the most experienced mounter, summed it up best when she said, "All three of us take great pride in doing this job; it's an art."

Progress in preparing a loan is naturally dependent on the state of the material, and this state has, at first sight, an odd and paradoxical relationship with its amount of use. It transpires that the more a particular set of collections is used, and especially loaned, the better its condition is actually likely to be. In effect, this is a natural consequence of the fact that it will have received more frequent scrutiny and repair. So, according to Rich, the much consulted and traveled Mexican material is generally "right up to snuff," while certain "old world" sections may never have gone out on loan and may, as a result, require a lot of work, including considerable remounting.

There is here both an interesting parallel and useful contrast with the "cottage industry" in the ELI (which was only abandoned in late 1996) of affixing small diagonally trimmed lengths of maize and blue ribbons (the university colors) under the gold university seal that adorns each of the "Proficiency Certificates" in English that the Testing Division awards every year to candidates from around the world. As there are several thousand of these issued per annum, there were months of the year when a call went out in the Testing Division for "all hands." Attempts to get rid of this old-fashioned craftwork were long unsuccessful. On the one hand, nobody was ever able to locate a machine to do the job; on the other, appeals to *tradition* (and fears of what new recipients might think if, in contrast to their predecessors, they were to receive "ribbonless" certificates) long prevailed. Unlike the Herbarium, however, and true to the different *cultures* of the two floors, in the ELI all members of the Division used to pitch in for this chore, from the Associate Director in charge and the Research Associate responsible for the Proficiency test, to the part-time undergraduate research assistants, and to the Certificate secretary. But in the Herbarium, the mounters get to do the mounting because they are, as Rich says, "most proficient" at it.

When the specimen sheets are done and ready for dispatch, they are placed within double newspaper sheets—the Herbarium is a keen collector of old newspapers of the right size such as *The University Record*. Bundles of newspaper-wrapped specimens a few inches thick are then placed within sheets of cardboard and tied with tapes. These packets are overwrapped with brown paper and finally packed in boxes for dispatch. The packers make sure that the cardboard overlaps the sheets so that no corner damage can occur, a practice which Rich again notes is not universally followed by herbaria elsewhere. The final stage in the process is reached when a triplicate form is typed up giving details of the loan: number of packages, number of sheets, brief descriptions of specimens, loan number (the Kew number is, in fact, 3065), and various other bits and pieces such as whether the loan is being sent by surface or air mail. The Herbarium retains the top, white copy. The instructions for the blue copy are: "Please sign and return immediately upon receipt of the material"; and for the pink copy:

> Retain for your records. In the case of a loan, the pink copy should be mailed under separate cover when the specimens are returned. It will be returned to you when the returned loan has been received and checked, indicating cancellation of the loan.

The preceding account is my reading of the Herbarium's system for outgoing loans. According to Rich, these normally number from 60 to 90 a year, ranging in size from a single specimen (as in the Kew request) to upwards of 2,000 sheets (as in the Alabama request). Rich reckons that around three quarters are sent to the United States or Canada; the rest, in declining order, go to Latin America (especially Mexico), Europe (especially Britain and Germany), and Asia (especially Korea). The standard procedure is for the loaning herbarium to pay for the outward freight (in Michigan's case out of its regular Current Account), and for the receiving institution to pay for the return costs. As a result, one of Rich's responsibilities is to follow developments in postal rates looking for the best deal (e.g., The United States Postal Service's "library rate" versus United Parcel Service's competitive rates with the advantages of insurance and "tracking"). In his seven years at the Herbarium, Rich notes with some relief that only two loan packages have gone irretrievably astray—half of a dispatch to Kansas in 1989, and one small two-sheet loan to Canada. He feels that "we've been fortunate so far," but it does not take a genius to note that the workroom's meticulous packaging and labeling have likely contributed to this excellent record. However, matters are not so simple with lending and borrowing "across the oceans" because of the much higher postage costs. One quasi-inevitable consequence is that certain cash-strapped Third World herbaria, such as the new one in El Salvador, require loan-requesters to pay postage both ways—a development that Rich understands and has some sympathy with.

If the foregoing accounts for how the Herbarium handles loan requests once they are received, it does not yet explain how a particular researcher might target the University of Michigan in the first place. For that we need first to return to the standard reference work, the *Index Herbariorum*, which lists the strengths of each collection. Here are selected extracts for "ANN ARBOR (MICH): Herbarium, University of Michigan," leaving aside the names and addresses of the people involved:

> *Status*: State university.
>
> *Foundation*: 1837. *Number of specimens*: 1 613 500.
>
> *Herbarium*: Worldwide, especially temperate North America; marine algae of e. North America, West Indies, Alaska, and Pacific islands; bryophytes of tropical America; vascular plants of n. South America, Mexico, sw. Pacific region, and se. Asia.
>
> *Important collections*: M. Bang, H. H. Bartlett, D. V. Baxter, D. E. Breedlove (plus 56 other names of collectors including D. Houghton, W. N. Koelz and R. McVaugh).
>
> *Exchange available*: From areas and groups of MICH specialization, by arrangement with appropriate curator. *Wanted*: Same.
>
> *Associated garden*: Matthaei Botanical Gardens, University of Michigan, . . .
>
> *Periodical and serial works*: Contributions from the University of Michigan Herbarium. Flora Novo-Galiciana. (*Index Herbariorum*, 8th ed., 1990, pp. 351–352)

Although Bill claimed in interview that Michigan was a "mid-size" herbarium, this strikes me as being a slight understatement. To be sure, there were in the eighth edition seven herbaria listed with collections with five million or more specimens. In order, and with their date of foundation, these were: Muséum National d'Histoire Naturelle, Paris (1635); Royal Botanical Gardens, Kew (1841); Komarov Botanical Institute, Leningrad (1823); Swedish Museum of Natural History, Stockholm (1739); New York Botanical Gardens, New York (1891); The Natural History Museum, London (1753); and the Conservatoire et Jardin Botaniques, Geneva (1864). On the other hand, Michigan is the seventh largest herbarium in the United States, and has the third largest U.S. university collection, only exceeded by Harvard and by the University of California, Berkeley. It is comparable in size to national collections in countries such as Scotland, China, Hungary, and Indonesia.

Consulting the *Index* is therefore one possible first move in targeting source material. Rich notes, however, that the large herbaria tend to have established specialized collections mainly created by the interests of past and sometimes long-past curators. For genera or species that are known or thought likely to occur in particular areas, it often makes sense to contact "very small places" in the vicinity, especially because they are likely to possess much more recent material. Clearly, intuition, "local knowledge" in the Geertzian sense, contacts, and networking also all play their part in the search process.

This section has offered an account of what is, at present, a five-person *community of practice* that supports and upholds the mission and reputation of the Herbarium's collection of vascular plants. Over this activity lies the organizing hand of the Director, Bill. Although, according to Tony, "there is really not a rigid chain of command," next comes Tony, whose curatorial office is not inadvertently nearest to the workroom, and who operates as some kind of "administrative curator" insofar as he has responsibility for personnel matters in the workroom. Then there is Rich, the Collections Manager, then Bev, and finally Betty, Jan, and Linda along with intermittent student assistants.

Rich and Bev strike Yu-Ying and me as having quiet and unassertive personalities (certainly they stand in contrast to Tony's ebullience or Bill's bursts of acerbic eloquence in college-wide fora such as faculty meetings), but equally, by either nature or nurture, they have that friendliness and helpfulness which, as an import myself, I have come to associate with the Midwest. The current mounters, in contrast, tend to form a more riotous subgroup, as indeed we discovered from their background laughter and camaraderie which infiltrated the tape of the recorded session with Rich, and this perhaps as a way of compensating for the finicky manual work they continuously undertake. Although this group as a whole processes new material and takes initial care of incoming loans, it seems pretty clear that their sense of achievement lies primarily in the *quality* of the outgoing product: its completeness (with nothing held back for local convenience), the meticulous (re)preparation of sheets that do not meet the high standard this Herbarium sets for itself, and the efforts that go into the safe arrival of a sturdy package. The system clearly works, but in a rather old-fashioned and perhaps patriarchal way. Rich fully concurs with this last comment, even if he consistently "mucks in" by doing a fair part of the packaging himself.

In the end, even beyond Bill and extending long into the past, there exists a lingering but powerful curatorial tradition here, an "invisible hand" of care for the vascular plants and of attention to traditional detail and accuracy. The concern for this last emerges when it becomes clear that the commitment to loaning out the material has its own peculiar and discipline-specific compensations:

> One of the things that the Herbarium really gets out of this loan activity is that the specialist looks at the specimen, and the specialist puts a name on it. Now, we have *a more valuable specimen* because we have got an authority to say what this specimen really is. (Rich, in interview; italics added)

These minute accretions of knowledge tokens, as witnessed by expert hand-written nominal annotations, thus underpin, if perhaps precariously at the end of the 20th century, the whole laborious merry-go-round of assembling, repairing, dispatching, receiving, unpacking, checking, and re-integrating loans. In Giddens' sense (1979, 1984), it is activities of this kind that, in their recursiveness, in their sedimentation through time, and in their slow evolution through long practitioner experience, bring human agency and institutional structure together. Further, these are activities that form cycles wherein the textual, visual, and physical components have their standardized precursors and successors (collection, mounting, inspection, study, annotation, and so on) and wherein the activities of the team are hierarchically distributed to maximize expertise in the service of the profession. In effect, these iterative activities *structurate* the service roles and purposes of this—and other herbaria—and *operationalize* the physical movement of data so that botanical works can be properly and competently composed.

Although there is much that is traditional about the procedures of "collections and loans," there is also change and evolution. The arrival of the massive compactor with its complex electronic circuitry is the most visible symbol of this, but also, as Tony notes, the Herbarium has been modifying its methods in order to accommodate the databasing of records and the computer printing of forms and reports. Furthermore, even the traditional apparatus used principally by the mounters has undergone certain changes. The use of small sandbags for pressing specimens was apparently an innovation brought in by Tony's predecessor, and my draft reference to the mounters' spraying apparatus brought forth this enthusiastic marginal note from Tony:

Actually, the spray method of glueing is a more or less radical recent innovation. Most herbarium staff glue labels only by hand. Bill and I worked out this method some years ago.

However, for radical innovation we perhaps should look to Bob, the technology-minded mycological curator, with his listing of the fungi collections by late 1995 already universally accessible—to those in the know—on his Home Page.

Addendum: The Long Story of Loan 478

In the main body of this section, I made brief reference to a 1959 loan to central Europe. I would like to close the section by filling out the details of this loan as far as I am able (the European botanist declined to give me permission to quote his correspondence). These details give some added perspective to the *modus operandi* described earlier; they show, for example, how the slow and regular rhythms of loans can, on occasion, decelerate to virtually imperceptible movement. But equally they show how the unruffled tenor of scholarly curatorial correspondence prevails.

As intimated, our long story starts with a correspondence in 1959 between the vascular plant curator at Michigan and an important European scholar regarding plant collections made in the Middle East by one of the Herbarium's curators. By October 15 of that year, Michigan had everything ready. Here are the last three paragraphs of the letter written by Rogers McVaugh:

> The bulk of the shipment comprises a set of Dr K____'s recent . . . collections. As far as we are aware, we have sent you an example of every number, approximately 1800 in all. Except for the 290 mounted specimens listed on the inclosed invoice, these are all duplicates which you may retain at your pleasure. We should like to have lists of your identifications at your convenience. I realize that this may be a matter of some years.
>
> The 290 unicates have been mounted and sent to you as our loan no. 478. The loan is made for a period of two years as a matter of form. If you would prefer to return the loan a part at a time, as your identifications are completed, this will be quite satisfactory. Please sign and return the blue slip as soon as you have verified our count.
>
> We are very pleased at your interest in this collection, and we consider ourselves very fortunate to be able to contribute in small part to such an important floristic study as yours. I hope that you may find something of interest among the K____ material.

We see here everything that the previous section has led us to expect: generosity, the careful mounting of the loan specimens, the hope for enrichment (and payback) in the form of expert "identifications," the patient recognition that this may be "a matter of some years," and the modestly expressed faith in collaborative utility.

As it transpires, 50 of the 290 sheets were returned in the 1960s, and the next significant item in the file, is a letter from McVaugh dated September 23, 1968, apparently in response to an exchange of correspondence that is now missing. The last paragraph reads as follows:

> Thanks also for your note in response to my letter about our loan. We are glad to have you work over the . . . material of K____, and return it family by family as you finish with it. My letter was one of a series of routine inquiries, and was not intended to hurry you.

Everything in 1968 thus seems in order, at least according to the slow pace of botanical work, as the clarification of the routine nature of the inquiry attests. The years passed, and, according to a handwritten entry on the original 1959 invoice, by July 1986 the situation was as follows: "Total 184 ret'd; 106 still out."

However, as the remainder of the loan approached its 30th year, Tony, as Associate Curator, on January 13, 1988, wrote another letter:

> Dear Dr. ____
>
> We have been reviewing our undistributed duplicates at MICH over the past year, and one of the sets is . . . material of K____. The first set of this material was sent as a gift to you in 1959 with the hope that eventually you might provide names for the material. We would like to distribute the remainder of this valuable collection. Do you have lists of even partial identifications compiled for this material? If so, we would be grateful for whatever you could send us.
>
> You may be interested in knowing that Walter K____ is still alive and well, in his 92nd year. I visit him periodically at his home near Ann Arbor.

The *system* of adding value via authoritative specimen determination might seem not to be working in this particular case, and the reader, as I did originally, might interpret this letter as dangling the enticing "carrot" of further gifts of material in the hopes of extracting some names from Europe. This, however, is not the case. Tony is in fact referring to further specimens of species which had already been sent to Europe and did not need to be retained in Ann Arbor for reference (triplicates and quadruplicates and so on) and which would be enhanced by expert determinations. Rich's marginal note on my first draft at this point offers confirmation of this interpretation: "This was an attempt to move some of the boxes of duplicates that need determinations from our back wall to other herbaria." However, the request was politely declined, principally because of a complete absence of secretarial help throughout the many years of the Middle East flora project. Here the long story essentially ends, except for two things. One is the return of a further 25 "unicates" (what a nice new word!) in October 1988 and one more in May 1994, still leaving 80 outstanding. The other is that Rich, by February 1996, had been able to find the time to extract the names for about a quarter of the loaned specimens from the published volumes.

The story of loan 478 in fact presages some of the themes that will emerge in chapter 3. These include the constraints under which many systematic botanists conduct their unremitting endeavors. A connected theme is the difficulty of not underestimating "the time and energy" needed to complete a project. A third is the surprising number of systematic botanists who have immensely long professional lives, with publications that may span five or even six decades. But if there is one message behind this account of loan 478, it would be that the seemingly interminable delay in providing the promised determinations has not ended in acrimony and recrimination, or in any increasingly heated exchange of correspondence, let alone in any suggestion that noncompliance with this "gentlemen's agreement" might require MICH to ask for the return of the outstanding material. In the 37 years that have—as I now write—passed since 1959, the one moderated request for recompense (". . . we would be grateful for whatever you could send us.") occurred in Tony's letter of 1988. If Rogers McVaugh's original "a matter of some years" has dilated into a matter of some decades, then the rather formal collegiality in the letters continues to maintain harmony among a rather special, and mutually supportive, circle of scholars.

A TOP FLOOR TEST-MAKING CO-OPERATIVE

> If you can't quell an item writer's zest for invention, send that individual to more congenial pursuits, such as sculpture, gymnastics or erotic dance.
> W. James Popham
> [Notice on the door of Room 3025]

A Little Background and History

In some sense, institutional language teaching and language testing operations are closely intertwined, if only because practically all language departments assess the language proficiency of their own students at various times and for various purposes. At Michigan, for example, the ELI runs a re-evaluation of the academic English proficiency of most of the incoming international students, evaluates—in conjunction with academic departments—the readiness of overseas graduate students for instructor roles, and produces end-of-course assessments for most individuals who take its classes. In these respects, the ELI is little different from equivalent units in comparable institutions in the United States and, aside from the second role, from those in other countries. However, in terms of the size, structure, and reach of its testing operations, the ELI is decidedly unusual. On the first count, there are a number of individuals who spend at least half of their work week on testing matters (three research associates, four research assistants, and three clerical staff). On the second count, these individuals, plus one or two more part-time people, are constituted into a separate "Testing and Certification Division" within the Institute. And in terms of reach, this division provides substantial English language testing services to the world at large.

The first of the Michigan tests to be developed was called the Examination for the Certificate of Proficiency in English (ECPE), which started in 1953 and is today given annually at more than 75 test centers in 40 or so countries, with a recent average of about 7,000 candidates a year. As the test brochure says, "The certificate is recognized in several countries as official documentary evidence of advanced proficiency in the English language for education, employment, career advancement, and business purposes." The most popular test centers are currently Thessaloniki, Athens, São Paulo, Rio de Janeiro, and Barcelona (in that order). The ECPE consists (as do most other Michigan tests) of an oral interview, a written composition, and multiple-choice listening, grammar, vocabulary, and reading sections. Partly in response to requests from the Hellenic-American Union in Athens, The Testing Division in 1995 developed a lower-level intermediate test entitled the Certificate of Competency in English (ECCE), which in 1996 was taken by 4,362 candidates. A major motivation for this development was a wish to provide an *American* English alternative to the hugely successful Cambridge First Certificate.

There is a third test which, like the ECPE, has a long history, but took on its present format—and title—in 1985. This is the *Michigan English Language Assessment Battery*, commonly known as the MELAB. The MELAB is another advanced test, but with a different purpose, being designed "mainly for [international] students who are applying to universities in the United States and Canada where the language of instruction is English" (from the brochure). Apart from the oral interviews, these three tests are all scored in Ann Arbor, which then reports the results to candidates and/or sponsors and admission offices. Altogether, some 14,000 external tests were given in 1996.

As succinctly as I can tell it, the necessary historical background to this soft-money testing enterprise is as follows. The first Director of Testing was Robert Lado, a pioneering applied linguist and professor of English. With ELI director Charles Fries, who was the force behind the establishment of the ELI itself in 1941, Lado was determined to put foreign language teaching and testing on a "scientific" footing. The essentials of their approach were:

The target language usage (in this case, American English) should be descriptively analyzed, rather than prescriptively judged; linguistic comparison of languages would predict many areas of learner difficulty; language was speech, not writing; language learning, at least by adults, was more a matter of acquiring habits than of cognition; and, in consequence of all this, teachers should teach language by drills, pattern practice, and chorus work. Set against the prevailing "grammar-translation" tradition, this was revolutionary stuff, and Lado was soon applying these principles to "scientific" language tests. The first of these was the *Lado Test of Aural Comprehension* in 1946, and here the choice of *listening* for a first demonstration of the so-called new "oral" approach was surely not accidental. Besides, the nomenclature is itself revealing. This is specifically a "test," not some woolly, liberal-minded "examination." Further, the technical and latinate "aural comprehension" phraseology asserts an identification with the burgeoning social science ethos of that era. Finally, this was a graded, discrete-item *multiple-choice* test with spoken *prompts*, a format that much more easily permits the employment of statistics for analyzing individual items. And statistics to this day continue to play a significant part in the Testing Division's activities, as perhaps most prominently illustrated by the 75-page *MELAB Technical Manual* (Briggs & Dobson, 1994), which, inter alia, contains no fewer than 60 statistical tables.

About 10 years after Lado's original initiative, a full suite of skill-specific tests had been carefully assembled into "an English language test battery" (*battery* being a term presumably borrowed from IQ testing), which was administered to incoming foreign students at Michigan and, by arrangement, to those entering other universities. However, by the end of the 1950s, the number of foreign students coming to study in the United States began to escalate rapidly, and "In 1961, at the conference on Testing the English Proficiency of Foreign Students held in Washington, D.C., the need for a large-scale overseas testing program was affirmed and guidelines were agreed upon concerning the nature of the test with regard to content and administration" (Briggs & Dobson, 1994, p. 67). Although Mary, the longest-serving member of the Testing Division, had only recently started work as a secretary at that time, she carries the institutional memory of that event. As she said in interview:

> We knew that we were not equipped to handle such large numbers . . . we didn't have the set-up to handle such a big thing overseas and ETS sort of got the contract, as it were, and made a lot of money on it. No one else, I think, was prepared to do a test like that.

As many readers will know, the test that emerged was the Test of English as a Foreign Language, or TOEFL, produced by Educational Testing

Service (ETS), and currently taken by close to 500,000 candidates annually. These emerging levels of activity were clearly of at least one order of magnitude greater than the ELI could cope with; even so, some 35 years later, the institute still produces its ECPE examination and a TOEFL equivalent in the MELAB. Because the MELAB can be taken on an individual basis in more than 100 countries, including some where the TOEFL is not given (such as Iran), it thus operates in a niche market as a small but useful testing service appropriate to a major public research university with a strong tradition of quantitative work in the social sciences.

The final piece of scene-setting concerns the evolving—or perhaps devolving—organization of the Testing Division during the five decades of its existence. For the first 30 years or so the testing directors were faculty or staff with strong psychometric skills who undertook, sometimes with graduate student assistance, the statistical analysis, and edited the trial items produced by others. Although there was and is an ongoing tradition of moving through the ranks—Mary, for instance, moving from secretary to research assistant to research associate over a 30-year career— the Testing Division remained somewhat hierarchical with jobs being allocated according to individual capacities and abilities. But, as we will see, over the last decade or so, the division has developed a more co-operative style of working.

Thus, the Testing Division continues to consolidate a number of traditions, some starting many years ago and others of more recent origin. One of the former is a global network of local examiners and test centers. More recently, this has been supported by a regular *Testing Newsletter* which is designed—through profiles—to introduce examiners to each other and so create a sense of "family," and to keep the examiners and centers abreast of developments at HQ. A second long-standing tradition concerns the elaborate procedures for producing reliable and equatable *new forms* of its tests (see below), and for introducing modifications and improvements to its processes and products. A third is financial self-sufficiency in a *nonprofit* context, with any balance of income over expenditure going into the rainy-day fund, to support research projects and conference trips, and to provide research assistantships for doctoral students from the Program in Linguistics. A final and more recent development has been a professional self-sufficiency independent of professorial technical expertise, aside from the occasional short-term consultant.

Managing on Their Own

The Testing Division occupies a series of rooms clustered along the west and northwest sides of the third floor. When visitors turn left on entering the ELI, the first room they will meet is that currently occupied by Sarah, a research associate and the Associate Director for Testing, and by Judy, a PhD student and part-time research assistant. The next room has a "dutch" half-door and a wooden shingle proclaiming "ELI TESTING (MELAB)." This is where local MELAB test-takers present themselves in order to hand in applications, pay their fees and (nervously) collect their results. (The local test-takers, averaging 30 or so every two weeks, provide important information about experimental items that are mixed in with the standard items on which they are actually tested.) Behind the half-door are two secretaries, Sherlyn and Maria, who not only deal with this local traffic but also handle international and domestic MELABs, respectively. The adjoining small room now has no permanent staff, but houses the coffee machine, files, sets of "retired" tests for sale to institutions around the world for student placement or practice, and the fax machine mentioned in the previous chapter. The corner room is occupied by Mary, the long-serving research associate we have already met, the ECPE/ECCE secretary, Renata, and Vicky, a relatively new research assistant (RA), who graduated recently with a joint concentration in Linguistics and Russian. Finally, the largest room—around the corner—houses on a regular basis, Barbara, the third research associate, Theresa and Eric, research assistants, and less regularly Chris and Maria, who have joint appointments in testing and teaching and who have their main offices further down the northern corridor.

There are therefore up to 12 people who have to occupy these four rooms, and every few years the division upheaves itself and tries to reconfigure its cramped space to better advantage. Apart from the space issue, another problem is the one Sarah characterizes as that of "body parts." This derives from the fact that most of the RAs have part-time appointments of 50% or less. Sarah, who makes up meticulous short- and long-term schedules in order to ensure that all the different jobs get done within their appointed calendar round, has thus to struggle to get these *body parts* synchronized, especially for the purposes of collaborative test-making.

Because I am (at the time of writing) Director of the ELI, I also have official responsibility for the Testing Division, but this does not normally amount to very much. I look at the accounts, suggest the occasional initiative, fuss a bit about publicity and research image, try to keep the testing and teaching operations on the same side, write the occasional memo or letter, and do a certain amount of what might euphemistically be called "managing by wandering around." I used to serve as an occasional British informant since the item-writing teams do not want to end up with test sentences or utterances that might be correct in British usage but incorrect in American, or vice versa, but this role has now been largely taken over by Judy, who is also British. If I have a real purpose, it is as a trouble-shooter, either within the university, such as when a senior administrator gets exercised about some "problematic" international student graduate instructor, or externally, as with the simmering "turf war" between our two important testing centers in Greece over expansion into the more rural northern areas of the country and over control of the new ECCE examination. This disharmony, during 1995–1996, has involved rival delegations visiting Ann Arbor, the mediation of the American Embassy in Athens, communications with one of the Regents who happened to be an ex-colleague of the director of one of the operations, and a 3-week visit to Greece by Mary and Sarah to try to hammer out an agreement that would "stick"—not to mention floods of faxes from and to Ann Arbor and Athens and Thessaloniki. On these kinds of special occasions I may have some supportive part to play, especially as a swift and practiced writer of memos and administrative letters, but a tester I am not.

If one impetus toward a collaborative work-style has been the recent absence of major testing "authorities," another has been changes in computer usage. Here are Theresa's observations on this topic from her "notes from within," a 1995–1996 diary that I asked her to write:

> One observation I've had is that it is only relatively recently that the procedures for doing the statistical analysis on our tests have become "shared" knowledge. In the past, Mary handled all of it, and had programs that ran through MTS [the mainframe system], with complicated-seeming instructions (most of which were in her head). So no one else really knew what she did, since that was part of her job and she just did everything. I think with the fading away of the old MTS and with our increasing "expertise" in computers, and with the increase in the kind of tests we do, that finally it was time for Mary to pass on some of her knowledge. So now it seems more reasonably distributed.

Further signs of this migration would be the spread of computers throughout the division, modem-linked computers for the three research associates in their homes, and the specification and procurement of customized test analysis programs, such as ITEMAN from *Microcat Assessment Systems.*

So far, then, we see a group of people—all but one of whom are women—who prepare ESL tests for the university and for the world. They differ greatly in their years of experience in doing this; their names, current positions, and starting years are as follows:

Mary (Res. Associate)	1971 (but from 1960 as a secretary)
Sarah (Res. Associate)	1983
Barbara (Res. Associate)	1991 (but also 1972–1978 as an RA)
Theresa (RA)	1991 (but from 1986 as a secretary)
Maria (RA)	1987
Chris (RA)	1992

Judy (RA)	1994
Eric (RA)	1995 (but part-time ug RA 1993–1994)
Vicky (RA)	1996 (but part-time ug RA in 1995)

The three research associates (Barb, Mary, and Sarah) are the true professionals of the division and have the main responsibilities for training the research assistants. The lower-ranking research assistants (RAs) fall into a number of discrete categories. Theresa (who obtained an MA in Teaching ESL a few years ago), as well as Chris and Maria, have dual expertise as teachers and testers—in fact, all three have co-authored textbooks to their names. Although this duality has obvious benefits, it also means that the ebb and flow of their teaching involvments over the calendar year further contribute to the "body parts" problem. Judy is a doctoral student in Linguistics with a very useful special interest in nonnative speaker difficulties in academic listening. Eric and Vicky are part of a new tradition of recruiting bright and energetic Linguistics concentrators in their junior or senior year and then hoping that they will stay on for at least a year before going to graduate school. Previous incumbents have gone to the doctoral program in linguistics at Berkeley and to the joint linguistics and cognitive science program at MIT, and Eric is lining himself up for a JD in International Law. As we will see shortly, this mix of technical experience, pedagogical expertise, and youthful energy provides a further rationale for group test-making.

The Testing Division has links with most regions of the world, especially with bi-national cultural centers, USIA offices, and university examiners, and has a close relationship with the ELI's broader administrative and teaching activities (further discussed in chapter 4). The research associates are active members of the *Language Testing Research Colloquium*, an association of experts in the field spread around the world; indeed, as it happens Mary co-chaired the 1997 annual conference.

On the other hand, there are links and contacts that do not exist—although not necessarily for lack of trying. A few years ago the Division (and I) tried to make its exceptional resources more widely available to the "Big Ten" consortium, and looked toward a Michigan-inspired collaborative and standardized test for re-assessing the English of incoming graduate students who were not native speakers of English. Despite goodwill from many quarters, especially from Fred Davidson at the University of Illinois (one of the very few tenure-track ESL testing specialists in the Big Ten), the initiative foundered on the fact that the other institutions did not have the right people in the right quantities to even administer—let alone participate in creating—a more sophisticated re-assessment instrument. The exceptional nature of Michigan's facilities is nicely brought out by the first two subsections from Barb's 1995–1996 annual report:

[Glossary: AEE = Academic English Evaluation (the test for incoming students); GVR = Grammar, Vocabulary and Reading]

Analyzed data from the fall 1995 AEE tests. These analyses included:

- Using Microcat to item analyze the multiple choice listening and GVR tests and the 10 experimental reading questions (included in the Fall tests) in order to check on how the tests were functioning (for grads, for undergrads, and for the total group), to identify which of any items might be excluded to make room for more reading questions, and to identify which of the experimental reading items would be appropriate to include in the next version of the GVR test.
- Using Excel and SPSS to get profiles of undergraduate performance on each section of the AEE. This study suggested, among other things, that giving the AEE listening test to undergraduates is not necessary (as VERY few get a score low enough to suggest they need a listening class—[only 2 out of 171 got in the "class required" category by their test score]; only 3 of 171 got less than 37 listening questions correct), but as of now, I have not recommended that we eliminate the listening test for them because of the practical problems in implementing such a policy.

This memo-extract, which is typical enough of the full document, is syntactically pretty complex. There are but four sentences in the whole excerpt, three of them heavily abutted by nonfinite clauses, and the last even including a parenthesis within a parenthesis. As is common in each community of practice, new specialized verbs tend to pop up; in this excerpt, *to item analyze*. These linguistic features, as well as others such as acronyms, formal temporizers (as of now), purpose statements, and complex modals (*might be excluded*), serve to reinforce the underlying message of the text: Barb is engaged in a statistically driven and professionally scrupulous search for greater *efficiency in the testing instrument*. (The "practical problems" alluded to in its close refer to the fact that graduate and undergraduate testees may be present together in some smaller test administrations.) These kinds of detailed analyses require knowledge, experience, and above all *time*, and are just not possible in ESL operations that do not have the luxury of dedicated positions for testing specialists. On the other hand, the ghost of Robert Lado, who produced the ELI's and perhaps the world's first *scientific* foreign language test half a century previously, would likely be nodding in silent approval in the background.

We have just seen the collapse—or perhaps abeyance—of a regional initiative. Another area where contacts are unexpectedly slight, at least *prima facie*, is within the university itself. There are quite large numbers of people on campus with expertise in social science statistics, with a large concentration in the Institute for Social Research, and other significant groupings in places like the School of Education and the large and prominent Department of Psychology. Somehow, contacts do not flourish with such colleagues; partly, I suspect, because of a missing professorial "authority figure" and partly because of the special requirements of psychometric work in language testing, as opposed to the statistics used in survey work and experimental validation. However, it is not so much the case that the Testing and Certification Division isolates itself from the wider statistical community, but rather that the problems and solutions that interest this wider community do not coincide with the Division's "nitty-gritty" issues. As Barb wrote in a marginal note on an earlier draft at this juncture:

> People with experience in social science statistics are different from psychometricians. In spite of looking on and off for years, Mary, Sarah and I have not found anyone at UM to advise us or work with us.

On the other hand, the lack of collaboration between the Testing Division and the foreign language teaching departments on campus is explicable in the same way as was the collapse of a regional EAP testing initiative: the gulf between a sizeable grouping of dedicated testing professionals and the single, if enthusiastic, amateur test-giver from a language department.

Around the Table

In the middle section of this chapter I took some pains to describe the workroom set-up in the Herbarium, with the mounters at their tables, Rich in his corner, and the curators barging through on their way to and from "the range." In the Testing Division, the central operating area is neither Sarah nor Mary's office, but the midsized table that occupies the center of Room 3025. The rest of this room is largely taken up with desks and computers facing the walls, where Barb, Eric, Theresa, and others do much of their individual work. The table has a green cloth and is the depository for sundry candies, snacks, breads, and other offerings that form the centerpiece of the division's food-bringing and food-sharing rituals. Aside from parties, this is the only place in the building with this gastronomic character, because elsewhere food is largely hidden in discreet brown bags tucked away in backpacks, briefcases, and refrigerators. This table then gets lots of visits from Division "regulars" and "visitors" (including the Director) to see what might be available. Food is a common topic of conversation in Room 3025, and its denizens are resigned to being teased about it.

The table's real purpose, however, is as the traditional locale for meetings, especially meetings for the group-editing of test items. Yu-Ying and I asked Mary in interview how this group work came about. She replied:

> I'm trying to remember how this sort of group editing evolved, because it wasn't always that way. I think we used to just write items and hand them over to the testing director for editing, who would edit them and hand them back to the secretary to type up. It could be that we got into the group work when we had no testing head as an authority figure; so we said "let's do it ourselves." Since I don't trust my own individual judgment, we might as well use someone else's judgment. It seems more efficient. Rather than to pass items around from person to person to person for them to make comments on and then come out with, you know, some final version of something . . . actually it is more efficient than going down the "assembly line." Instead of an "assembly line" technique, we got ourselves a group.

This consistent teamwork has its own stresses that need to be countered. Here is one of them, again described by Mary in interview:

> You have not to be defensive or to have too big or fragile an ego, because when we do item editing or writing, we are very critical of the item. And as long as writers realize that we are not being critical of them, but the item, then that's fine. So, you know, we must be critical [laughs] about these items because we want *good* items.

However, as the number of people employed in testing has increased, and the number of tests grown, an informal kind of specialization has occurred. And here another kind of pressure has also played an important part. Here is an extract from Theresa's diary (1/17/1996):

> But in the writing process, time pressure is often a big consideration. But I don't think it means that the items are better or worse for it; it just means we often work up against deadlines, despite real efforts to plan and stay ahead. Although I'd say these days we are much better at the planning and distribution of work. Maybe here I can mention that last year we started working in mini-teams, based on item type, and that has helped focus and I think helped us make better items. For example, for this year's ECCE, Judy, Sarah and I have been responsible for Listening items. Other mini-groups have worked on reading, on speaking, and on gram/vocab. Of course anyone can contribute to the others, but this team set-up has reduced the sense of panic that often set in before deadlines.

This time pressure may need a word of explanation because, in a large-scale testing operation, it exerts its influence beyond the item writing process itself. Once the items for a particular test have been assembled, they need to be sent to the printer and proofed on return. The test booklets, answer sheets, and administrative instructions are then printed and re-turned to the division for shipping in appropriate quantities to the remote test sites. Like magazine editorial staff, everybody is aware of the need to have everything ready for the final "day," and of the slip-ups and delays that always threaten to intrude.

There seems, in fact, to be a remarkable consensus within the division about individuals' particular talents and abilities. Mary's meticulous sense of detail and documentation is widely seen as indispensable to the op-eration, as is her vast experience. It is Mary who can say "déjà vu" to a proffered item, remembering a similar one at some time in the fairly recent past. It is Mary who controls test security, an important aspect of the operation that is not easily appreciated by outsiders; for example, she is famous for spotting "ringers," that is, examinees who attempt to im-personate less-English-proficient others for either personal or pecuniary motives. She is also "GQ" (grammar queen), and "can wring more ques-tions out of a reading passage than anyone can" (according to Theresa's diary). Sarah is both a strong mid-term planner and a serious questioner of the rationale behind decisions to include certain kinds of test items and exclude others. She is interested in and knowledgeable about second language acquisition as well as test theory, and she has a strong ethical sense of the potential *impacts* of testing decisions on individual test-takers. Barbara is seen as having growing mastery of statistics and of their underlying logic, and as being a great item-editor. (Recall that Sarah and Barbara were the primary authors of the *MELAB Technical Manual.*) The-resa is recognized as having immense patience, so she can often be relied on to get some recalcitrant computer subprogram to work long after all the others have given up on it. According to the others, she also has a particular knack for finding reading passages, something Barb says she cannot do. However, Theresa assigns this ability to a particular kind of awareness that language testers have:

> We are not safe even at home. Once an item writer, everything we come across has item potential. So while reading at home the perfect passage might appear. (from her diary)

Despite his relatively short experience, Eric has developed a reputation for being very fast; as Mary said in interview, "he tends to do things magically—you know, sort of getting things done without seeming to be working on them." Of course, these individuals are not total paragons of virtue, and each doubtless has quirks that can prove exacerbating, but they are a group "who know each other and know how to work with each other and each knows their own strengths/weaknesses in item writing" (Theresa's diary).

Mini-team item writing is a somewhat chancy business, and most thoughts scribbled down on the ubiquitous half-sheets of scrap paper come to nothing tangible. Sometimes, a group will struggle with a reading passage or listening script for a half-day and then have to relegate it to the "cold storage" file-box as not being "doable" at the present time or for the present purpose. Sometimes, a promising item will be judged as being too easy or too difficult for the particular test. Sometimes it will be too similar to another item, or fall victim to "déjà vu" memories of earlier tests. When I asked Theresa to describe a "good" mini-team session, she instanced the occasion in her diary when she observed Chris, Mary, and Barb work for two hours hashing out seven questions for a reading passage, each with one correct answer and three distracters (incorrect answers). This might not seem like much (seven questions for six person-hours), but all those who have tried their hand at this kind of task will not, in fact, question this level of productivity. However, even such successful collaborations are not yet assured of ultimate achievement, because the seven-question reading passage now has to be *caboosed* to a test (i.e., answered by a group of examinees, but not included in their actual results). The ensuing statistical analysis may yet reveal that one or more of the seven questions are not "good" items. (They hope it will be not more than two, because they ultimately need five items for the final version.) Eventually, perhaps, some version of that two hours' work by the reading mini-team, based on a passage that Theresa had contributed to the file-box of potential items a year previously, will make its way into a secure test, and then later become released for sale as part of a practice test, emerge as illustrative material in an updated brochure, or find its way into a preparation manual. As Theresa observed, "the loop is endless."

For various reasons, the division has been developing in the last few years improved *item specifications* (usually known as "specs"), which are collated in a big green ring-bound notebook in Room 3025. One of these reasons is to meet recognized professional standards: "Test publishers *should* have these standards," according to Sarah. Another perhaps reflects Sarah's own deeper concerns: "Actually, the process of writing specs . . . has had the purpose of forcing us to examine *what* we are assessing" (original emphasis). Others include their use as training materials for new item writers, as criteria for judging the quality of a particular item, and as a means for increasing chances of item-writing success. For example, the *specs* for ECPE/MELAB vocabulary items consist of four pages of explanations and instructions, followed by two pages of references to dictionaries, word lists, and other kinds of vocabulary studies. The subheads for this particular spec are as follows (other specs may have additional subheads):

GD (General Description)
PA (Prompt Attributes)
  HA (Head Attributes)
  KA (Key Attributes)
  DA (Distracter Attributes)

The first and last sentences in the GD are:

Items are designed to measure knowledge of lexis common in academic discourse. . . . Items should not assess spelling (e.g. pair vs. pear), punctuation (e.g. it's vs. its), pronunciation (e.g. personal vs. personnel), grammar (e.g. quarter vs. quartered), register (e.g. buddies vs. friends), or dialect (e.g. make a decision vs. take a decision).

As the preceding extract shows, the specs are written in a straightforward way and without an excessive amount of testing jargon. They set the bounds of possibility in a way that is likely particularly helpful to new (or newish) members of the team. Typical test items are the following:

I don't care which hotel we stay in as long as it's _____ one.

   a. a reputable
   b. a prevailing
   c. an attributable
   d. a contractual

The investigators are sure Eric _____ the crime.

   a. committed
   b. executed
   c. produced
   d. achieved

We can notice in the first case that choosing the correct answer requires understanding of the general context expressed in the "head" sentence and matching it with a knowledge of the meaning of *reputable*, whereas in the second, the item is essentially testing a recognition of the fixed phrase or *collocation* "commit a crime." In general, the answer choices in the second type are, according to the spec, permitted to have a higher frequency of use, that is, above the 5 to 20 times occurrence per million words of English recommended for the first type.

   An acknowledged difficulty in item-writing is coming up with appropriate distracters. So here is the DA spec:

There are three distracters, each of which is grammatically correct but clearly wrong given the context of the head. All distracters should be "attractive" and similar to the key in the following ways:

- the same part of speech as the key, e.g. noun, verb (same tense), adjective, adverb
- all a single word or all a phrase
- all same register. (If key is colloquial, all distracters are colloquial too.)
- all approximately the same word frequency

All distracters should be "useful" words, that is, worth testing as the key in another item. Sources of distracters may be NNS essays, NNS speech, word frequency lists, lexicons.

This, then, is the "standard practice guide" to writing vocabulary items. It has ostensibly a number of immediate functions—as opposed to the broader purposes enumerated earlier. It uses—and explains to neophytes—the terminology used to describe the structure of what might seem at first sight to be a simple kind of mini-text—that of a humble vocabulary question. It stresses by enumeration and illustration what *not to do* when trying to write a vocabulary item; and it provides some suggestions for where to find *keys* and *distracters*. It does not attempt, however, to describe the typical *process* by which a typical vocabulary item might get written, either because there is no typical process or because this process is deemed to be subjective or intuitive. Nor, as we have seen, do the *specs* provide any historical context or attempt to justify the decisions that have been made. For example, it would be quite feasible to question the decision to exclude testing differences between formal (e.g., "eliminate") and informal (e.g., "get rid of") registers, because making appropriate choices here would seem to be of some importance in academic and professional contexts. But this is not done. At this point in my draft circulated to the division, Sarah noted: "It *was* discussed during the writing of the spec, but we do not use the spec to document rationale." This is an interesting comment both in terms of her previously cited comment about the specs "forcing us to examine what we are assessing," and in terms of my original following observation, by which I stand. Like most Standard Practice Guides, the item specs project a calm and self-evident rationality—one that frames the boundaries of human creative efforts but leaves unchanneled their well-springs.

In the foregoing I have stressed the development of organizational routines, beautifully glossed for my purpose by Cohen and Bacdayan as "multi-actor, interlocking, reciprocally-triggered sequences of actions" (1994, p. 554). This emphasis might be seen as corroborating the section's epigraph with its tongue-in-cheek suggestions about how to handle "an item writer's zest for invention." Indeed, the arrangements I have been describing, such as *mini-teams* and *specs*, are clearly designed to secure potential "loose cannons." But the actual situation is clearly more complicated than this. Here is Eric's *Projects and Research in Testing* from his first annual report:

> NOTE: most testing projects are collaborative, so unless noted, these are group efforts
>
> - Revised outdated test forms, and compiled bibliographic information, item statistics for the ECPE study book
> - Created a new form of the AEE Undergraduate Writing Test and revamped scoring system
> - Created a new form of the AEE Data Commentary
> - Administered ECPE and ECCE comp rater calibration
> - Produced grammar and composition item specifications
> - Developed and pretested ECCE grammar, vocabulary and reading tests
> - Compiled and formatted experimental MELAB tests and restructured the x-test keys
> - Assisted in administering IGSI tests
> - Assisted in consulting Chemistry departments regarding IGSIs
> - Arranged ISGI tests in Sarah's absence
> - Updated AEE grammar, vocabulary and reading section
> - Developed ECPE/MELAB and ECCE composition topics
> - Conducted MELAB oral interviews
> - Wrote and edited all types of ECCE, ECPE, and MELAB items
> - Scored ECCE, ECPE, MELAB, and AEE compositions
> - Proofed ECPE score rosters
> - Proctored AEE, ECPE, and MELAB tests

This then is what Eric ostensibly *did* under this, the main entry for his report, in and for the Testing Division in 1995–1996. We find here in this summary 23 past-tense verb forms invoking a whole host of activities, only four of which are repeated (just once): *assisted, compiled, created, developed*. The last two of these repeated verbs project a sense of considerable imaginative energy, as do *produced, wrote,* and *edited,* to which we can also add those that reflect a more incremental kind of improvement—*revised, revamped, pretested, restructured, updated*. Eric's elaborate list of descriptors thus underscores the multifunctional roles of even relatively junior members in the testing cooperative. There is a clear parallel here with university research laboratories wherein development and innovation is similarly *routinized* for the purposes of project completion and creative control.

No Time for Other Roles?

In the previous subsection I offered an account of test-making practice in an unusual university setting toward the close of the century. This is a practice that has evolved over 50 years, and one that has warmly embraced both the word-processing and analytical powers of the modern PC. It has also transformed itself from a traditional university lab set-up (expert in charge, research assistants, a technician or two) into a largely self-regulating and self-managing group of test-makers, which breaks itself down into smaller teams (typically trios) for the actual item-writing tasks. This is certainly a more democratic and probably a more collaborative community of practice than we can find elsewhere in the North University Building. Like similar groupings, its discussions abound with acronyms (MELAB, GVR, AEE, etc.) and abbreviations (e.g., specs, comps, ports, stats). The around-the-table meetings engender a fair amount of constructive criticism, but everybody seems careful to depersonalize this and to soften it wherever possible with humor or, especially in Mary's case, by casting comments in the form of literary allusions. The test-makers also have some weird adjacency pairs (standard utterances and responses such as "Thank you," "You're welcome") that derive from memorable earlier test items. Just one example must suffice. The common—almost inevitable—response to "Good idea" is "I don't want to stay home," which in fact derives from a venerable listening item:

F: Let's go to the football game.
M: Good idea. I don't want to stay home.

Other common weird responses include "It's good to be with Arthur Miller" (the title of a famous student composition) and "It can become 10 pizzas."

Although the work in the Division can be quite varied, going from what the testers call "chimp work" such as signing a large batch of certificates, through dealing with examiners, admissions officers, and printers, and on to statistical analysis, the core activity is unremitting test production and scoring. The humor, the food, and the collegiality thus all serve to lighten this labor. But here, too, the relentless pressure of the calendar, increased by cries from Greece and elsewhere for "more tests," constrains opportunities, especially among the research associates, for vacation time, or "thinking time," or "writing time" or mini-sabbaticals, all of which the ELI as a whole thinks is their due.

Meanwhile Carolyn, as Associate Director for Curriculum, would like more teaching contributions from the Testing Division, over and above the couple of courses Theresa teaches each year. Among other things, this would help her (and me) cope better with the imbalance between Fall and Winter semester enrollments. She also holds the view, which everybody in both the teaching and testing divisions in principle shares, that an occasional opportunity to teach will usually turn out to be an enlivening and enriching experience. But the Testing Division often finds itself compelled to say that it is too busy. At the same time, as director, I am often trying to nudge the division into raising its academic research and publication profile. In response, the testers quite accurately insist that they *are* in fact authors. As they remind me, they write and *publish* language tests. They do this in groups, several times a year, and these tests are very carefully and very professionally done, and with more pretesting and "norming" than any other outfit in the world with the exception of the Educational Testing Service. It just happens, they counter, that convention dictates that they do not put their actual names on the tests. Further, they remind me, they go to conferences, where they participate in discussion, network and present papers—and they say that even doing this already takes much valuable time away from a tough production schedule. They are professionals not academics, and if they author an academic article, as they occasionally do, this is *lagniappe* and should not considered part of their normal activities.

The cooperative thus keeps itself on track by imposing a certain kind of discipline on itself. We have seen this in the emergence of more complex item specs and planning schedules. We have seen this by the division (mostly) turning a deaf ear to siren voices from outside its own corner of the North University Building extolling the seductive delights of either teaching or academic publication. In addition, and more subtly, the cooperative imposes restrictions on its own members through its mutual concerns and felt responsibilities about the inexorable running of the calendar. One consequence is that the longer-serving members *feel bad* about taking anything but short vacations, and so rarely take longer ones. Even overworked and underpaid as they probably are, they tend to worry about whether everything is OK at the office, or how their mini-teams are coping without them. There are no professorial summer months away at the cottage here; indeed, as Director, I am dunned with communications from the Personnel department advising me once again that so-and-so has accrued more than her allowable maximum vacation time.

The obvious answer of hiring another research associate or senior research assistant, especially given the fact that the current budget situation would allow for this, turns out not to be so obvious. Apart from the practical—and intractable—problem of where to house another body, there are issues of compatibility with the distinctive work-style, finding the right expertise in a very narrow field, and slotting a new professional into the constrained salary structure. However, as author of this account, as observer of the Division, and as co-participant in its decision-making, I would conclude that this is a community of practice that has become something of a prisoner of its own test-making and certificate-issuing success. The outside world of test-takers wants predictability in the tasks ahead of them, and their numbers are increasing as the ECCE begins to spread across those countries where Michigan Tests have an established foothold. The test-makers and test-scorers have, in consequence, their regular and onerous duties that tend to proscribe other activities. Meanwhile, out of sight, the accounts slowly accumulate and, in principle, offer a means of breaking the circle. But more in principle than in practice, for any solution involves undertaking initiatives viewed as peripheral to the main community enterprise, or thought to be at odds with that community's vibrant collaborative spirit.

Robert Lado Remembered

This section opened with a selective account of the history of ESL testing at Michigan, in which I stressed the pivotal role of Robert Lado, who left in 1960 to become Dean of the School of Languages and Linguistics at Georgetown University, who spoke at the 50th anniversary celebration for the ELI at the TESOL National Convention in 1991, and who died at an active and advanced age in 1995. Unlike Botany, with its ancient traditions, ESL, at least as a professional activity, is very much a phenomenon of the second half of the 20th century, wherein it has had a meteoric rise in commercial and professional significance. Lado was a pioneer in at least three aspects of ESL: in his emphasis on English as a living, *spoken* language; in his advocacy of the need to compare languages in the preparation of national English language courses; and in his interest in appropriate and well-constructed tests of English language proficiency. (A comprehensive account of the history of ESL testing is given in Bernard Spolsky's *Measured Words*, published in 1995.)

Exactly 50 years after Lado's first major venture in the last area, one final way of reflecting on an evolving community of practice is by once again invoking its originator. When Lado died, Alan Davies, a leading British expert in ESL testing and himself close to retirement, wrote a eulogy for Robert Lado, based on a poem by the British poet Francis Thompson (1859–1907) in which Thompson recalled two famous cricketers of his youth. The version I have, which Alan Davies has kindly given me permission to use, was circulated via E-mail. On re-reading it yet again, I was once more struck with thoughts and feelings about how a vibrant *interpersonal and professional life* can exist within a community of practice engaged on what most people would assume to be a series of humdrum pursuits. (*Strevens* in the last line refers to Peter Strevens, a much-loved and equivalently pioneering British applied linguist, who died in 1989.) Here is the eulogy:

> It is little I repair to the meetings about real life tests,
>   Through my own test data I have shown;
> It is little I repair to the meetings about real life tests,
>   Though the test data fit the scales I've known.
> For the room is full of shades as I near the shadowy coast,
> And a ghostly tester scores discrete items host on host,
> And I hear through my tears one more voice we used to toast,
>   As the stakeholders bicker to and fro,
>   To and fro:
>   O my Strevens and my Lado long ago!

The testers in the North University Building may indeed be scoring "discrete items host on host" in their diurnal round, but they certainly do not lack corporality and humanity as they interactively undertake their pursuits, and in so doing exchange food and beverages, banter, joshing, and jokes.

ENVOI

If we briefly reflect on these accounts of three "communities," we can see some clear tendencies to differentiation. To start with one of the most obvious, they differ greatly in the extent to which they are publicly accessible. On the one side, the CRS, despite its half-door to the consultant area and other physical barriers, has its staff ready and waiting to be of service to members of the university. On the other, the Herbarium Workroom reacts to written requests that filter down from the director himself and are often orchestrated in mid-passage by Tony or Rich. My research assistant and I, and the staff journalist from *LS&A Magazine* (Beadle, 1996), may have been the only nonbotanical *outsiders* to enter this space during the period of the project (aside from the reception for the inauguration of the Compactor). As is often the case, somewhat intermediate is the Testing and Certification Division of the ELI. Although the clerical staff behind *their* half-door—but one that never opens (for test security reasons) to admit test candidates—do deal with the general NNS public on a regular basis, other contacts are uncommon. In Room 3025, one can sometimes find international students, because Theresa and Eric often tutor such people. Mary, in her room, may deal with the occasional obstreperous recently tested customer, and Sarah may see students from Social Work and allied disciplines because she has a project designed to help such students interact with the general Michigan public when they go on internships and so on. All in all, though, these contacts are limited.

Another differentiation involves fluidity. Although all three "communities" have embraced modern computer technology, they differ in its effects and consequences. For the CRS, upgrades, modifications, and changes of name are both endemic and integral to the activity. The Testing Division has followed this march of technology as best it can, but struggles with issues such as whether it should purchase a scanner, and looks a little concernedly at ETS's plans to put the TOEFL test online. In the Herbarium, the new equipment is in place, and, as far as I can tell, is designed to remain in that place for some time.

Other differences involve how long members of the "communities of practice" stay in their jobs, and whether their present positions are "stepping stones" to something else. For the younger members of the CRS and the ELI, this is certainly the case. For the more mature members of the ELI they are certainly in it, paradoxically, "for the long haul"; elsewhere, matters are more uncertain. Overall though, the most striking differences are those with which we began—the wild disparities among temporal horizons of expectation on the three floors: close to instantaneous in the CRS, annual in the Testing Division, lustral and beyond in the Herbarium Workroom.

Text and Text-Life
in the Herbarium

STUDYING SCIENCE WRITING

This is the first of two chapters that deal, directly or indirectly, with the written discourse of individuals. Here I provide personal and selective accounts of the writing—and its associated activities—of four members of the Herbarium: Bill, Tony, Ed, and Bob (in that order). The general processes whereby these accounts have been written have already been described in chapter 1. However, at this juncture, I probably need to say something more—by way of preview—about the particularities and peculiarities of the methods used to study these writerly lives. In this chapter, the writers are all scientists *tout court* (whereas those in the next are more tenuously positioned between the applied and the descriptive and between the social sciences and the humanities).

Scientists are somewhat notorious in some quarters for their writing style, and the few distinctive voices among them, such as that of Stephen Jay Gould, are typically thought to be the exceptions that prove the pedestrian rule. This style has been closely studied in recent years by sociologists of science, rhetoricians, and discourse analysts. Here is one of the more eloquent of its characterizations:

> Scientist or not, one hears the persona of univocity, unbroken statement, the single voice of the scientific style. But how achieved? How constructed? For the most part, through a series of grammatical and syntactic strategies that attempt to depersonalize, to objectify all premises, such that they seem to achieve the plane of ahistorical essence: "Recent advances have shown

...."; "Analyses were performed ..."; "The data therefore indicate ...."
The narrative is driven by objects, whether these be phenomena, procedures, earlier studies, evidence, or whatever. These are the subjects that perform the crucial action, that absorb the responsibility of what happens. (S. L. Montgomery, 1996, p. 13)

We have here a rhetoric that attempts to achieve its objectives by making itself invisible, by allowing "the facts to speak for themselves," and by being in Geertz's (1988) distinction "author-evacuated" rather than "author-saturated." In such contexts in particular, the analyst's gaze needs to address small matters as much as large ones, partly in order to bring to light the *consequences* of Montgomery's "syntactic and grammatical strategies." Further, within this depersonalized, univocal style, there will likely be odd moments when the personal and the heartfelt will ruffle the smooth rhetorically machined textual surface, and these fleeting instances need to be investigated to see what they might reveal of larger concerns. Overall, then, I have focused on the noting of odd and unobserved features as a kind of method for uncovering the particularities of discursive landscapes. More widely, I hope that highlighting particular discoursal features of certain fields and of their genres, especially ones that have been hitherto little analyzed, and then relating those features to wider sociorhetorical characteristics, can make its own contribution to the communal enterprise of reaching a better understanding of writing in the disciplines.

Although the foregoing paragraph rightly suggests certain commonalities in my practice, it is also true that I have tried to view each case as a vehicle for telling a particular story. First up is Bill, for many years the Director of the Herbarium. For Bill, I have focused on three aspects: his involvement in the enormous *Flora Novo-Galiciana* project, his expert knowledge of one large tropical family of plants, and his languages. Tony follows, and there my interest has been engaged by the contrast between his practical day-to-day life and his role as a primary researcher and as a writer of *treatments*. In the case of Ed, I could well have concentrated on his *Michigan Flora* volumes, but the flora aspect is already covered by Bill. Instead, therefore, I have used Ed's contributions to nomenclature as a vehicle for discussing the extremely significant role of terminology in systematic botany. And finally, in Bob's case, I have tried to explicate a rather more complex research agenda (which is why I have placed him last) involving fungal systematics, methodological innovation, and ecology. At the halfway point in this chapter, as a kind of theoretical interlude, I turn briefly aside to discuss the one rhetorical account known to me of taxonomic discourse. The differences between Alan Gross's ornithogical text and the botanical ones discussed in this chapter serve to further underscore the textual particularity of scholarly work emerging from a Herbarium.

BILL

It is as perfect a representation of its genre as can be presented to the botanical public. (review)

Bill is in his 50s. He has a PhD in Botany from the University of Michigan and, apart from his first three years after graduation, he has spent his working life there. Since 1986, he has been a full professor and Director of the Herbarium. In 1993–1994 he was President of the American Society of Plant Taxonomists, a professional organization with some 1,200 members. Bill takes the curatorial side of his work very seriously:

I take the meaning of curator from the classic Latin to be someone who cares for something. And I think the role of a curator, as divorced from a researcher, is to see that the specimens are given good care, and preserved, and made available to whoever needs to study them. (in interview)

And in response to the question of what makes a good curator: "You need someone first of all who loves plants, loves plant diversity, and has enough experience working with herbarium specimens to see them as something other than dried weeds" (in interview).

Although the curating and the researching cannot really be kept apart, as a scholar-researcher Bill is both a *floristician* and a *monographer*. In terms of the first, he edits, compiles, and writes floras, which are elaborate, complex, and structured regional inventories of plants. It turns out that regional floras and systematic monographs (authoritative accounts of all species in a particular taxonomic grouping of plants, such as "a family") are the two *big* genres in the field. Bill explained the relationship like this:

Floristicians whenever possible base their floras on monographs, as being the authoritative source of information about a group . . . The problem is that there are so many plants and so few people to do monographs that if you waited for all the monographs to be done before we did any floras there wouldn't be anything left . . . The floras are important because they make it possible to know what we have, and we can't begin to decide what to save until we know what we have.

For many years now, Bill, a colleague (now emeritus), and others have been working on the *Flora Novo-Galiciana*. Nueva Galicia is a biogeographical area of western Mexico which includes all of the states of Jalisco, Colima, and Aguascalientes, as well as some portions of adjacent states. The *Flora* project actually dates back to 1949, when his colleague first began collecting and studying the plants of western Mexico, and the project has been continuously supported by the National Science Foundation for more than forty years. The first actual volume appeared in 1983, and so far seven volumes have been published, treating about half of the species of Nueva Galicia in a remarkable total of some 4,087 pages. At the time of this writing, the eighth and ninth volumes are in preparation. Seventeen volumes are planned altogether. The volumes are now published by the Herbarium itself and are illustrated by a much-respected in-house botanical artist; indeed, her work for the flora was featured in the 1996 calendar distributed by the College of Literature, Science, and Arts. When I messaged him about a likely completion date of the project, he replied:

> I have no clue when the Flora will be completed. We're working now on the eighth, ninth and tenth volumes (of 17), and revising the first. There is some prospect that a revised edition of another of the early volumes will come out in the next five years. If it takes us 2–3 years for each new volume, I'll be fortunate to see the Flora finished in my lifetime. Perhaps we'll be able to pick up the pace some, but at best I can't imagine the first edition of all 17 volumes coming out in less than another 15 years. As for second editions, they will happen as need dictates and opportunity permits.

As briefly mentioned in the last chapter, in 1995 the Herbarium held a reception to celebrate the completed installation of the *Compactor*. As part of this celebration, a poster display about the *Flora Novo-Galiciana* was assembled. One of the sheets included excerpts from reviews of six of the seven volumes published to date. I include them here as an indication of how this decades-long project is not only a massive quantitative effort, but also a very remarkable quality achievement. Indeed, everybody I have spoken to about this flora always says that there is nothing like it anywhere for any region of the Third World.

> VOL. 5: "The style, the comprehensive, critically revisionary scope of the taxonomy, and the perfectionism evident in every detail of presentation . . . have received universal and deserved acclaim from reviewers in the botanical press."—R. C. Barneby

> VOL. 12: "It is as perfect a representation of its genre as can be presented to the botanical public."—M. C. Johnston

> VOL. 14: "This volume provides an authoritative treatment of about half of the Mexican grass species. It will be essential to anyone needing to name western Mexican grasses, and it will be basic to further research on Mexican grasses in general."—S. D. Koch

> VOL. 15: "This volume continues the high standards set in the previously published volumes . . . , and it also merits the uniformly favorable reviews that these have received."—M. Nee

VOL. 16: "This is the best orchid flora yet produced for any part of the Americas."—E. W. Greenwood

VOL. 17: "It is, beyond any doubt, the most carefully written and highly detailed flora of any tropical region."—D. B. Lellinger

The volumes of this flora consist essentially of *treatments* of genera and species (at completion, estimated numbers of the former are 1,400 and of the latter very approximately 6,000). Treatments are descriptions of one or more species and comprise the working genre of the systematic botanist, just as the research paper is the working genre of the experimentalist, and the essay that of the humanist. Although treatments will be considered in further detail when we look at Tony's writing, a first look at part of a genus-treatment is offered here as a scene-setting to what is to follow. After giving the name of the genus (in this case, *Eriocaulon* L.) and a botanical description, the authors provide the following "notes on the genus":

> A genus reportedly of 350–400 species in the tropics and subtropics, in America represented by many species in Brazil and elsewhere in South America, and in Cuba, but by fewer than ten in Central America and still fewer in Mexico. Our species are confusingly alike, with identification depending upon microscopic characters, and crowded flower heads that are difficult to dissect. Lectotype-species, *E. decangulare* L. (McVaugh & Anderson, 1993, p. 202)

This is a smooth and succinct two-sentence account, in which the first would seem to encapsulate, despite its bland matter-of-factness, a quite remarkable amount of work and knowledge. The second, in some small contrast, opens with a first person pronoun usage ("Our species") and this, along with the quasi-confessional "confusingly alike," shifts the mood to one of affiliation with and propinquity to the plants themselves, remarkably so perhaps when we recollect that the sentence was presumably written in the decidedly untropical environment of the Great Lakes region of the Midwest.

These notes are then followed by a key to the identification of the four species found in Nueva Galicia:

1. Scapes mostly less than 10 cm tall; heads 2–4 mm wide, glabrous to moderately and finely gray-pilose; receptacle glabrous or essentially so.
    2. Heads glabrous or essentially so, gray to black; anthers white; ♂ flowers without petals.   *E. bilobatum.*
    2. Heads at least thinly beset with fine stiff hairs, from blackish to nearly white (because of the hairs), anthers blackish; ♀ flowers with petals, these lacking a gland near apex.   *E. jaliscanum.*

1. Scapes mostly more than 10 cm tall; heads 4–10 mm wide, densely beset with very stout cylindric blunt white trichomes; receptacle glabrous or copiously long-pilose with silky hairs; petals of ♂ flowers present, usually with a black gland at apex.

    3. Sepals of the ♀ flowers distinct, not connate into a spathe; receptacle pilose.   *E. benthamii.*

    3. Sepals of the ♀ flowers connate into a spathe split along one side; receptacle pilose or glabrous or nearly so.   *E. ehrenbergianum.*

(from McVaugh & Anderson, 1993, pp. 202–203)

As can be seen even from this extract, the key is a kind of stepped algorithm that a botanist will work through in order to identify a specimen. (The one just illustrated is a relatively simple instance, as there are only four species; with many more species, the key can extend over several pages.) The key is dichotomous and is made up of a series of paired but contrastive statements describing one or more features of plants in the genus. As the two halves of each pair are mutually exclusive, the specimen to be identified should fit under only one of the two descriptions. Each statement leads either to a subsequent pairing (indicated by the numeral 1 in the sample text) or to an actual species identification (numerals 2 and 3). As Bill's colleague, Ed, wrote in the introduction to the first volume of his *Michigan Flora* (Voss, 1972, p. 32), "A key is simply an efficient way of rapidly narrowing down the possibilities. It is like a highway system with no crossroads but only forks."

One of the curiosities of Systematic Botany—at least to this observer—is that all the keys I have seen are in smaller type than the descriptive text, even though botanists insist on their central value and importance. Here is Tony in interview on the centrality of keys:

> The keys are important because there are a lot of botanists, and I guess I'd count myself among that group, that believe if you can't distill your systematic arrangement into a concise summary of characteristics by which others can tell them apart—if you can't do that, then your systematic arrangment is suspect. In other words, you may be seeing things that aren't really there if you can't translate what you're seeing in words to somebody else . . . (a key is) a form of repeatability . . . it's the equivalent in systematics of repeating experiments.

The usual explanations that have been furnished to me of how this apparent paradox (small print but great importance) has come about either involve reference to "convention" or to "print economy," or sometimes to both. Although neither of these (or even both) strikes me as a fully convincing rationale for the customary practice, mismatch between font size and significance is not only confined to botanical keys. Doubtless, a similar conundrum exists with article abstracts which, as Hartley (1994) and many others have pointed out, also conventionally appear in smaller type than the body of the paper, even though there is much evidence (e.g., Bazerman, 1988) that an abstract often operates for the harried reader as a kind of "identification key" as to the merits or otherwise of reading the longer text. Bill, however, in a marginal annotation to my draft, offered the following convincing rationale for the practice:

> We do it [use 10-point] to keep the key as compact as possible, in order to facilitate comparison of contrasting leads and backtracking. Because of the ways we set our keys (there are other methods), such comparison and backtracking are easier if more of the key is in view at a time. So our motive is one of making the key easier to use. After many years of using keys, I am convinced that this really does help the reader and justifies the small size, which I would otherwise avoid.

Thus, in the opinion of someone who has thought about these matters long and hard, the rationale for small-print *keys* turns out to be different from that of abstracts (whatever that is) by virtue of the key's instrumental and referential purposes.

Because of his area of specialization, Bill makes regular field trips to Latin and Central America, especially to Brazil and Mexico. Unlike most of the other denizens of NUBS, he is a considerable linguist. He is highly proficient in Portuguese and Spanish—and can correspond with fellow botanists in those languages; and he also has—at the least—a very good reading knowledge of French and German. He is an opera buff and has taught himself to follow sung libretti in Italian; indeed, on most visits to his office I am greeted by Italian opera emanating from his CD player. He is also the leading expert in the Herbarium in yet another language. Here is part of a 1993 *treatment* written by Bill, and partly in that "tongue." The literal interlinear translation (in *italics*) is my own:

Bunchosia itacarensis W R Anderson, sp. nov.—TYPE: BRAZIL. Bahia: Mun. Itacaré, 3 km S of Itacaré, forest at edge of ocean, Dec fl, *Mori et al. 13081* (Holotype: MICH!; isotypes: CEPEC, NY, not seen).

Frutex vel arbor parva 2–3m alta, ramis permox
Shrub or tree small   2–3m high, with-stems very-soon

glabratis. Lamina foliorum majorum 14–21 cm longa,
becoming hairless. Blade of larger leaves 14–21 cm long,

6.7–9.2 cm lata, permox glabrata, abaxialiter
6.7–9.2 cm wide, very-soon hairless, on the back side

biglandulosa prope basim; petiolus 10–12 mm longus
two-glanded near base; leaf-stalk 10–12 mm long

eglandulosus; stipulae 2–3 mm longae. Inflorescentia
glandless   ; stipules 2–3 mm long.   Inflorescence

saepe ternata. Sepala utrinque glabra,
often 3-branched. Sepals on-both-sides hairless,

margine saepe ciliata. Gynoecium bicarpellatum;
on-the-edge often fringed. Gynoecium two-carpelled;

ovarium dense sericeum; styli 2, 1.4 mm longi, liberi.
ovary densely silky; styles 2, 1.4 mm long, free.

Fructus (siccus) 10–11 mm longus, 12–14 mm diametro,
Fruit   (dry)   10–11 mm long,   12–14 mm in diameter,

glabratus, laevis.
hairless,   smooth. (Anderson, 1993, p. 355)

As of today, the International Rules of Nomenclature in Botany still require that any species new to science be first described in a Latin diagnostic paragraph. Even so, the preservation of this tradition remains highly controversial. Here is Bill once more:

> There have been proposals at every Congress for the last twenty years or so to replace Latin with English . . . and that has not flown because people from other countries who are not Anglophones have resisted this—to the point where Anglophone botanists have said "Look, we are not going to suggest this any longer; if non-Anglophones want to propose something we can live with, fine; but any such proposals have got to come from non-Anglophones", and one did come this year—from India—and he proposed that one be allowed to publish the diagnosis in either Latin or English. (in interview, 1994)

Even though the proposal did not pass, Bill believes that Latin "may be on its way out." However, whatever its official future, Botanical Latin is and will doubtless remain very much part of Bill's working life, partly because a diagnostic paragraph in Latin will presumably remain at least for some time to come as an option, and partly because Bill's most-used reference (a reprint of a 1928 monograph) has the main text entirely in Botanical Latin—although the geographic notes are in German.

There exists, in fact, an outstanding volume entitled *Botanical Latin* by William T. Stearn, originally published in 1966 and now in its fourth edition (1992). The book-jacket to the latest edition quotes the following extract from *The Journal of the Royal Horticultural Society*: "This remarkable work has evoked worldwide esteem and affection. Encyclopedic and erudite, extraordinarily interesting and packed with detail." And I also have found it to be so, even if I have wished at times that the author might have been a little more of a rhetorician (or even better, some kind of pioneering discourse analyst) with subsequently more to say about the textual *arrangement* of botanical descriptions.

According to Stearn, "Botanical Latin owes its present utility, together with its divergence from classical and mediaeval Latin, largely to Linnaeus" (1992, pp. 14–15), the famous Swedish botanist who lived from 1707 to 1778. Indeed, systematic botanists divide the history of their subject into pre- and post-Linnaean eras; for them, Linnaeus is as much one of Foucault's (1984) "founders of discursivity" as Freud has been claimed to be for psychoanalysis, or Marx for socialist thought, or Darwin for studies of evolution. Stafleu, in his book *Linnaeus and the Linnaeans*, describes this achievement as follows:

> Victory for binary nomenclature was almost complete by the time of Linnaeus's death in 1778. It is impossible to say which of his activities and innovations did most towards the ultimate victory of his works. The major publications, such as the *Genera plantarum*, *Species plantarum*, and *Systema naturae*, would have created order in plant taxonomy and its literature even without the help of binary specific names. On the other hand, this apparently simple and obvious device was so successful and of such direct help towards achieving stability in nomenclature that its role in making Linnaeus's work the generally accepted basis for future taxonomy should not be underestimated. (1971, p. 110)

Stearn noted particularly how Linnaeus in his Latin eliminated verbs, opted for the nominative case, used punctuation to separate treatments of different organs, and insisted on clear typography. Indeed, on the first of these changes, Stearn mordantly commented, "Botanists manage verbs best by avoiding them altogether" (1992, p. 130). Not surprisingly, we can see these features displayed in Bill's Latin text. There are indeed no finite verbs. Compare the "moodless" *Inflorescentia saepe ternata* with the schoolchild's *Inflorescentia saepe ternata est*. Aside from a single genitive (line 2), one accusative following a preposition (line 3) and an ablative (line 9), the phrases and moodless clauses are in the nominative case—with the following two exceptions: *ramis permox glabratis* and *margine saepe ciliata*. These are remnants of the ablative case, which used to be prevalent in pre-Linnaean botanical description, and which only persist here in secondary phrases, dependent on prior nominative-case structures. Punctuation is careful and exact: as Stearn again noted, "Procedure varies, but it seems best to separate the account of one organ from that of another by a full stop and to use semi-colons to mark off the parts of an organ which are separately described" (1992, p. 194).

Another interesting feature of the part-genre (whether in Latin, English or some other language) is that the object under description, in this case *Bunchosia itacarensis*, is never directly referred to in the text either by name, abbreviated name, or even by pronominal reference. Rather, it has a kind of ghostly immanence that hovers over the textual proceedings—a feature, in fact, of many other kinds of technical descriptions and instructions. Recall, for instance, the frequent "missing" complements in many cookery instructions of the "bring to boil, stir and serve" type. Another feature of the text is that the Latin translates easily and quite literally into botanical English, at least once the morphological complexity of the Latin and its post-modifier position for adjectives are taken into account. This phenomenon presumably occurs because the diagnostic short Latin paragraph and a more detailed English description have co-evolved over time as a matched response to the stable descriptive exigency which provides professional botanists with the form and content that they need.

I have so far stressed, as genre analysts are prone to do, what is *not* there in the text. When we do turn to look at what *is* there in abundance in botanical descriptions, we see above all else a complex and immense adjectival resource stock, much of it of latinate origin, and much of it devoted to specifying the shape and texture of plant parts. For a nonbotanist (like myself) this lexical richness is both a frustration and a delight. When I started this project I kept on coming across adjectives that I felt I *ought* to have known, but somehow I didn't quite manage to resurrect their meanings (and I suspect that I am not alone in this kind of annoying discovery). Typical words of this sort were *glabrous*, *pinnate*, and *sessile*. There were, of course, many others that resounded to my nonnaturalist ears with a splendid, sonorous anonymity, words that I liked—and still like—to roll around my tongue. Although my botanical word-stock has perforce grown somewhat over the life of this project, I remain entranced by adjectives such as *cespitose*, *trigonous*, *involucral*, and *serrulate*.

Further evidence of this adjectival predominance can be extracted from glossaries to botanical works. Consider the case of Ed's three-volume *Michigan Flora*. The glossary for Volume I (Voss, 1972) has 228 entries which, in terms of parts of speech, break down as follows:

Adverbs	0
Verbs	1 (subtend)
Suffixes	2
Prefixes	3
Nouns	90
Adjectives	132
Total entries	228

It would be hard to imagine such a skewed grammatical distribution of glossed items in fields outside the descriptive life sciences. Here, for example, are the items glossed under the letter D which, in this case at least, are *all* adjectives:

Decumbent
Decurrent
Deflexed
Dehiscent
Deltoid
Denticulate
Depauperate
Dichotomous
Dilated
Dimorphic
Dioecious
Diploid
Dissected
Distal
Divaricate
Divergent
Dorsal

So, after this excursion, we can see in this extract of Bill's text the maintenance of a highly specialized variety of an ancient language in which form has so followed function as to render it largely unintelligible to Classical Latin scholars. All we see today are clumps of highly technical nouns and adjectives organized according to one of several possible and overlapping schemata (*root* to *flower*, *big* to *small*, *known* to *new*, etc.). The famous 19th-century botanist, Alphonse de Candolle, perhaps epitomized best the felicitous nature of Linnaeus' Botanical Latin:

> Une langue aussi universelle, aussi précise, aussi bien adaptée par un homme de génie aux besoins de la science ne doit pas être abandonnée [A language so universal, so precise and so well adapted by a man of genius to the needs of science that it ought not to be abandoned]. (*La Phytographie*, 1880, p. 35)

We are, however, not quite finished with the extract from Bill's 1993 treatment. As readers may have noticed, there is also some abbreviated front matter to be glossed. First the name of the species itself in bold (**Bunchosia itacarensis**), named after the place where it was originally collected, and then Bill's name as the person responsible for writing up the description of a new species. Geographical information follows, as well as the name(s) of the collectors. On the last line we see the oddly punctuated "MICH!." "MICH" is the conventional abbreviation for the University of Michigan Herbarium; in fact, the exclamation point is a highly specific convention indicating that the writer has personally examined the specimen from the designated herbarium (note that Bill follows "NY"—the New York Botanical Garden—with "not seen").

At this point my procedure may need a bit of explaining. I have so far focused the textual analysis on the key and the diagnostic paragraph, as two elements in a treatment. In effect, I have deliberately chosen to start with extracts that are in Becker's sense (1995) "distant." The extracts so far are very likely to appear "distant" to the inhabitants of the English Language Institute on the floor above the Herbarium, or to the occupants of the Computing Resource Center below it, and this despite the fact that, in terms of time and space, they are both contemporary and geographically adjacent. In contrast to Becker's own texts from classical Malay or the remote Burmese countryside, they are not from far-off times and places. Becker, following Ortega y Gasset, suggested that there are "two apparently antithetical laws, which are involved in every utterance we make, spoken or written—that all languaging is deficient and says less than we wish it to, and that at the same time all languaging is exuberant and says more than we know ..." (1995, p. 5). Becker was at pains to clarify that such deficiencies and exuberancies are not matters to be analyzed and then rectified, but are "a basic necessity of all human languaging" (p. 5) in response to different turns and twists in linguistic evolutionary history. A similar phenomenon is apparent in very distinct stylistic varieties *within* a language. Thus, these botanical texts are alien and mysterious, and distant from our expectations in having their exuberancies in adjectives and their deficiencies in verbs, but perhaps also, in the case of the key, by the way it seems to the noninitiate to be a set of instructionless instructions (in marked contrast to Tung's text about the unfreezing of the computer workstation). Further, in the case of the diagnosis, we find evidence for the perpetuation of a language otherwise commonly thought to have but vestigial life in the Catholic Church, or in the tags of old-fashioned lawyers.

By now I hope to have given a broad account of Bill and the *Flora Novo-Galiciana*, and a narrow account of a couple of Bill's paragraphs. We next need to try and put these two together better by establishing the contextual middle-ground of institutional practice. The first part of this *bridging* story is that Bill gets sent thousands of specimens a year to name, because he is a specialist in a big tropical plant family, the Malpighiaceae. Indeed, his second major multiyear project, alongside the flora, is to write a comprehensive *monograph* of this complex and showy group of plants.

So, for Bill, it is part of his research to name and study these specimens, while it is his role as curator to make sure any donated specimens in his family are added to the herbarium collection and given the care they need. In interview, he explained the situation in the following way:

> ... in the New World and especially in the New World tropics, there is just a lot more plant diversity than there are people. So each group of neotropical plants tends to be sent to one person, or a small number of people who are, at any given time, the specialists most likely to get things and name them. There are not good modern treatments of most tropical groups, so that it is a lot of work, and in many cases impossible, for non-specialists to name things. So, the standard practice is to send specimens to specialists for naming. In my family those come in here to me.

He went on to say that he and other specialists identify specimens in any way they can; using any available references, using their own accumulated experience with the group, or by comparing newly arrived and as-yet unnamed specimens with old and named ones in the extensive file cabinets of their herbaria. Typically, however, the identification process involves "some combination of these." When all is done, the names are written on the specimen sheets, and this information is sent back to whoever submitted the specimens for identification in the first place. Unless the specimens are sent on loan, "we then keep the specimens—that's our pay for the service." Bill usually deals with "a cubby hole" of specimens (typically 30–40 sheets) in a session that extends over several hours. Occasionally, however, a plant arrives that is apparently new to science. This he will put aside for detailed study. He may, as a result, end up publishing a treatment of this new species, an activity that may take him several days.

This, then, is the generalized context for our "**Bunchosia itacarensis W. R. Anderson. sp.nov.**" textual extract, replete with its "MICH!" and its opening Latin paragraph. The second aspect of the contextual middleground begins with the fact that this extract does not come from the *Flora Novo-Galiciana*. First, as is obvious, this piece describes a plant discovered in Brazil, not in Western Mexico. Second, even if it were to occur in the latter location, it would not have come from the flora itself because the volume dealing with the large *Bunchosia* genus has yet to be published, although it is in preparation. It comes, in fact, from the 19th volume in an approximately annual series entitled *Contributions from the University of Michigan Herbarium*. The size of these volumes—and of Bill's contribution—can be gauged from the fuller cited reference: *Contr. Univ. Michigan Herb.* 19: 355–392. 1993. The title of Bill's contribution is low-key and unassuming, or certainly seems so to me. His "Notes on Neotropical

Malpighiaceae—IV" looks like a slowly unfolding story of careful work in the family for which he is "responsible for the names."

The last piece of the macro–micro connection is textual rather than contextual, because it deals with the *text* that lies between this title and the now-familiar *B. itacarensis* treatment. The relevant paragraph is reproduced here:

> The notes that follow are a true miscellany, published here for diverse reasons. It would be much better, of course, if they could appear in the context of complete monographic treatments of these groups, but monographs of large genera like *Bunchosia, Byrsonima,* and *Heteropterys* are years in the future, and much of what follows cannot wait that long. Several of the new species are needed for floras, or have already been cited as *nomina nuda* in floristic lists. In other cases, notes of explanation are needed for actions taken or soon to be taken; for example, non-specialists seeing my recent annotations on specimens may reasonably wonder why I have abandoned a well-established name like *Heteropterys beecheyana* Adr. Juss. for *H. brachiata* (L.) DC., and why I am using *Mascagnia divaricata* (H.B.K.) Nied. for the species traditionally called *M. ovatifolia* (H. B. K.) Griseb. Moreover, a number of the entries supplement Niedenzu's 1928 monograph by clarifying problems that he had to leave unresolved, usually because he did not have the opportunity to study critical collections in Paris and London. I trust that the relevance of each entry will be obvious to informed readers. (1993, p. 355)

This paragraph reinforces a number of traits that are becoming increasingly apparent. One is the bedrock role of the competent monograph, as illustrated by its adjectival use in "complete *monographic* treatments." A second is the time pressure exerted on a group of historically minded and historically trained scientists in an age of rapid ecological change largely caused by humankind. A third is Bill's revisionist stance, as is most clearly indicated in the middle of the paragraph. Indeed, we will later see further examples of how this nomenclaturistic intertextuality (or, fiddling about with previously assigned names) emerges as a central if controversial transaction in the systematic botanist's conceptual and textual trade. However, there may be also a subtext here, which I believe to be revealed by another section in the interview with Bill, and where we can again see the centrality of terminology:

> I have been involved in a ferocious controversy about nomenclature, that is ways of treating and stablizing plant names. I have been one of the outspoken opponents to a European school ... that essentially wants to freeze plant nomenclature. It is basically saying that names in current use shouldn't be overturned, and I simply feel that that's going to make more problems than it solves.

The renaming sections of a 42-page contribution thus look like an oblique challenge to those stick-in-the-mud Europeans, and, to my mind, give an added—if wry—charge to the concluding sentence: "I trust that the relevance of each entry will be obvious to informed readers."

My final observation concerns the penultimate sentence, which deals with Bill's major reference work. I present it first in its original form (5) and then in an alternate phraseology (5a):

> 5) Moreover, a number of the entries supplement Niedenzu's monograph by clarifying problems that he had to leave unresolved, usually because he did not have the opportunity to study critical collections in Paris and London.

> 5a) Moreover, a number of the entries correct Niedenzu's 1928 monograph by resolving problems that he failed to solve, usually because he did not study critical collections in Paris and London.

The original is a "kinder, gentler" rhetoric that reinforces systematic botanists' sympathetic understanding of the arduous conditions under which their direct predecessors worked, and here we need to recollect that the direct predecessor in a particular family may have been active several decades ago (as is the case with both Bill and Tony). My alternative version is reminiscent of the "create-a-research-space" for yourself approach common in contemporary research articles (Swales, 1990a; Paul & Charney, 1995), but finds apparently little place in the monographic, floristic, and treatmental traditions of classic botany. Although it is true that all fields have their Young Turks, to "seasoned" botanists (a common epithet which appears to refer to both the number of years spent out in the "collecting season" and to the empathetic maturity that accompanies such trials), appreciation of prior work is so much the norm that it tempers inescapable contemporary revision of it. And if we need further confirmation of this attitude, here is Bill's annotation of my draft at this juncture:

> I hope that, if I am unfair to Niedenzu, my successors will be merciful in correcting the errors I am certain to make. Niedenzu did most of his work between 1895 and 1920, when it was politically difficult or impossible for him to get to England and France. He was a professor in a high school ("Lyceum") in East Prussia, not a pampered full-time researcher in Berlin. It's remarkable that he did so much, and did it so well.

What more can one say?

Bill then is a classical botanist in several senses. He loves plants and is dedicated to the *Flora Novo-Galiciana* project, a project that is likely to occupy him throughout his remaining working life, as a collector, specialist, grant-writer, contributor, and editor. In the big tropical family in which he specializes, he is slowly constructing, as and when circumstances permit, a definitive *revision* of Niedenzu (1928). He typically identifies every year for other people hundreds, often thousands, of specimens that he is sent—for no payment or gain except for knowledge itself or for the possibility of being able to keep the specimen and add it to the Herbarium collection. He knows all the languages he needs to know. As he said in an interview, "I reply to the Brazilians in Portuguese, but mostly I reply to the Spanish letters in English. I could reply in Spanish but it is not so easy for me. There's generally an agreement that you write in your language and we'll write in ours."

As again we have seen, he writes other pieces, such as treatments for the annual herbarium volume, as well as occasional articles for the standard academic journals in his field. But like most people who write in the classic genres of systematic botany, his work tends to be more used than cited, because these genres function more as manuals than as experimentations or conceptualizations. He also does some advanced training of students, but as he says of apprenticeship in his field, "it's something you learn by doing it with someone looking over your shoulder," and this again is part of the Herbarium story. He is committed to writing, both in terms of the time he devotes to it and to its ultimate quality. He is equally a tireless and meticulous editor; referring to his doctoral students, he commented "so when they leave me they may not be great writers, but anything they did with me tends to be pretty good."

This concludes the first of seven profiles of a writing life. As in some of the other cases, the account of Bill Anderson has been presented in a largely inductive manner as I attempt to engage the reader in a co-exploration of the discourse of systematic botany and of a particular systematic botanist. The turns and returns of this individual textography have, among other things, introduced a particular genre-set, dealt with a remarkable examplar of one genre, discussed the linguistic and termino-logical particularity of the field, and related the curatorial and scholarly life. The inductive sorting through of bits of evidence of various types and of various textual sizes has perhaps led to a somewhat leisurely narrative pace, but one that may also have helped to live up to some of the methodological promises made at the chapter's outset.

TONY

It is easy to describe specimens, but our *aim* is to describe species. (Tony, in a marginal note)

In the previous section I offered some account of the textual practices and products of a senior professor from the second floor of the North University Building. In this, I turn to another member of the Herbarium who is not classified in the university hierarchy as "a professor." Tony is a curator with an unfunded courtesy appointment as a lecturer in Biology. However, as we will see, in both Tony's case and in that of Carolyn from the ELI, the lack of professorial status has not apparently inhibited their being given positions of considerable responsibility within the system, nor prevented them from developing influence and reputation outside it. Although Tony and Carolyn's publications differ considerably in quantity and type, they match, as far as I know, what might—across some national average of varying types of institution—be expected of professorial faculty in their respective fields of Botany and English as a Second Language.

Tony is in his mid-40s with a PhD from the University of Toronto. Since coming to the Herbarium in 1978, he has moved steadily through the curatorial ranks. Although he does relatively little regular teaching, he is active in many other ways, such as serving on doctoral committees, running the workroom, and identifying specimens of Great Lakes flora for the public (typically hundreds a year). He recently served for three years as Director of the university's Botanical Gardens. A further sign of his status is that when Bill was on sabbatical in Winter Term 1994, it was Tony who was appointed Interim Director of the Herbarium rather than one of the professorial members associated with the unit. Additional evidence of the regard in which he is held can be seen from the positions he has occupied; as of March 1994, some of the more significant of these were:

- President, Great Lakes Chapter, American Rock Garden Society
- Director, Michigan Botanical Foundation
- Chairman, Endangered Species Technical Committee for Plants, Michigan DNR
- Director, Michigan Natural Areas Council

He also, on occasion, does consultancy work for both public and private organizations.

As a person, Tony exudes bonhomie and infectious enthusiasm, and his "large" personality is amplified by his strikingly resonant voice. Given these personal attributes and professional involvements, it comes as no surprise to find that Tony is invited several times a year to give presentations to a wide range of groups and organizations, and that he is much in demand as a leader of botanical field trips. He also publishes short articles in more popular journals such as *Blue Heron*, *Plant Press*, and *Wildflower*.

From the story so far, we might well conclude that Tony is an excellent administrator and organizer, a leader in raising civic consciousness about the natural world, and a determined and effective lobbyist for plant protection and preservation. Although we do indeed see here the biography of somebody (like Joan in the ELI) who has conscientiously devoted professional expertise to public service and public education, the story of Tony (again like that of Joan's) does not end at this point. For another perspective on Tony, we can look at the "Current Research Interests" section from his c.v.:

> My current research interests are two-fold. My major interest is the systematics and evolution of the large and complex genus *Carex*. Here, I emphasize a multi-level approach concentrating on several aspects, including development of new characters useful in systematics, monographic studies of major groups, sectional classification and nomenclature, and processes and patterns of evolution. The goals of this research, in addition to monographing difficult groups of *Carex*, are to produce a revised sectional classification and phylogeny of the genus. A longer term goal of my work is the production of a monograph of the New World species of *Carex*, but at this point, I am particularly interested in Mexican species. I am also conducting research on the phytogeography of the northeastern North American flora, concentrating on the Great Lakes region. My primary interests here are plant migration and colonization, the origin and persistence of relict plant communities, and the determining factors of species richness in plant communities. I am also gathering materials towards a book on the phytogeography of the Great Lakes region as a long-term goal.

There are several points of note in this eight-sentence summary. The earlier Tony, the educator, the infuser of love for plants, the conservationist, has retreated into the background (except perhaps for the clues contained in the phrase toward the end about "persistence of relict plant communities"). Rather, his major interest, as described in the opening five sentences, falls centrally within the field of classic systematic botany, and deals with the "large and complex genus *Carex*" or sedges. Indeed, the parallels with Bill's research (identification keys, sectional classification, and nomenclature) are close. We can note too the emphasis on the crowning professional genre in this field—the monograph—and observe in passing how Tony centralizes the concept by using it as a verb: ". . . in addition *to monographing* difficult groups of Carex."

So, in addition to the more popular kinds of writing he does for amateur botanists, Tony is a primary researcher. In fact, by the end of 1994, he had an extensive list of 65 refereed publications, plus another six in press. Seventeen of these are single-authored and 35 co-authored with just one other colleague. A little over half of this output is devoted to his major research area, with titles that include the words "sedges," "Carex," or "Cyperaceae." These publications vary in length from a single page to 76 pages. Text-lengths break down as follows:

Number of Pages	Number in Group
1–5	29
6–10	19
11–20	7
21–40	6
41–80	4

In order to get a handle on how this extensive textual production gets accomplished, Margaret and I asked Tony in interview to estimate how his time is distributed among his many activities during a typical year. The approximate proportions look like this:

a) Administration, planning, curatorial mat-   4 months
   ters, committees, grant applications
b) Writing and "all the associated things"   2 months, 10 weeks
c) "I give a lot of lectures, and I do a lot of   2 months
   identification material for people all over,
   probably I get sent and identify for people
   somewhere in the order of 1500, 2000
   sheets, collections of sedges mostly but
   also other things, a year"
d) Processing material from the field   1 month, 10 weeks
e) Field work (somewhere in North Amer-   1 month
   ica, including Mexico)

Tony, therefore, manages his life in order to spend some annual time in the field and to produce several papers a year. As he said, "I try to plan, and I try to make sure that I get certain amounts of time at certain periods for certain things."

Apart from these rather more distinct activities, Tony has also the Herbarium to "manage" on a regular basis, as well as to cope with a fluctuating stream of identification requests. The first of these tasks was already examined in the previous chapter; now let us have a brief look at the second, because doing so provides another useful window into Tony's textual world, and also provides some extension to Bill's identification practices.

The process typically starts when some botanist elsewhere inquires whether Tony could look at some specimens, a request to which Tony usually agrees. When the specimens arrive they are typically in the form of duplicates so that if Tony wants to keep them and add them to the Herbarium, he is, like Bill, free to do so as some small repayment for his service. When he initially examines the material, he makes "a first pass through the specimens" and names those that he can by ordinary (if exceptionally skilled) observation. For many of the remaining specimens, he can reach an identification by using a microscope "to double-check characters that I can't see with my eye." This leaves a residue of specimens that, for various reasons, requires considerably more work. Those reasons may include the fact that the specimen happens not to contain its most identifiable features (it may be in flower when it is easiest to name in fruit); or it may be a representative of a difficult and complex taxonomic group; or it may belong to a group that has not been well studied or one where the available monographs "are darn near unusable."

In one or more of these situations, Tony's normal recourse is to go back to "the range" and examine a sizeable number of specimens in the group—a process that, as he says, "often gives me a fairly clear picture of what's going on, and then after I learn them that way, I can often go back and say 'yeah, that's so and so,' and it all works." However, even a comprehensive examination of range material may not suffice. At such an impasse, for Tony if not for Bill, quantitative methods may be invoked, ranging from simple one-dimensional scales, through two-dimensional scatter-plots, and perhaps eventually extending to "extremely time-extensive" and complex mathematical operations, such as *discriminant function analysis*.

As an example of such methods, we can consider the case of the specimen listed as Rolfsmeier 5025, which was one of a number of problem plants sent to Tony in 1996 by a botanist working on a treatment of the sedge family for the State of Nebraska. Tony simply observed to me that he got sent them because his colleague "just couldn't work out what some of these things were with the material he had available" (shades of Bill's sympathetic understanding of Niedenzu's difficulties!). Tony also observed that Rolfsmeier 5025 belonged to a very difficult group of sedges— "even nastier than usual"—where the most easily used and easily measured characters show a great deal of overlap. However, Tony was able to resolve this difficult identification problem in about 30 minutes, but only because, once he recognized that 5025 had to be either *Carex tenera* or *C. normalis*, he *already* had the relevant data on his computer.

Figure 3.1 is the first of two scatter-plots that he has developed to distinguish these two species. Using mostly material from the Michigan Herbarium, Tony has entered the key pairs of measurements for about 80 identified specimens of *C. normalis* (dots in the scatter-plot) and for about 30 of *C. tenera* (triangles in the scatter-plot), to which he has now added a square for Rolfsmeier 5025. Figure 3.1 also shows Tony's hand-drawn tracings of how the characters of the two species are distributed. As can be seen, in this difficult case, there is a considerable overlap zone, and the mystery plant unfortunately abuts the edge of it. Tony then observed, as he clicked onto his second scatter-plot (Fig. 3.2):

Carex tenera var. echinodes vs. C. normalis

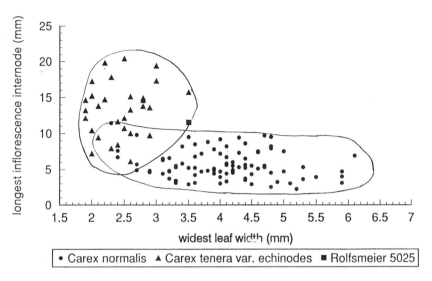

FIG. 3.1. The first scatter-plot.

Carex tenera var. echinodes versus C. normalis
Overlap zone only

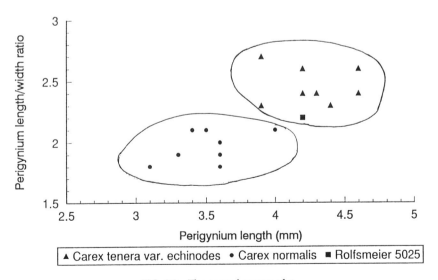

FIG. 3.2. The second scatter-plot.

Within this overlap zone you can actually apply characters that might not work in other instances. So, for example, the perigynium length and shape do not differ all that much among these two species, but confining yourself strictly to the zone of overlap does produce a difference because the ones of this species [pointing to the dots] are the very smallest individuals, and the ones of that one [pointing to the triangles] are somewhat larger than normal individuals . . .

J: So you decided it was *Carex tenera*?

T: Yes, even though the specimen was pretty ambiguous.

I also asked Tony whether he was unique or unusual in having such a computer database for difficult identification problems. He replied that for this particular group of sedges he was collaborating with a colleague in Indiana, but for many of the others he was the only person who "has a lot of this data compiled in usable form." He added that one of his long-range goals was to make his work on this group of sedges available in ways that take advantage of modern technology. He noted with some animation that computers are exceptionally good at running operations like search algorithms, techniques that have clear advantages with material that tends to be intractable for dichotomous key treatments because of "character overlap."

While the story of Tony's multivariate approach to the couple of thousand specimens he identifies each year for others has a certain intrinsic interest, it also has a broader message. At an immediate level, it reinforces Bill's comment that the curatorial and research work cannot really be kept apart. Indeed, Tony's very considerable investment of time, thought, and energy in developing computer-driven quantitative methods of identification, to a considerable degree motivated by a concern to provide a better service, is now leading him toward a new conceptualization of what a more interactive 21st-century sedge monograph might look like and how it might be used. On a wider level, we see here, as we will see in our discussion of the top floor, enough evidence to once again question all those widely held opinions that service (whether curatorial or pedagogical) and research are in dire competition and conflict. At least for some inhabitants of NUBS, academic life is not a zero-sum game in that regard.

One of Tony's Texts

In order to discuss Tony's writing, I have focused on just one of Tony's many texts. Not surprisingly given his major interest, I have chosen for this purpose a paper dealing with sedges: *Revision of Carex Section Ovales (Cyperaceae) in Mexico* (Reznicek, 1993). This is recent, single-authored, and substantial (running to just under 39 pages). Like Bill's **B. itacarensis** text, it was published in Volume 19 of *Contributions from the University of*

Michigan Herbarium. As the title suggests, this publication is central to his major research area. For those whose knowledge of biological writing derives from such recent publications as Myers' *Writing Biology* (1990), Killingsworth and Palmer's *Ecospeak* (1988), Selzer's 1993 edited volume devoted to an "opinion piece" by Gould and Lewontin, or the relevant parts of Williamson (1988), Berkenkotter and Huckin (1995), or Gross (1990— apart from his Chapter III to be discussed in the *Interlude*), Tony's paper will come as a considerable surprise. Although Tony does write a fair number of biological research articles of the type analyzed by Myers (1990), Thompson (1993), and others, especially in his second area of interest, the *Revision* text is not much like any of the genres discussed to date in rhetorical studies of writing in biology.

On more than one occasion Tony's paper describes itself as a *treatment*. This common genre-label in Plant Taxonomy and Systematic Botany appears to be a somewhat elastic term designed to cover the description, classification, and discussion of a variable number of plant species. If we recollect that one of Tony's major "longer-term goals" in his c.v. is a monograph of the New World species of *Carex*, then this paper can be seen as a contribution to that undertaking. In it he describes 14 species from Mexico in the "Section ovales," there being another 60 or so in the section collected elsewhere in North America. A complete monograph of all New World Carex would need, according to Tony, to *treat* about 800 species.

Tony's *treatment* has a number of features that place it within the specially evolved genres of systematic botany. There is no Abstract (despite its length), and there is no Discussion or Conclusion section (again despite its length). On the other hand, there are some treatment-specific elements, such as a list of "Excluded Names" and some paragraphs in Botanical Latin. Another intriguing aspect of the paper is its handling of the literature. Quite large numbers of references within the text are designedly not included in the *Literature Cited* section toward the end. Even so, the literature that is included is, at least to the outsider, peculiarly historical. Of the 32 citations, only 15 are after 1980, whereas the other 17 were more than 14 years old at the time of publication. There is one from 1850, two each from the first two decades and the next two decades of the present century, three from the 1940s and 1950s, and nine from the 1960s and 1970s. Exceptionally venerable is the list of five *Excluded Names*, the first dates assigned to these being 1837, 1915, 1842, 1858, and 1892.

There are a number of other features that set the *Revision* apart from most kinds of academic writing, while reinforcing its affinities with Bill's written discourse. For one thing, there are three paragraphs that Tony has written in Latin in order to comply with the traditional nomenclature rules, which require that all species new to science be briefly described in that language. He says of his Latin writing, "it's slow, but I don't especially find it difficult." For another, both the syntax and lexis of the species descriptions are highly unusual and highly conventionalized. For a third, the text is peppered with those exclamatory signs of personal examination resulting from that postal merry-go-round whereby specimens are circulated among the denizens of herbaria. Consider the effusive nature of this short partial extract:

> *Carex egglestonii* var. . . . .
> . . . .
> 25 Jul 1938, [Schneider] 954 (holotype: MICH!;
> isotypes: F! GH! ILL! MO! NY! US!)

The paper itself consists of a three-page introduction, a 32-page taxonomy containing a short overview of Ovales species, a key to identification and 14 species accounts, and about four pages of end matter (Excluded Names, Acknowledgments, Literature Cited, Index to Numbered Collections Cited).

The Introduction. The Introduction is divided into 13 paragraphs of normal length. In the list that follows, I illustrate the character of this opening section by giving the first sentences of the paragraphs (or in some cases "skeletal" reductions) accompanied by a marginal gloss:

1. *Carex* L. Section *Ovales* . . . is the largest and most difficult section of the genus in the New World.   PROBLEMATICS (1–3)

2. The section is considered very difficult taxonomically and treatments of local areas vary considerably in the number of species recognized.

3. Essentially nothing is known about the reproductive biology of Mexican members of section *Ovales*.

4. This treatment represents a considerable amplification of past treatments of the section in Mexico.   JUSTIFICATION OF PRESENT WORK (4, 5)

5. Subsequent to Hermann's (1974) treatment, many new collections have accumulated.

6. All the Mexican members of section *Ovales* are montane plants: . . .   PLANTS, DISTRIBUTION IN MEXICO, REJECTION OF M'S SCHEME (6–8)

7. Mexican members of section *Ovales* are in no way a natural group; ...

8. Mackenzie (1931) divided the section into 11 unranked groups based on ...

9. The primary taxonomic characters that have proved useful in the systematics of the section reside in ....

   I.D, PROBLEMS, NEED FOR NEW KEY (9–12)

10. An additional complication with species occurring in alpine sites is that ... all tend to become dwarfed ...

11. Most keys to the section (e.g. Hermann 1970, 1974) are very difficult to use, because ...

12. Immature specimens ... can sometimes be recognized, if complete, but cannot be keyed ...

13. All names based on Mexican specimens are typified here.

    STRUCTURE OF ACCOUNTS (13)

In many ways, Tony's Introduction superficially resembles the character of research article introductions, as by now widely discussed in the discourse analysis literature. The opening three paragraphs set up the problematic state of current knowledge, while the next two provide explanations for why the present treatment, though still "preliminary," represents an advance on earlier efforts. Paragraphs 6 through 9 discuss the plants, their distribution in Mexico, and why Mackenzie's classification has not been followed. The next four discuss identification problems and then explain why the new key may be easier to use than Hermann's. The final paragraph outlines essential features of the forthcoming accounts, concluding with: "Specimens are arranged alphabetically, and all Mexican specimens that were examined are cited, arranged alphabetically by states and by collector and number." We seem to see here a number of the expected rhetorical moves in their expected textual place, such as Establishing the Field, Indicating a Gap (with at least one recycling), and Outlining Structure.

There are a number of factors, however, that suggest that we might want to be cautious about interpreting it as a standard "create a research space" text. First, as we have seen, this is a stand-alone introduction without a subsequent Discussion wherein the central issues initially raised can be reprised, reinterpreted, and further cogitated upon. This is not to say that the taxonomic *treatment* is devoid of commentary dealing with decisions made and alternatives rejected; rather, as Tony observed in interview, "The discussion associated with it is typically fragmented, and it follows under each of the species." Indeed, the fact that there is no opportunity for general reflection at the end of the paper explains why Tony's account of the geographical *distribution* of Ovales appears in the middle of the Introduction (Paragraphs 6 & 7), as it will turn out that lack of information about phytogeography has led to many of the earlier difficulties with the section. Under the "normal" circumstances of a research article, we might have expected this important consequence of the study to have been reiterated in a later section and to have been discussed more explicitly (as, for example, Luebs & Coon [1997] show for Social Psychology).

As far as I am aware, nobody with an interest in discourse has published any studies on this kind of "prefacing" introduction, although Bhatia (1997) has offered a preliminary survey of the "mixed genre" (description and promotion) of the initial matter in textbooks. However, even a little reflection seems to show that such introductions may be fairly common in the academy. They will provide the front matter not only to taxonomies, as we have seen, but also to specialized bibliographies, *catalogues raisonnés*, anthologies, textbooks, reference books (such as dictionaries and field-guides), scholarly editions of literary works of all kinds, collections of historical documents, and monographs accompanying special museum exhibitions. The reasons why my own field has neglected this large class of introductions I imagine to be essentially two. First, the main texts to which they are introductions tend to have descriptive, fragmentary, and technical characteristics unlikely to be of immediate interest to rhetoricians and discourse analysts. Second, with few exceptions, of which Botany and Library Science may be the principal ones, these inventory-type genres are rarely required of graduate students, but are rather the outcomes of years of work by seasoned scholars. Therefore, in our present state of uncertainty, it would be rash to immediately assume that such introductions fall simply and easily within the rhetorical frameworks now fairly well established for research articles and scholarly papers. Indeed, in the following chapter I present a fairly extensive account of a book introduction that has a highly distinctive purpose and character.

Another reason for caution follows from the first. There may be a somewhat different relationship between introduction and main text in inventory, reference and pedagogic genres than in research articles. Here is Tony again:

> Most people try to keep the introductory matter as crisp—which is a euphemism for boring—as possible, and concentrate their loving care on the descriptions and maps and illustrations, and I guess I'm no exception there. . . . Taxonomic monographs tend to be judged as good and bad by whether other people can make them work, in the long run.

There would seem, in consequence, to be reduced pressure to offer "news value" (Berkenkotter & Huckin, 1995), or to "establish the field" (Swales, 1990a). Introductions to taxonomies, in the eyes apparently of both authors and readers, may turn out to be more rhetorically and informationally tangential than they are in many other genres.

A third reason for hesitation derives more specifically from a particular characteristic of Systematics. Systematic Botanists, as noted on several previous occasions, have exceptionally deep time-lines, partly deriving from the fact that botanical nomenclature is based on priority of publication. Although Miller and Halloran (1993), in their chapter on the Gould and Lewontin "opinion piece," discussed Biology as "a historical science," they did so in terms of relationships to "intellectual forebears." They commented:

> The adaptationists claim to be strict Darwinians, but Gould and Lewontin claim to be *more* Darwinian by being truer to the spirit if not the letter of his work. Darwin must be read and reread, interpreted and reinterpreted. We find this attention to a body of work that is well over a hundred years old to be highly unusual and worth investigating. (1993, p. 108, original emphasis)

However, in Systematics the relevance of history is better conceived of in terms of archival imperatives rather than in intellectual allegiances. As we have seen, the great Linnaean divide of the mid-18th-century places any writings since that epoch as having potential relevance for Plant Systematics. Further, several informants have stressed that in this field a 50-year-old monograph may be the latest comprehensive text available. Recall that Bill's main reference is a Latin work (with the notes in German) published in 1928. Chris, another member of the Herbarium, has recently completed a monograph on an 89-species family that has been dealt with on just two previous occasions: first in 1840 and then again in 1928! Tony himself consistently uses the most recent complete monograph on North American sedges, which was, in fact, published as long ago as 1935.

However, there does remain one aspect of Tony's Introduction that *will* be familiar to those who know the Rhetoric of Science literature, or are themselves academics. As with the researchers described by Knorr-Cetina (1981) in *The Manufacture of Knowledge*, there is a disjunction between the carefully constructed rationale of the published introduction and the adventitious reality of how the research project came about. However, in this particular case, the "facts" of the matter are disclosed by Tony at the end of the Acknowledgments, rather than requiring extensive ethnographic effort. Tony writes: "This work originated out of frustrated attempts to provide the correct names for the two species in section

Ovales occurring in Rogers McVaugh's *Flora Novo-Galiciana* area, and I am grateful to him for forcing my confrontation with these plants." As is so often the case in scholarship, a minor problem (the correct names for two species) leads to a larger study (revision of section *Ovales* in Mexico), and once again reconnects curatorial and research roles.

The Rest of the Text. After a short overview, the taxonomy leads straight into Tony's extensive 68-line stepped key, which a botanist will work through in order to unlock the identity of a putative specimen of Mexican *Ovales*. The major portion of the text is then devoted to the species accounts. Of the 14 species, three are new to science and have, as we saw with Bill, the now-customary opening paragraph in Latin. The text is supported by one plate of drawings and one plate of photographs, plus a number of maps showing the distribution of the species.

In the *Revision* the species accounts follow a standard arrangement:

a. Name plus bibliography
b. Very dense and highly technical description (see below)
c. Habitat in Mexico
d. List of specimens examined (!)
e. Distribution in North America (including Mexico)
f. Commentary discussing previous identifications etc.

The second element (b. in the preceding list) is again written in that very striking lexis and syntax that we have already met in Bill's text, and which is quite distinct from the style of the later elements. Here are the first two sentences from the first species account (*Carex athrostachya*):

> Densely cespitose in large clumps, fertile culms 15–80 cm tall, erect, trigonous, scabrous-angled; bladeless basal sheaths pale brown, disintegrating into short, dark brown fibers. Leaves 2–5, on the lower ⅕–⅓ of the culm; blades 3–30 cm long, 1.2–4 mm wide, plicate, glabrous, the margins and midrib antrorsely scabrous distally; leaf sheaths ca. 1.5–9 cm long, tightly enveloping culms, glabrous, green; the inner band of sheaths glabrous, whitish hyaline, sometimes prolonged up to 4 mm beyond the leaf bases, the apex concave, whitish hyaline; ligules 1.5–6 mm long, rounded, the free portion entire to +– erose, up to ca. 1 mm long.

Such structural descriptions have, as we now know, regular kinds of order. Depending in part on the kind of plant, some may start at the ground and work up through the vegetative to the reproductive parts; others progress from the inside out, or from the outside in. Yet other schemes, such as the one Tony uses for sedges, follow a sequence from the largest to the smallest element. The order chosen seems to be partly determined by the different foci of attention required to describe one kind of plant as opposed to another, and partly by the inherited conventions for structuring descriptions within a genus or family, although one may, of course, hope that these two determinants are connected.

This opening extract from *Carex athrostachya* consists of only two sentences, the second extremely long. In this subgenre, as we now also know, punctuation has come to take on particular significance. Periods mark divisions between the basic parts of the plant; semi-colons separate important elements within the parts; and commas handle the separate items of descriptive detail. Once again, there are no finite verbs and no pronouns, and the topic (*Carex athrostachya*) does not itself appear in its own description. The vocabulary for shape and texture is heavily derived from classical Greek and Latin (*glabrous, hyaline, scabrous, cespitose, trigonous*), even if everyday adjectives and modifiers are used for colors (*dark brown*). As far as I can discover, this kind of writing is rarely, if ever, directly taught, but acquired via long and close exposure to the species-description literature. Although sometimes described by botanists as formulaic, Bill, for one, does not see writing in this subgenre as that simple:

> ... being able to boil down descriptive data into something that's clear and concise turns out to be very difficult; and it requires a feeling for words and an understanding of the proper placement of modifiers that many people don't have, and have to learn to do.

Tony concurs. He wrote the following marginal note, which I have chosen as epigraph, at this point in a draft of the section:

> I agree fully; it is easy to describe specimens, but our *aim* is describe species.

Another parallel with Bill can be seen in Tony's handling of revisions. As we have already seen, the long intervals between revised treatments not only mean that long-past work retains relevance for long periods of time, but also that experienced and "seasoned" systematic botanists are sensitive to the difficulties under which their predecessors may have worked. As Chris observed, "It isn't that people are kind; it is just that there isn't too much focus on people; the focus is on the problem or the plant." For example, Tony ended his first species account with the following short paragraph:

> *Carex athrostachya* was first reported from Mexico in Hermann (1974), based on *Balls 4202*. Gonzalez E. (1990) reported two additional collections, *Gonzalez E. 1151* and *1142*. These collections, all from high elevations in the Transvolcanic Belt, are here referred to as *C. orizabae*.

After some hesitation, I finally took the last sentence to be a correction, or perhaps better "a revision" because that is the first word in Tony's title. Here is Tony (in interview) commenting on our comments on his commentary:

> ... that's a very nice way of saying that they were wrong (all laugh) ... it turns out that there were elevational differences, one species is lower èle-vation and one is upper, but none of this was known because nobody had pulled all the material together and discovered these things, so there was no way in fact that either of these people could come to the right conclusion.

Another area of revision occurs in the Excluded Names section, which falls between the species accounts and the Acknowledgments. The Excluded Names are a final bit of tidying up in a treatment. There are five such exclusions in the *Revision*. One is a simple *nomen nuda* (a "naked" name because it has been assigned without any accompanying description of the plant), but the other four have all been reported in the literature as belonging to the section *Ovales* and occurring in Mexico. Tony, therefore, needs to explain for future researchers why he has not used them. Here is part of his final exclusion:

> *Carex xerantica* L. H. Bailey, Bot. Gaz. 17:151. 1892. -
> TYPE: CANADA. [Saskatchewan]: . . . .
> The two Mexican specimens referred to this species by
> Hermann (1974) are *C. lagunensis*.

As we can see, this is a bald re-identification; for example, there is no attempt to press the matter by saying that "this is not *A*, but *B*" or to point out that Hermann was in error. All the botanists I have spoken to in the course of this project readily admit to making errors themselves, and having to correct them at some later date. The underplayed nature of these correction processes offers us a glimpse, I suspect, of the strong collegiality of this community, however dispersed its members may be in both time and space.

The final aspect of writing in this area that is worth a further comment is the tradition that only a smallish proportion of the internal citations are gathered together in the *Literature Cited* section in the end. Tony explains this anomaly by referring to the way "conventions have evolved in the field," although, somewhat ruefully, he does admit that "it kills us in citation indices and stuff like that." But then again, and unlike other genres such as research papers, citation *per se* of taxonomic treatments seems less relevant to their authors and less pertinent to the work's value or visibility. As Tony remarked, "these kinds of things are generally used, they're not cited. I mean nobody cites a dictionary."

I hope the foregoing account has indicated something of the complexity of the *Revision of Carex Section Ovales (Cyperaceae) in Mexico* text. It deals with technically demanding material and its creation has involved more than one field trip to Mexico and meticulous scrutiny of many specimens from many places. It is complex because it has to wrestle with a botanical history of a section that extends back more than a hundred years. For instance, it has, as we have just seen, to account for all the names that have ever been assigned and explain why some have been "excluded" as no longer valid. It takes up the responsibility of critiquing and rectifying prior work, but does so with patience and understanding, and with a degree of academic tactfulness that has traditionally been more closely associated with Asian academic cultures (Ballard & Clanchy, 1984; Scollon & Scollon, 1995) than with North American or European ones.

In essence, there is in the *Revision* a distinctive air of intertextuality— "the web of texts against which each new text is placed or places itself, explicitly or implicitly" (Bazerman, 1993, p. 20). In this case, however, this web exceptionally extends itself in two ways. First, it goes back deep in the past, not so much in search of history *per se*, but as part of the pragmatics of checking and assessing the primary botanical record. The web of texts also extends beyond the published texts to the collection sheets. These, after all, contain textual information in the form of labels, annotations, and the names of botanists. Further, the specimens themselves are not exactly "raw data," but detached from their context, dessicated, distorted, and displayed according to a determining set of traditions and conventions (as discussed in chapter 2). The parallel with the attempts in my own field of linguistics to use transcription to capture the essentials of living speech on paper is interestingly close. Assembling specimens, like transcribing conversation, turns out to be part of theory (Ochs, 1979) and thus represents an early-analysis rather than a data-gathering stage in investigation (Luebs, 1996).

The *Revision* is also complex because it contains within its compass several distinct types of writing: rhetorically crafted scholarly prose, as in the introduction; highly structured annotated material, as in the key; and meticulous technical description, as in the species accounts. Above all, though, Tony's treatment is complex because of its set of communicative purposes, which are not merely concerned with consolidating present knowledge, but rather with assisting botanists in the future to identify material in a section known for its taxonomic difficulty. In the end, we see here an *instrument* to be used in the herbarium or perhaps in the field, yet an instrument in which the elaborate history, the developing phytogeography, and the highly intertextual discursive commentary are not mere adornments of scholarship, but components that are essential and integral to the enterprise.

Interlude: Alan Gross on Taxonomic Language

In the previous section I observed that rhetoricians and discourse analysts have not discussed the kinds of texts I have been illustrating from the writings of Bill and Tony. There is one ostensible exception to this: the third chapter of Alan Gross' *The Rhetoric of Science* (1990), which is both entitled and devoted to "Taxonomic Language." As we are now at the halfway point in the discussion of the Herbarium textways, this seems an appropriate moment to assess Gross' contribution. However, when doing so, two difficulties quickly emerge, although of very different kinds.

The first arises in connection with Gross's aim in his third chapter, which ultimately is more demonstrative than descriptive. In effect, his purpose is to use taxonomic description (and its role in and relationship to evolutionary taxonomy) as a *vehicle* for establishing what a "complete" rhetoric of science would be like, that is, one which, once the analysis was completed, would leave no unrhetorical remainder such as some "hard 'scientific' core" (p. 33) to be further or otherwise accounted for. Gross produced a number of ingenious arguments, often impressively supported by philosophical sources, for his ambitious purpose, and these arguments were used to set up a basic contrast between "a rational reconstruction of species" (as one of several possible variants that biologists might adhere to) and his own "rhetorical reconstruction of species." The former, he argued, is premised on *identification* and the latter on *creation*. His "theory hope" (my borrowed term, not his) thus emerges as follows:

> By means of rhetorical reconstruction, evolutionary taxonomy is transferred into an interlocking set of persuasive structures. *Sub specie rhetoricae*, we do not discover, we create: plants and animals are brought to life, raised to membership in a taxonomic group, and made to illustrate and generate evolutionary theory. If a rhetorical reconstruction describes rhetorically every aspect that a rational reconstruction describes rationally, a complete rhetoric of science becomes possible. (1990, p. 34)

These arguments, as we may be beginning to suspect, have their own further purposes directed toward establishing—or perhaps re-establishing—rhetoric as a discipline in its own right. Completeness of account is thus equated with disciplinary status. Further, there is, for Gross at least, a crippling corollary: "without disciplinary status, rhetoric of science is not a field but a bundle of techniques, an adjunct to fields" (p. 49). However, as the Sociologists of Science were soon to discover (e.g., Ashmore, 1989), this assertive stance immediately raises *tu quoque* ("you also") concerns about self-reflexivity, which Gross did not in fact address. In effect, any *complete* rhetorical account (as, for instance, the one proposed by Gross) is itself inevitably socially constructed and created, ultimately "persuasive" only in defiance of its own unannounced contingencies, and thus remaining as much a prisoner of its own circumstances and ethos as any other account, rationalist, rhetorical, reductionist, or whatever.

In contrast to Alan Gross, I see no problem with rhetorical or discoursal analysis offering only a partial account and would, contrary to Gross, support the quotation from Gusfield that he attacks: ". . . thus an analysis of a scientific work *should* . . . include its rhetorical as well as its empirical component" (Gusfield, 1976, p. 31). Indeed, in fear of hubris, I would prefer to set my sights even lower than Gusfield's and argue that an analysis of a scientific or academic work can, under propitious circumstances, *potentially* be illuminated by a rhetorical component. I would also diverge from Gross in his assumption that only rhetoric-as-discipline has the hermeneutic capacity to generate knowledge. Rather, I would argue that "adjunct" work, if done with serendipity and skill, can show us ("us" hopefully including the disciplinary or professional practitioners whose very texts fall prey to our analysis) alternate perspectives that are revealingly ironic, thought-provoking, and genre-interrogating, and so possibly even emancipatory for their disciplinary authors. As both teacher and researcher, the general value of rhetorical consciousness-raising has long seemed self-evident to me. And here, at the last, I fully agree with Alan Gross' advocacy of rhetorical analysis.

The second difficulty in aligning Gross' chapter with the present one is to outsiders likely trivial, but turns out to be crucial. It happens that Gross' primary text for examining the rhetoric of species identification and/or creation is "A New Species of Hummingbird from Peru" (Fitzpatrick, Willard, & Terborgh, 1979). It also turns out that the rhetorical/scientific demands placed upon experts in their efforts to establish a new species in ornithology as opposed to botany are very different. In consequence, Gross' detailed, intricate, and powerful account of how a new species of *bird* is established in the ornithological literature has its own self-evident verisimilitudes for *that* rhetorical situation, although it happens to fit ill with the rhetorical situations of systematic botanists. This is because "species new to science" are extremely variable in their occurrence within the higher taxonomic categories. A new mammal, such as the one reported from Vietnam in 1995, makes all the newspaper headlines; one or two new bird species are still reported each year and, as we have seen in Gross's specimen text, their attestation can make a splash in the ornithological literature—and then be picked up by the "serious" birding magazines. In Botany, and probably even more so in Entomology, descriptions of "species new to science" are a dime a dozen. Bill responded to my messaged query about the numbers of new botanical species described each year with: "... it must be thousands, but how many thousands I haven't a clue. Nor, I suspect, does anybody else."

At this juncture, it is worth recollecting the downbeat title of Bill's contribution "Notes on Malpighiaceae—IV," even though its opening description was of a species new to science, *B. itacarensis.* In contrast, Fitzpatrick et al.'s title, "A New Species of Hummingbird from Peru," is both severely nontechnical and highly newsworthy (Berkenkotter & Huckin, 1995, have many valuable things to say about the appeal to "newsworthiness" in scientific papers). Further, Fitzpatrick et al. occupies ten pages in Volume 91 of the venerable and highly esteemed ornithological journal *Wilson Bulletin,* and includes, doubtless at considerable expense, no less than a full-page, full-color plate of the male and female of the new species in their typical habitat. In contrast, describing a new botanical species is almost quotidian. We may further recollect, as just one example, that Tony slips in three new species among the 14 sedges he describes in the Mexican *Ovales* section, for which, apart from the muted abbreviation "sp. nov." in the head matter, the primary signal to the botanical world of *discovery* continues to be that short diagnostic paragraph in Latin.

Another difference that affects the rhetoric of species identification in ornithology as opposed to botany is the criteria that contribute to the undertaking. Gross, from the perspective of his ornithological text, opens his detailed account with the following statement: "In contemporary biology, species cannot be defined classically, by genus and differentia" (p. 34). This statement is largely true for ornithology (and at this juncture I offer the passing observation that I am coincidentally a fairly serious amateur birdwatcher). There DNA, vocalizations, habitat preference, migration patterns (if any), evidence of non-successful interspecific breeding, and several other "characters" can all play their part. On the other hand, while DNA can be relevant in Botany, the "genus and differentia" *key* remains the primary—and classical—instrument both for established species identification and for the identification of new species that fall outside its rigorous algorithmic confines.

Gross went on to claim that, for his rhetorical reconstruction, "The first stage, the creation of the potential species is best elucidated by the New Rhetorical concept of 'presence'" (p. 42), seen as the foregrounding of certain elements in the reader's consciousness. In consequence, the reader's mind becomes occupied with this emerging "'creature so as to isolate it, as it were, from (the reader's) overall mentality' (Perelman & Olbrechts-Tyteca, 1971, p. 18)" (p. 43). Gross further suggested: "In the description and depiction of the potential species of evolutionary taxonomy, presence is created by two devices: overdescription and multiple sensory perspectives. The first, overdescription, is the characterization of sense objects in detail beyond a reader's ordinary expectations" (pp. 42–43).

As I have intimated, Gross' account of "A New Species of Hummingbird from Peru" can indeed make use of these characteristics, such as *presence* being established by the title, the illustrations, and the complex multisensory description (appearance, habitat, behavior, vocalizations, and the like). And, of course, any description of a new species is likely to go beyond "a reader's ordinary expectations" because, even in botany and entomology, clear differentia must be established. Further, in ornithological and bird-watching circles, to get even a *locally unusual* species accepted by a state *Birds' Record Committee* requires extensive and elaborate descriptive work in which "excellent details" is the highest accolade and in which the swiftest path to dismissal is to observe that "the bird I saw looked exactly like the one illustrated on page so-and-so of such-and-such field guide." This set of genres is thus not premised on the "ordinary expectations" of some decontextualized reader, but on the extraordinary ones established by the particular communicative purposes at work in the genre set.

Moreover, in botany, there is little that can be multisensory in the depiction of a set of dried herbaric specimens, especially as the presence-invoking named object is rarely, if ever, iterated in the actual description, and the whole enterprise is, in Bill's words, designed "to boil down descriptive data into something that's clear and concise . . . ." In fact, in terms of "a reader's ordinary expectations" of what he or she might hope to find, the new species are, if anything, *underdescribed*.

There are more contrasts that could be drawn between Gross' account and the ones presented in this chapter, but I fear to belabor the essential point that the rhetorical exigencies of producing a viable account of a new species differ greatly from one area of the biological sciences to the next. Gross has many intelligent and perceptive things to say about texts in his chosen areas, but they do not work in those I have chosen, just as my observations do not pertain to his. Therein perhaps lies a lesson for all those of us who are interested in the discourse of academic disciplines, whether we take the high road to that discourse via a complete rhetorical reconstruction (*pace* Gross), or take the low road of a modestly adjunctive reading of sets of individual texts (*pace* myself).

ED

The Nomenclature Committees, bless their hearts, are all volunteers. Nobody gets any pay, stipends or anything, for it. . . . Mostly it's entirely volunteer work by people who think it's important to do, and are willing to put time in on it . . . . Of course, there is some criticism of this; it's the same old people all the time who are sitting on the committees and doing all the work. It's an esoteric in-house field and the public doesn't have a democratic opportunity to affect things. Well, they can always come to the Nomenclature Section. While that's important, it's also excessively expensive. To go to a Botanical Congress and to participate in the Nomenclature Section takes an extra week. (Ed, in interview)

Ed officially retired in August 1996 after he finished his traditional summer teaching at his beloved Biological Station in the forests, lakes, and swamps of Michigan's Northern Lower Peninsula. However, he also notes—with some satisfaction—that the director of the station has offered assurances he will be welcome to continue if demand for his course continues. So, as he says, "I will probably teach up there for a few more summers anyway." Here is another example of the long botanical working life, to be added to those mentioned in chapter 2. Indeed, like most other botanists I have encountered during this project, Ed's professional interests are as likely to intensify as to diminish once he is free of the standard teaching and administrative duties associated with being a regular faculty member in Ann Arbor. His future plans include revising the earlier two volumes of his *Michigan Flora* and, in collaboration with Tony, producing a condensed one-volume manual that people "can take into the field." He is also intending to take up once again his long-standing interests in lepidoptera.

It was, in fact, moths and butterflies that attracted him to botany in the first place:

I got started saving great big caterpillars that fell off the trees in our yard in Toledo [Ohio] when I was growing up, and my parents suggested I put them in a carton with a screen over the top and watch them make cocoons and big moths hatched out. And my grandparents had a summer cottage up in Mackinaw City on the straits just west of where the bridge takes off from now, and so I've spent at least part of almost every summer of my life up there. It's mine now. And so I started collecting butterflies and moths in Emmet and Cheboygan counties. And then as a junior 51 years ago [I had] a full year of high school Botany, and we had to make a collection in the fall and we had to make a collection in the spring. So I started collecting that summer and documenting what my butterflies were visiting, and that turned out to be a much bigger task . . . so that got me off in Botany, but I haven't really abandoned the lepidoptera.

Ed has been at the University of Michigan since 1950, first as a graduate student, later as a faculty member and curator of vascular plants, becoming a full professor in 1969. In contrast to Bill, however, his scientific interests are primarily local; indeed, we have already seen that he has spent part of "nearly every summer" of his life up-state. As a natural consequence, in the *Field Experience & Collections* section of his c.v. Michigan occupies pride of place and is glossed as "extensive field work since 1945, collecting on mainland of every county plus many islands in the Great Lakes." Over this half-century or so, Ed reckons that he has deposited about 26,000 plant specimens into MICH and other herbaria, and examined around a quarter of a million Michigan specimens collected by others. At least part of the motivation for this collecting and examination effort can be directly related to his major project, a three-volume flora of Michigan, Part I appearing in 1972, Part II in 1985, and Part III in 1996. Ed reflected in interview—albeit a little ruefully—that when he started work on *Michigan Flora* in about 1956, it was originally conceived of as a five-year project. In fact, it has taken him, as he precisely and immediately calculated it, "eight times that." This dilation is one further example, if one still be needed, of the extremely measured pace of floristic publication.

The vast collecting and study experience that underpins *Michigan Flora* not only means that the volume itself contains important distributional information (for example, dot maps of species occurrence or otherwise for each of Michigan's 83 counties plus seven major island groups), but also explains some of his taxonomical beliefs:

> I have very little use for a lot of these named varieties and so on of species; they all grade into one another. I think in many cases it comes down to many people looking at too small a sample . . . so they can put them into two neat piles. But when I look at all the stuff I have, I can't put them into those two neat piles any more. Some people will admit that "Well, we looked at the first 20 specimens and saw each of these species," and then they wrote their key. Well, I look at every specimen I can get my hands on, and that makes it much more difficult actually, but I hope more accurate.

I also asked him in interview about Linnaeus's observation that genus and species exist in nature, but higher orders are a combination of nature and art:

Ed: . . . there is a question of whether a species is a real thing or an artifice of the taxonomist. Sure. That question still comes up.

John: And where do you stand on this?

Ed: I think they vary. Some are good and some aren't. I mean something like *Calypso*—there's no doubt about it at all. It is the only species in its genus and it's absolutely distinctive right around the world. There is no question about it. But then you come into some of the hawthorns and serviceberries, *Antennaria* (pussy-toes), even the sunflowers, and they all seem to run into each other; so it's hard to know where to draw the line. Evolution has not produced equal species, so you can't expect to be able to tell them apart with equal ease.

John: So Linnaeus was wrong when he said that "nature makes no jumps"?

Ed: Well he crossed that out in his personal copy of one of his volumes. I think he changed his mind. (interview)

Ed is very much a field taxonomist, a person who prefers to let the plants tell at least part of their own story, especially their own Michigan story. He commented, for example, that the classic manual originally written by the 19th-century botanist Asa Gray was based largely on New England plants to which "specimens from the Great Lakes region, ours, just don't fit." Another aspect of this pragmatism is his approach to the diagnostic keys for genera: "The key is simply an artificial device for identifying an unknown, and if flower color works best I'll use flower color [although] that might be completely irrelevant to any other critieria for classification" (interview). A final illustration of this orientation comes from the introduction to Volume I of *Michigan Flora* itself:

> Realizing that there may easily be differences of opinion as to the proper disposition of some of our taxa, I have often indicated taxonomic and nomenclatural alternatives, especially when they seem to have almost or quite as great merit as the ones adopted here. But it has not been desirable or possible to call attention to *all* of the recent taxonomic and nomenclatural innovations proposed for our plants. Keeping a flora in manuscript up to date and also within bounds could be a never-ending task of re-evaluation; somewhere the work must stop and be prepared for publication. When differing treatments for our plants exist in reliable manuals and monographs, I have pragmatically based the disposition of our plants on the treatment which seems to deal most satisfactorily with specimens from this region. (Voss, 1972, p. 29; original emphasis).

As earlier parts of this chapter have amply demonstrated, systematic Botany is desperately intertextual, and here we see Ed trying, on the one hand, to acknowledge the previous botanical record—and this in a region where that history is only about 150 years old—while, on the other, trying to extricate himself from the massive weight of Becker's *prior texts*. He emerges as prudent, pragmatic, and selective, acknowledging that some cited alternatives may have "almost or quite as great merit" as his own *dispositions*, and yet declining to cite others in an effort to bring a first volume of just under 500 pages to completion in a span of years that was now three times that originally set aside for the whole project. There is a palpable sense of pressure in this paragraph deriving from the complex and often contradictory exigencies of floristic text-work, but there is equally a sense of affinity with the material, as witnessed most strikingly by the four uses of that affiliative little pronoun "our."

As we saw at the beginning of this section, Ed has "never really abandoned lepidoptera," and, in addition to his floristic activities, earlier in his career he co-authored several short articles on uncommon or rare Michigan butterflies. More recently, he has been publishing an extensive series of papers on "Moths of the Douglas Lake Region (Emmet and Cheboygan Counties)" in the *Great Lakes Entomologist*. In addition to being a floristician and a lepidopterist, a third strand to Ed's busy and committed life is the remarkably large number of societies and organizations to which he belongs, and sometimes serves in some administrative capacity. According to his c.v. these number about 40, and still exclude what he describes as his "church, community, and fraternal activities." Some of these societies and organizations are umbrella professional groupings like the *International Association for Plant Taxonomy*, but more are regional such as *The Federation of Ontario Naturalists* or local (*The Little Traverse Conservancy*, for instance), and still others are concerned with conservation issues, such as *The Sierra Club*. Regarding these kinds of involvement, Ed is more like Tony and less like Bill or Bob, and indeed again like Tony, he is also a member of several technical or advisory committees concerned with rare or threatened plants. When I asked him about this, he responded with his customary modesty:

> I get involved in one thing and that leads to another. I was with the Little Traverse Conservancy on their board up north, and then the Nature Conservancy asked me to serve on their board, and so I'm on both. I think it is basically just a difficulty in saying "no."

The final entry in Ed's *Miscellaneous Positions and Activities* c.v. section reads "Member, Working Party on Author Abbreviations, Royal Botanical Gardens, Kew, 1985–". As this looked like a highly discipline-specific and intriguingly arcane enterprise, I asked him about it. He explained that the purpose of the Working Party was to provide a revised and expanded alphabetical listing of the full names along with unambiguous abbreviations (plus all known or relevant dates of birth and death) of all the people who have described flowering plants, algae, fungi, and so forth new to science. He went on to comment that he kept finding disagreements in the various sources about when botanists were born and what their full names were. Eventually, the job got done, even though "the list is still sort of temporary because we didn't have time to do a decent job with it." On the other hand, he also noted that most people now follow it as a standard even though it has no official "authority." When I asked him how many names were on the list, he laughed and said "about 30,000." I confess I had been thinking of something along the lines of three—rather than five—figures. Often in my conversations with him, Ed stresses how much he enjoys everything he does. Doubtless to many people, checking the biographical details of often obscure and long-departed botanists would seem like a research assistant's worst nightmare, but not to Ed. As he remarked in interview, "it was fun working on it."

So far, we have looked briefly at three of the elements that have made up Ed's professional life: his work as collector, curator, and floristician; his interest in lepidoptera; and his commitments to organizations that promote understanding and protection of the natural world. In the main subsection on Ed, I turn not to the flora, since this genre has already been explored in the earlier sections of this chapter, but look at yet another—and important—strand in Ed's career.

Nomenclature and a Nomenclaturist. As we have already seen, Systematic Botany is an ancient science of great descriptive and terminological rigor. It perhaps comes not as a total surprise, then, that issues of nomenclature figure large in the official affairs of botanists and plant taxonomists. The International Botanical Congress meets every six years, the 15th and latest such gathering having taken place in Tokyo in 1993. At each congress, a new edition of the *International Code of Botanical Nomenclature* is adopted, and published one or two years later. As might be expected, the processes of revision are elaborate. Here is the relevant section from Ed's preface to the 1983 code:

> The procedures for producing this edition of the Code have followed the well established outline in use since the Stockholm Congress of 1950. Published proposals for amendment, with technical comments by the Rapporteurs and various relevant reports, were assembled in a Synopsis of Proposals (Taxon 30: 95-293. Feb. 1981). Results of the Preliminary Mail Ballot on these proposals, a strictly advisory but very helpful expression of opinion, were made available at registration for the Nomenclature Section of the XIII International Botanical Congress, in Sydney, Australia. The Section met August 17–21, 1981, just before the regular sessions of the Congress, and made the final decisions on all proposals, often with some modifications of text. These decisions were adopted by resolution of the closing plenary session of the Congress on August 28 and became official at that time. (Voss, 1983, p. xii)

Ed was the Rapporteur-general for the Bureau of Nomenclature at this 1981 Congress, this position being the culmination of a 12-year involvement that (summers aside) he calculates as consuming about a quarter of his time during those years. And here we would do well to note that the "Synopsis of Proposals" published in *Taxon* extended to just under 200 pages, as well as to remember the volunteer aspect of this activity as decribed by Ed in this section's epigraph. Ed's description of how he became involved in nomenclature work is yet again one of his happen-stance stories:

> I had no idea of going into nomenclatural activity until the person who was in charge of international nomenclature work [the Rapporteur at that time] was here visiting Dr. McVaugh some years ago [prior to the 1969 Seattle Congress], and said, "Well, would you like to be Vice Rapporteur?" and I don't know he even gave me the option (laughs).

In fact, Ed's opening comment "I had no idea of going into nomenclatural activity . . . " is a little disingenuous. Although he asserted in interview that he had had no prior or longstanding ambitions to work on nomen-clatural *committees* per se, there is already evidence of this kind of interest in his *publications*, as in a 1966 paper entitled "Nomenclatural Notes on Monocots." And this kind of interest may have been known to or brought to the attention of the Rapporteur-general. Whatever the precise align-ments of cause and effect here, issues of nomenclature certainly find their place in Ed's introduction to Part I of *Michigan Flora*, published a little later in 1972. There are doubtless a wide range of topics that need to be addressed in a floristic introduction, especially one designed to be used by amateur as well as professional botanists and naturalists. For example, there are the sources of data to be covered; accounts of pioneering col-lectors and of postglacial vegetative history to be written; and decisions about habitat-types and plant distributions and relative abundance to be explained. In addition, the introduction will also need to contain detailed explanations about how the flora is organized and can be used to best advantage. Yet in Ed's 35 pages of introductory text, he managed to devote as many as seven pages (one fifth of the total) to "Taxonomy and No-menclature." From all this, we can well conclude that Ed was, after all, a natural and sensible choice for a major international nomenclatural role; no wonder he was apparently given little option.

The Sydney Code (Voss et al., 1983) consists of front matter, a five-page preface written by Ed, the code itself published in English, French, and then German, and then some appendices, some of them extensive. The whole volume amounts to 472 pages, including the index. The code proper, about 80 pages in length for all three languages, has a ten-point Preamble, six Principles, 73 Articles, and over 50 Recommendations. The first element in the Preamble provides its own justification for the Code:

> *1*. Botany requires a precise and simple system of nomenclature used by botanists in all countries, dealing on the one hand with the terms which denote the ranks of taxonomic groups or units, and on the other hand with the scientific names which are applied to the individual taxonomic groups of plants. The purpose of giving a name to a taxonomic group is not to

indicate its characters or history, but to supply a means of referring to it and to indicate its taxonomic rank. This code aims at the provision of a stable method of naming taxonomic groups, avoiding and rejecting the use of names which may cause error or ambiguity or *throw science into confusion*. Next in importance is the avoidance of the useless creation of names. Other considerations, such as absolute grammatical correctness, regularity or euphony of names, more or less prevailing custom, regard for persons, etc., notwithstanding their undeniable importance, are relatively accessory. (Voss et al., 1983, p. 1; emphasis added)

While the *flora* and the *monograph* represent the big genres of the field from the perspective of the individual botanist or of a small group of same, the *code* (its name immediately inviting associations with the Napoleonic traditions of Civil Law) is the big genre for the international collectivity of systematic botanists and taxonomists. This is disciplinary legislation of a force and of a character that goes well beyond, say, the efforts of the American Psychological Association to organize its members' activities through the APA Publication Manual (Bazerman, 1988, provides an excellent account of the manual's evolution). Further, the regulative effort articulated in the code is not confined to the here-and-now, as the fourth element in the Preamble makes clear:

4. The object of the Rules is to put the nomenclature of the past in order and to provide for that of the future; names contrary to a rule cannot be maintained. (Voss et al., 1983, p. 1)

Further, because "The Rules of nomenclature are retroactive unless expressly limited" (Principle VI), all the ramifications of any particular rule-revision are hard to foresee and thus have the potential to "throw science into confusion." In consequence, although "Botany requires a precise and simple system of nomenclature," precision is not easily reconcilable with simplicity—hence the 80-page structured listing of Principles, Rules, and Recommendations.

One decidedly nonsimple matter deals with the conservation of names. Indeed, I have had my own protracted struggle with the issue, at least partly because I long labored under the misapprehension that "conserving a name" must be a conservative or traditional move, rather than a radical one. Recollect that Preamble Item 4 states in part that "names contrary to a rule cannot be maintained." But now consider the first two subsections of Article 14:

14.1. In order to avoid disadvantageous changes in the nomenclature of families, genera, and species entailed by the strict application of the rules, and especially of the principle of priority in starting from the dates given in Art. 13, this Code provides, in Appendices II and III, lists of names that are conserved (*nomina conservanda*) and must be retained as useful exceptions.

14.2. Conservation aims at retention of those names which best serve stability of nomenclature (see Rec. 50E). Conservation of specific names is restricted to species of major economic importance. (Voss et al., 1983, pp. 13–14)

As with the precision versus simplicity disjunction, we can see emerging another polarity here: that between a wish to tidy up or improve upon the past, on the one hand, and a wish to preserve some stability in the established nomenclature, on the other. This issue was of sufficient importance, perhaps because of its controversial nature, to form a large part of the second paragraph of the preface that Ed wrote on behalf of himself and his committee. Having announced at the outset that "This 'Sydney Code' will for the most part look quite familiar to those who have used the 'Leningrad Code' " he went on to observe:

Many botanists will consider the major alteration to be acceptance of conservation of names of species. This authorization was adopted cautiously, with severe warning that it is not to be abused, and with an explicit restriction to names of 'species of major economic importance' (Art 14.2). No new machinery is established to handle proposals for names of species, which will be considered by the same committees as names of other ranks . . . (Voss, 1983, p. xi)

Here then is the Rapporteur-general admonishing his fellow botanists, in his plainest no-nonsense style, not to abuse the exception, by asking them in effect not to let the genie out of the legislative bottle too often or too easily. In the epigraph Ed described nomenclature as "an esoteric in-house field," which it undoubtedly is, but botanists are consummate and inveterate revisers, and Ed confirmed my suspicion that conserving the old names of "species of major economic importance" was ultimately a pragmatic concession to seed-purveyors, horticulturalists, foresters, and the like, who are likely disinclined to be changing their products' names—and labels—at the instigation of Botanical Congress resolutions.

This genie did in fact get out of the bottle. At the 1987 Congress in Berlin, it was decided that "In addition to 'species of major economic importance,' conservation of species names is now possible in two other situations" (Greuter & McNeill, 1988, p. vii). Further, according to Ed, "at Tokyo [1993] they threw it wide open and now any species name can be conserved" (in interview).

Ed spoke long, fluently, and earnestly in response to my somewhat hapless questions about the conservation of names, thus again suggesting that this was an issue that had preoccupied him for a long time. Here is part of what he said:

> It [conserving a species name] has to go through committees which will make the decision as to whether this *does* promote stability, or whether that's your provincial attitude in North America, while all the rest of the world calls it so-and-so anyway. So somebody is going to have to change ... So it will have to go through committees to get this stuff sorted out, and one of the arguments against conserving specific names was always that it would be too much work for the committees. But it hasn't turned out to be that anyway; so far we seem to be able to manage it. If committees are willing to do it, I am not opposed in principle. I just didn't want committees to get too much to do so that nothing else would get done, including the bigger issues of generic names and so forth. So I was never enthusiastic about widespread conservation of species names. But it's there now and I guess so far it is working. (in interview)

As Ed said, "nomenclature can get very complicated," and my foregoing account has selectively focused on one of several possible topics. Even so, that account does, I believe, bring to the outsider a renewed sense of the character of this field. That character includes its continuing dialogue with its prior texts; its divided loyalty between preservation and revision (as we have seen, Bill—for one—is strongly against "freezing nomenclature"); its struggles with botanical latinity (Principle V states rather enigmatically that "Scientific names are treated as Latin regardless of their derivation"); its quasicompulsive concern with terminology (as witnessed by its hexannual recodification of its naming practices); and its hard-held beliefs in the virtue and value of the complex administrative processes that underpin its nomenclatural decision-making. On this last, Ed can be much more eloquent than I can. Here is the concluding sentence to his Preface:

> The truly international and cooperative nature which characterizes the nomenclature committees, the broad democratic way in which the Code is subject to modification, and the common consent by which its decisions are accepted throughout the world, all make it a pleasure as well as a privilege for each of us to serve in these endeavours. (Voss, 1983, p. xv)

The foregoing has been an account of Edward Voss as a regional floristician, and also as an internationally minded nomenclaturist. (And note here the British spelling of the final word in the preceding extract.) But before we leave him to his active and well-deserved retirement, our subject has one further, if minor, voice in those matters of identification and nomenclature in which he is truly expert. Over the last few years, I have noticed that Ed is assiduous in writing to newspapers and magazines in order to correct misidentifications and/or nomenclatural errors. These texts, I believe, reflect the redoubtable and no-nonsense side of his character to which I have already referred. In the following example, JPW stands for *The Jack Pine Warbler*, the newsletter of the Michigan Audubon Society, an organization to which (of course) he belongs:

Dear Editor,

The butterfly depicted on page 16 of the Jul/Aug (JPW) is *not* a "Satyr" but is in a totally different family. It is a Silvery Blue, *Glaucopsyche lygdamus*, which is much smaller than a satyr and blue rather than brown above (although neither scale nor color can show in the photo).

On the same page, incidentally, the Petoskey stone coral is *Hexagonaria percarinata*, not *"Pexagonaria"* as the heading (not the text) has it. And there are no circumstances whatsoever under which a semicolon or other punctuation may be placed in the middle of a scientific name.

Sincerely yours,
Edward G. Voss
Herbarium, North Univ. Bldg.
University of Michigan

So that science be not *thrown into confusion*, sloppy work, both textual and nontextual, and whether produced by specialists, journalists, or amateurs, must be vigilantly exposed and rectified.

Coda: English Ascendant. As we have seen, the Code published in 1983 was offered in a trilingual (English, French, and German) format. After its publication, Ed did not continue as Rapporteur-general and hence *ex officio* Chairman of the Editorial Committee, but did continue to serve as a member. It transpired, in the preparatory work leading up to the publication of the 1988 "Berlin" code, that this multilingual policy was abandoned. In fact, this change is signaled in the very first sentences of the 1988 Preface:

The most striking difference between this new "Berlin Code" and previous editions of the international Code of Botanical Nomenclature is that the text is in English only, lacking the French and German versions that have been a feature of the International Code since the very first, the Vienna code of 1905. This reflects a recommendation made by the Nomenclature Section of the Berlin Congress, which also encouraged publication of the principal text in other languages. A French text is currently in preparation and a German and a Spanish are being considered. (Greuter & McNeill, 1988, p. vii)

Given my interests in academic languages, it was inevitable, I suppose, that I should ask Ed for a behind-the-scenes account of the reasons for this important policy change. He began by saying that "it was nothing that I initiated, even though I voted for it with everybody else in the Editorial Committee." He then went on to observe that he thought that there were three issues involved. The first was the fact that the code was getting very expensive, especially as few people really needed to have it in all three languages. The second was a matter of speed. Because translation into other languages was contingent upon the English version being completed, a trilingual version inevitably slowed the pace of publication. The third issue was increasing doubts about whether French and German continued to be the most appropriate alternate languages for botanists. A stronger case could perhaps be made for Spanish, and a reasonable one for Russian. "So everybody agreed 'let's just stick with one in the first version' and then have authorized translations whenever persons can get them done."

My own reactions to this development are mixed. Certainly, the arguments of the editorial committee are logical and pragmatic, and here Ed diffidently confirmed that his own pragmatic bent may have been conspicuous in the discussion. However, this policy change does add fuel to the emerging debate about the positive and negative effects of English's inexorable march across the global academic landscape. Tyrannical English (Swales, 1997) is already proving a serious obstacle to efforts to develop and sustain scholarly varieties of languages like Arabic, Hebrew, Malay, Pilipino, and Swahili. At the same time, longstanding scholarly varieties in smaller scientific communities are threatened with diminution and, in some cases, with extinction. In the land of Linnaeus himself, for example, it is no longer possible to publish original medical research in Swedish (Gunnarsson, Bäcklund, & Andersson, 1995), but only in English. Translation, as an "encouraged" but inevitably delayed secondary activity, is a palliative rather than a solution. Maher (1986), in a broad historical commentary on medical scholarly languages, shrewdly observed that "language is maintained or declines in response to the amount of [new] information it carries" (p. 208). Current threats to biodiversity are rightly of concern to biologists and ecologists, just as threats to small languages are of real concern to many anthropologists and field-linguists. The consequences of threats to non-English scholarly registers are only belatedly coming to be recognized (Mauranen, 1993). Loss of academic linguo-diversity can certainly reduce the range of scholarly traditions, rhetorical styles, and reading expectations available. An Anglophone global professional culture may be efficient, in Botany as in other fields, but it may also stifle verbal and textual creativity. And if my own reactions to this development are mixed, it is principally because (as chapter 4 briefly discusses) I have spent a major part of my professional life trying to advance the understanding and use of academic English.

BOB

As part of my alternative service as a conscientious objector . . . I went to work on a forest ecosystems project as a technician and studied decomposition in the forest. At the same time I was doing my PhD thesis at night and at weekends—a systematic monograph. So I was on kind of two parallel tracks that were not related, except that . . . I wanted to do more than just put names on things. I wanted to understand the truffles and false truffles and their biology and ecology. I knew that truffles and false-truffles were mycorrhizal and therefore important for forest systems. . . . I couldn't convince the forest ecosystem people that that was something they really needed to study. They eventually told me to go away and get my own grant—which I did. So, that's what got me into ecosystems stuff. (Bob, in interview)

The fourth and final member of the Herbarium "quartet" is Bob, who is in his late 40s. He is a westerner in origin, educated at Oregon State University (BS and PhD) and the University of Colorado (MA). He has been a curator in the Herbarium and a member of the Biology Department faculty since 1978 (thus arriving in Ann Arbor the same year as Tony), becoming a Full Professor in 1995 (like Joan). He is a systematist in fungi, an area in which he is now the sole remaining curator following a recent retirement. This retirement, coinciding with his recent promotion, has further increased Bob's considerable curatorial responsibilities. As of early 1996, he commented in interview "It means I have less time to be as diverse as I have been—I am starting to shed some kinds of research because I just don't have time."

In addition to his systematic work, Bob is a fungal ecologist and a broad-based soil biologist with a keen interest in innovative techniques and methods. He has his own extensive "wet" laboratory corner of the Herbarium, which now occupies, as it transpires, the space that at one time used to house the ELI administration. This lab and its setting, plus perhaps his own self-characterization as being "a bit of a loner," tend to separate and distance him from the activities and inhabitants in the main "curator corridor." At least in physical terms, the different ambiances are striking: The contrast between Bob's expansive and instrument-dotted space and Ed's tidy but totally encumbered office (photo 8) is quite palpable, as is the contrast between the somewhat gloomy corridor plus its book-jammed office off-shoots and Bob's brightly lit rectangle, within which his own office is comparatively spare in traditional books, but has two computers, several "peripherals," and lots of folders. His personal working environment is thus, on immediate aspect, most reminiscent of the Computing Resource Site.

Bob teaches a number of courses, ranging from large introductory classes in *General Biology*, to more advanced offerings for biology concentrators in subjects such as *Ecology of Forest Fungi*, and on to doctoral-level seminars. The most recent of these last was on *Geographic Information Systems for Systematists and Ecologists* in 1995, and this opportunity to involve advanced graduate students in sophisticated GIS applications in his major areas reveals well enough his interest in technical advances, and again places him at some remove from most of his immediate colleagues. His own investment in GIS can be seen from this "Materials and Methods" sentence from one of his recent papers:

> Distribution maps were created by overlaying coordinates of localities on a digitized base map using C-map Geographic Information System personal computer software (Center for Remote Sensing, Michigan State University). (1994, p. 797)

However, with a 1996 hire of an assistant professor in molecular plant systematics, who will be occupying a lab next door to Bob's, his somewhat isolated situation may change. As Bob observed, "some of the techniques are the same" even though the organisms and the problems are different. An inevitable consequence—at least these days—of Bob's technical skills and interests is the added fact that he is highly computer-literate; and it was Bob, in late 1995, who took a month off from his research in order to construct for the Herbarium an extensive and impressive WWW Home Page, replete with color photographs and biosummaries of staff, and containing the Herbarium's loan policies for fungi and, at that time, a (partial) inventory of its collections in that area.

As is customary with botanists, Bob's c.v. has a section dealing with "Field Experience and Collecting Expeditions." If we exclude a trip to the Canary Islands and Madeira, which took place before his coming to Michigan, the list is as follows: extensive field experience in Colorado, Michigan, Nevada, Oregon, and Utah; short collecting trips to Alaska, Arizona, California, British Columbia, New York, North Carolina, Washington, and Italy. The strong "western" orientation, especially in his major field work, is very apparent here, as it is in one of his major publication strands. The "Italy" entry looks vaguely anomalous, but stems from his interest in *hypogeous* (i.e., underground) fungi and the subsequent research connection with a professor from L'Aquila University in central Italy over the important matter of "truffles." His other major international connection is with a professor at the University of Aberdeen in Scotland on broader issues of "root-soil biology."

At the time of writing, Bob listed, excluding "abstracts," 55 publications on his c.v. About two thirds of these (36 in fact) are journal papers (two also reprinted in volumes); 12 are book chapters; five are technical reports, most of these being written at the beginning of his professional career; and two are book reviews. The biggest single outlet for his published papers is the long-established journal *Mycologia*, which has carried ten papers written or co-written by Bob over the last 20 years. He also publishes in other mycological and soil biology journals, as well as in Canadian serials such as *The Canadian Journal of Forest Research*. In addition, there is a joint *Letter to Nature*, but only a single paper in the *Contributions from the Herbarium* series. The book chapters tend to appear in scientific volumes with fairly general titles such as:

- Root Ecology and its Practical Applications
- Plant Root Growth: An Ecological Perspective
- The Rhizosphere and Plant Growth
- Ecological Interactions in Soil: Plants, Microbes and Animals

Two of these volumes were co-edited by Professor Atkinson of Aberdeen, who also was co-editor of another earlier volume which carried one of Bob's reprinted papers, thus underscoring the textual nature of this collaboration.

Twenty-five of Bob's 55 publications were written by himself alone, 16 were co-authored with just one other person, and 14 co-written by two or more people. Scrutiny of the publication record shows a very clear authorship trend: when Bob writes on fungal systematics, such as "Studies on *Hymenogaster* (Basidiomycotina): A Re-Evaluation of the Subgenus *Dendrogaster*" (Fogel, 1985), he typically writes alone. In contrast, as he moves further and further into broader, more methodological, or more interdisciplinary areas, the number of authorial collaborators accrue. In consequence, Bob usually joins one or two others in fungal ecology or root biology papers, but in a wide-ranging 1993 paper in *Plant Soil* entitled "Elevated Atmospheric CO_2 and Feedback Between Carbon and Nitrogen Cycles," there are, in addition to Bob, as many as five other authors listed (Zak et al., 1993). When I asked Bob about my perceptions of his co-authorship patterns, he concurred, observing:

> That's a function of the disciplines. Systematics to me tends to be kind of a solitary occupation . . . kind of like solving a puzzle, whereas the ecosystem stuff is done in collaboration with people because no one person probably holds enough information to realize all the ramifications.

As a publishing scientist, Bob has, as we have seen, a number of areas of interest. The systematic work itself is one important element, as it accounts for about half of the published papers. Although this work seems to go in "bursts" of published activity, such as in 1976–1977, in 1985, in 1989–1991, and again in 1994–1995, the real situation for Bob is that the *taxonomic treatments* are the baseline "steady state" work. What essentially happens is that the major externally funded projects become, as it were, superimposed on this baseline and it is the pressure to finish these projects that squeezes the systematics publications into the intervening "down" periods.

Although fashions come and go, taxonomists in most branches of biology tend to be either "lumpers" or "splitters": in the former case they are inclined to argue, superficial differences to the contrary, that two (or more) species are really one; and in the latter case that, superficial similarities to the contrary, one species is really two (or more). Bob can go either way at the same time, as can be seen in the abstracts from the two 1985 systematics papers. In the slightly earlier one, as many as six species get "lumped" into one:

> Type specimens of *Hymenogaster brunnescens, H. diabolus, H. subcaeruleus, H. sublilacinus, H. subochraceus,* and *H. subolivaceus,* originally described in *Hymenogaster* subgenus *Dendrogaster,* plus a variety of other collections were reexamined. Particular attention was given to variability in spore dimensions within specimens, among populations, and the effect of stage of development on mean spore size. The conclusion is that the six names represent but one species, *H. sublilacinus.* Reexamination of *Dendrogaster* revealed that the type specimen has spores possessing an apical beak characteristic of members of the subgenus Hymenogaster, that it differs insignificantly in other characters, and is thus synonomous. (Fogel, 1985, p. 72)

However, the abstract of the second paper (Fogel & Trappe, 1985, p. 732) tells the opposite story:

> A new genus in the Hymenogastraceae, *Destuntzia,* is created to accommodate two species formerly placed in *Hymenogaster, H. ruber* and *H. subborealis,* and three previously undescribed species, *D. fusca, D. saylorii* and *D. solstitialis. Destuntzia* is characterized by the locules lacking an organized hymenium and being filled with a gel containing pigmented, verrucose to rugolose spores.

So in this case, a new genus is created to take account of similarities among three new species and two re-examined old ones, one of these being venerable in the botanists' time-scale for the western United States (Harkness, 1899), and the other comparatively recent (Smith, 1966). Bob was totally unsurprised when I pointed out these opposing tendencies. On several occasions, he observed that the taxonomy of the group of organisms he studies is "badly known" or "very badly known"; no wonder then that re-examination of old material and examination of new material can cause researchers like Bob to propose shifts in classification. But it is not the case that Bob is somehow cavalier or precipitous about changing these *orders* of things. In interview, he volunteered the following revealing comment about the reflective thinking that lies behind this aspect of his work: "I have a new genus right now that I am working on that I am going to describe and it's taken me three weeks ... to feel comfortable with the fact that it *is* a new genus."

Observations on Fogel and Trappe (1985). This is a ten-page article, printed on high-quality paper, consisting of seven pages of text and three pages of scanning electron micrographs (with magnifications of up to × 8200). After the abstract (already given), there is an untitled introduction of about a page, divided into four paragraphs. Then follows a *Materials and Methods* section, given here in its entirety, but in exploded form and with sentence numbers added for ease of reference:

1. Methods of collection and study were essentially those of Smith (Smith and Zeller, **1966**).
2. Color names were given by the ISCC-NBS names (Kelly and Judd, **1955**).
3. Dried herbarium material was prepared for scanning electron microscopy by pressing the gleba against the surface of double-coated tape affixed to aluminum stubs.
4. Spores adhering to the tape after removal of the sporocarps were coated with approximately 200 A of gold prior to microscopy.
5. Herbarium names were abbreviated according to Holmgren and Keuken (**1974**).

Although the section is thus extremely short, it remains interestingly variable. While it is true that the past passive dominates, as is the case with most such sections in many fields, the first, second, and last sentences are very different from the third and fourth. The former are short summations ascribing all the detail to previously published works in exactly the manner that Gilbert and Mulkay (1984) have discussed for biochemistry. Although in the case of the last sentence the operating procedure referred to is clearly unproblematic, in the first two the situations were likely to have been more complicated and complex than the uninformed reader might have supposed. For example, the straightforward statement, "Color names were given by the ISCC-NBS names" seems to suggest that selectivity and judgment had no part to play, but rather that the names were somehow automatically imposed on nonrecalcitrant material by the

ISCC color chart. (The color chart is used to match a specimen or specimens with a color panel in exactly the way we might try to match a paint
flake with a chart color in a paint store.) Indeed, the apparent automaticity
of Bob's color assignment is reinforced by the somewhat unusual quick
repetition of the word *names* in an eight-word sentence. An alternative
formulation such as "Color names were chosen according to the ISCC-NBS
nomenclature" would presumably make some greater allowance for any
subjectivity in the procedure, even if still falling short of a more "contingent" utterance like "Attempts were made to align colors as closely as
possible with those in the ISCC-NBS."

The preceding commentary is, in fact, what I (more or less) wrote about
the odd and striking use of "given" in the second sentence of the extract
before I had an opportunity to discuss the Fogel and Trappe paper with
Bob. But now consider this exchange—an exchange, incidentally, charac-
terized by riotous laughter from both parties:

Bob: I don't actually like color as a character, which I shouldn't admit,
        but I'm partially color-blind.

John: Well, actually, that's very interesting because there's a little
        sentence in one of your methodologies that's a little strange and
        that might actually explain that! . . . Oh, wow, that's brilliant . . .
        I will write it up—glad you told me about that.

As the reader can see, I have in fact not so much "written the revelation
up," but rather "set it down" in its verbatim original form. The moral of
Bob's admission for a supposedly "clever" discourse analyst is clear
enough: Linguistic choices may have obscure physical origins, and their
rhetorical over-interpretation thus remains an ever-present danger. Bob's
"attempt to depersonalize, to objectify . . ." (Montgomery, 1996, p. 13)
was, in this instance, not so much an invocation of the scientific style *per
se* as a protection against visual uncertainty.

In contrast to the opening and closing sentences, sentences three and four
are much longer (23 and 21 words respectively), considerably more explicit
about details, and unsupported by the literature. And here it is easy to see
that the contrast is a contrast between the modern microscopic techniques
described in this "meat of the method sandwich" and the classic, established procedures of the subject that surround it, as witnessed, not least, by
the far-from-contemporary nature of the three given dates—1955, 1966, and
1974. The dates are also interesting for the fact that *Mycologia* required (at
least until 1994) all dates to be entered in bold, except for those in the
"Materials Examined" subsections and in the "Literature Cited" close. This
journal-specific convention serves, probably inadvertently, to further highlight the long citational lifetimes of systematics literature.

The main body of Fogel and Trappe is then subsumed under the general heading of *Taxonomic Treatment* (that word again). As we have learned from Bill, this opens with the standard textwork for a new genus: in this case, five "verbless sentences" in Latin, a slightly longer description in English, and a key to the five species. This framing account is then followed by the five separate species descriptions (on average, each about a page in length). The species descriptions are broadly similar to those of plants, except that measurements (especially of minute parts such as spores) are taken down from the millimeter to the micron level, and that there are some additional characters such as *chemical reactions* and *odors*. These last, of course, do lend some support to Gross' claim that the projection of a new species can be rhetorically enhanced by marshalling "multisensory" evidence.

The one feature of this text that I now focus on concerns its etymological choices, because with a new genus being proposed, along with descriptions of three new species, much is likely to be happening *Nomenklaturweise*. In each of the six cases, the (new) name plus other details is given as a subheading and then, following the description, there is a note on *Etymology*, which typically precedes other notes such as those on *Other References* and *Habitat and Season*. Here are the double extracts from Fogel and Trappe, 1985 (entry numbers have been added):

1. **Destuntzia** Fogel & Trappe, gen. nov.
   ETYMOLOGY: In honor of Prof. Daniel E. Stuntz.
2. **Destuntzia rubra** (Harkness) Fogel & Trappe, comb. nov.
   ETYMOLOGY: Ruber = red (L.) possibly in reference to color of peridium in alcohol.
3. **Destuntzia subborealis** (Smith) Fogel & Trappe, comb. nov.
   ETYMOLOGY: Subborealis = nearly boreal (L.)
4. **Destuntzia solstitialis** Fogel & Trappe, sp. nov.
   ETYMOLOGY: Solstitialis = pertaining to summer (L.), the season of collection.
5. **Destuntzia fusca** Fogel & Trappe, sp. nov.
   ETYMOLOGY: Fuscus = very dark blackish brown (L.) Refers to color of gleba.
6. **Destuntzia saylorii** Fogel & Trappe, sp. nov.
   ETYMOLOGY: For Herb Saylor who has been so willing to share his collections of hypogeous fungi.

For the descriptive names (entries 2 through 5), Bob says that he just tries to use "a distinctive character." For the two attributed names, the origins are both more complex and somewhat at odds with each other. I asked him about Professor Daniel E. Stuntz. Here is part of his reply:

He was the mycologist at the University of Washington . . . my major professor, Jim Trappe, my Ph.D. professor, was a quote "student of his"—a
rather involved lineage—, but he worked with Dr Stuntz, and Trappe was
the one who wanted to name it *Destuntzia* . . . My personal preference would
not be to name it after somebody . . . especially as at that time Stuntz was
alive . . .

On the other hand, Bob's response to *Destuntzia saylorii* was, on the surface
at least, very different:

He's an amateur who has a very good knowledge of hypogeous fungi and
has spent a lot of time collecting . . . and was never able to realize his
ambition to become a mycologist because of family situations and because
he could make more money as an engineer working for the Caterpillar
Corporation.

In terms of attribution, therefore, Bob apparently treats professionals and
amateurs very differently. If professional scientists are to be recognized
and honored in this way, then this should only occur posthumously;
dedicated and knowledgeable amateurs fall into a different category and
perhaps *should* be recognized, where appropriate, in their lifetimes.

The Soil Biotron. The University of Michigan's Soil Biotron is now
part of its Biological Research Station situated in a forested location in
the northern part of the state's Lower Peninsula. The Soil Biotron is
essentially a tunnel-like underground chamber fitted with reinforced glass
walls for observing root growth and other associated activity (photos 23
& 24). With a colleague as Co-Principal Investigator, Bob received around
$200,000 from the NSF in the second half of the 1980s for the construction
and equipping of this facility. So far, Bob has co-published about seven
papers based on the biotron work, mostly written in collaboration with
a colleague from the University of Illinois and another from Michigan
State University.

The paper that I use to illustrate this very different aspect of Bob's
activity was published by this trio—Bob is the second author—in the 1991
volume of *Agriculture, Ecosystems and Environment*, an Elsevier journal.
The title of the paper itself suggests that we have moved quite a long
way from traditional taxonomic *treatments*: "A New Dawn for Soil Biology:
Video Analysis of Root-Soil-Microbial-Faunal Interactions." (Bob no
longer recollects who originally came up with the "new dawn" phrase.)

Right from the beginning of the introduction, problems with existing
methodologies are emphasized:

Most students of rhizosphere processes must study organisms or processes
by isolating them from the complex web of interactions in which they occur.

Photo 23. The Soil Biotron.

Photo 24. Bob in the Soil Biotron.

Roots are sieved from soil or grown in plastic pouches, bacteria and fungi are cultured, and invertebrates extracted from soil—all without ever actually observing them in place. Thus the whole spatiotemporal aspect of rhizosphere interactions is poorly known because each group of organisms is removed from its setting for study. (Lussenhop, Fogel, & Pregitzer, 1991, p. 235)

The introduction, which closes with the affirmation "We believe that new methodology will partly solve the problem of studying rhizosphere processes at the intermediate spatiotemporal scale" (p. 236), is followed by four pages of discussion of the rhizospheric complexities. The second half of this 15-page paper is then devoted to exploring new ways of studying the medium spatiotemporal scale. At its onset, we learn that the title of this chapter's subsection is itself a neologism:

Observations at this scale have been made directly with boroscopes, minirhizotrons and "mega-rhizotrons" which we will term soil biotrons. The term soil biotron is used to emphasize the value of these facilities in observing all of the soil biota, not only roots. (Lussenhop et al., 1991, p. 240)

The paper then concentrates first on video, especially time-lapse video, as an observational tool, and then in combination with image analysis, on its value for quantitative study. Here is one illustration from the earlier stage, which, as it were, frees up the human observer from having to watch some interminable Andy Warhol–type film:

As an example of the value of time-lapse video, seasonal variation in grazing intensity of collembola on a single root was demonstrated by filming it for 30 s every half hour for 3 months. A 100-fold increase in grazing was observed in April when roots begin to grow (Table 4). (p. 245)

The patent advantages of the biotron-video methodology are iterated in the *Conclusions*, as in this final paragraph:

Data collection and analysis with boroscopes, minirhizotrons, or soil biotrons is labor intensive. For this reason video recording coupled with image analysis offers the exciting prospect of reducing the labor of data analysis, increasing accuracy, and allowing direct measurement of rates and turnover. Our inability to observe roots directly has surely resulted in fewer students of, and many false assumptions about, root processes. The opportunities presented by boroscopes, minirhizotrons and soil biotrons, if used with video and image analysis, truly represent a new dawn for soil biology. (p. 247)

As readers will have noted, the very first phrase of the paper's title is reprised as the very last phrase of the paper itself, thus opening and closing on the same fervent note, one that makes a strong appeal to *kairos*, or timeliness, via its reference to the metaphorical yet temporal image of a "new dawn." (*Kairos*, however, turns out not to be an important rhetorical device in Systematics, because practically everything, at least after Linnaeus in 1753, is always "timely.") There are some further linguistic choices that add to the rhetorical momentum of this concluding paragraph, which I have italicized here:

- *exciting* prospect
- *Our* inability
- *surely* resulted
- *truly* represent

This text, and especially this passage, is an unusual kind of published writing from the Herbarium, however much it may be commonplace on the floor above, and its distinctiveness (in its context) further draws the reader's attention to the authors' *enthusiasm* for the methodological and technical breakthroughs they describe or anticipate.

Bob is an "ideas" person; as he said, "I have always felt that I have ideas, and my problem is not [in] coming up with ideas; my problem is usually finding enough time to do something (laughs) about the ideas." In fact, this ideas aspect of Bob has already been discussed in print by the Director of the Biological Station in a chapter from a 1992 volume appropriately entitled *Inventive Minds: Creativity in Technology*. Here is the most relevant paragraph:

> Dr. Fogel considers the process of scientific inquiry to be an ongoing series of approximations. When he approaches a problem he considers and discusses many different methods of inquiry. If a method appears promising he attempts to employ it quantitatively. He uses a trial-and-error approach. For example, he tried building small soil windows early in this project. Later he spent considerable time attempting to modify the minirhizotrons to suit his purpose. Standing in the East Malling rhizotron convinced him to abandon that approach and scale up to the biotron approach. As part of the search process he feels it is very important to know when to abandon a particular approach and when to seek information in other disciplines. (Teeri, 1992, p. 152)

Bob himself said that he does not have a "linear" mind and added that he has been told that his "logic is hard to follow" at times. Teeri also commented on his "ability to conceptualize in a spatial context" (p. 152).

So, "Standing in the East Malling rhizotron" (in Kent, England) could provide him with an epiphany of a bigger and better set-up, and spatial conceptualization has presumably contributed to the ecosystems work, just as spatial renditions in the form of charts, diagrams, and maps are integral and important elements in his ecology papers. And here we can usefully recollect that the topic of his most recent seminar was Geographic Information Systems.

"Materials for a Hypogeous Mycoflora of the Great Basin ..."

So far, we have investigated Bob's work in fungi systematics and his involvment with observations and experiments in the Soil Biotron. These two investigative areas represent the two poles of his interests. Lying between, and in many ways straddling these two poles is Bob's third research specialty—that of fungal ecology, particularly the role of hypogeous fungi in the woods and forests of the western United States. As the epigraph indicates, this interest started while he was a graduate student and predominates among his earlier papers, such as "Ecological Studies of Hypogeous Fungi II. Sporocarp Phenology in a Western Oregon Douglas Fir Stand" (Fogel, 1976).

This also was the area of Bob's work that I focused on in 1987 when I examined the "administration" of his publications, particularly the role of Reprint Requests (RRs) in the distribution of offprints (Swales, 1988). At that time, I focused on the following two papers:

R. Fogel and J. M. Trappe. (1978). Fungus consumption (mycophagy) by small animals. *Northwest Science* 52: 1–31.

R. Fogel. (1983). Root turnover and productivity of coniferous forests. *Plant and Soil* 71: 75–85.

The reason for this focus was obvious enough since, according to his files, these were the two papers that had generated the most RR traffic (46 and 57 requests respectively). At the time of the 1987 study, Bob had a positive attitude to such requests and would also typically include in his return package "papers on related topics," especially if requested to do so and if he had offprint supplies still available. Additionally, at that time Bob maintained a mailing list for Fungal Ecology consisting of 113 names and addresses. Not surprisingly, it was not uncommon for Bob to order as many as 300 copies of his ecology papers. Bob believed that responding to Reprint Requests was in general "good advertising"; more specifically, he observed that if colleagues had his reprints easily available, the papers would have a higher probability of being cited than would be the case if they had to be chased down in a library. Today, however, nearly a decade later, demand for reprints has fallen off, except from overseas, for three main reasons: the emergence of E-mail; the fact that "most people Xerox stuff now"; and the fact that he is no longer publishing on mycorrhizae (close physical associations between fungi and plant roots from which both apparently benefit, and a "big" research area with important ramifications for agriculture).

In fact, over the last 20 years, Bob has authored or co-authored close to 20 articles or book chapters on various topics in this third area of Fungal Ecology. Right from the outset, and as also indicated in this section's epigraph, Bob was concerned to further undermine "the fallacy of regarding fungi as either saprophytes or parasites in natural ecosystems ..." (Fogel, 1976, p. 1161), and has continued to stress that underground fungi provide an important food resource for forest rodents such as squirrels and chipmunks, who in turn play a role in the spore-dispersal of these fungi (because those cannot, like open and emergent taxa, rely principally on the wind for that key function).

His latest paper in this area was, once again, published in *Mycologia*, which by 1994 had converted to a double-column 8" × 11" format and dropped its practice of printing dates in bold-face. The title is long, but it captures well the coming together of his ecological, evolutionary, and taxonomic interests:

> Materials for a hypogeous mycoflora of the Great Basin and adjacent cordilleras of the Western United States II. Two subemergent species *Cortinarius saxamontanus, sp.nov.*, and *C. magnivelatus*, plus comments on their evolution.

The first paragraph of the *Introduction* is as follows:

> This is the second in a series containing materials for a hypogeous mycoflora of the Great Basin and adjacent cordilleras (Fogel and Pacioni, 1989). The region has received little attention from mycologists despite its potential for studies of fungal biogeography, evolution and coevolution. The Great Basin itself is an area of 714 854 square km as defined by Cronquist et al. (1972). Composition of the vegetation and availability of suitable ectomycorrhizal hosts for hypogeous fungi in the region reflects the interaction of environmental optima for species, soil factors, preglacial flora, extent of glacial advance, pluvial lake levels, and subsequent reinvasion from glacial refugia (Wells, 1983). Another significant factor affecting the presence of hypogeous fungi is the efficiency of mycophagous rodents, and perhaps insects, in spore dispersal. (Fogel, 1994, p. 795)

Right away we see in these extracts, as we saw in Tony's *Revision*, aspirations toward one of the two primary "big" genres in botany—a *flora*, on which I comment further later. Indeed, "This is a second in a series containing materials" for such an end, a 1989 paper by Bob and his Italian colleague in fact constituting Part I. After this announcement, the introduction takes on a familiar cast with its identification of an area of *undeserved neglect* ("... received little attention from mycologists despite its potential ..."). There follows a brief definitional clarification, whereupon the introduction invokes a host of factors that might affect the distribution of underground fungi, and the paragraph closes with a now-customary reminder about the significance of the activities of fungi-eating rodents.

The evolutionary aspects and implications, earlier discussed in more detail in a joint *Letter to Nature*, are too complex to summarize here, and take up a good part of one of Bob's longest introductions (nine paragraphs, some extensive). It is clear, however, that for Bob a mycoflora needs to do much more than simply state which species occur in which habitat, but also provide some reasonable and principled account of how they got there. And doubtless this explains the necessity for "extensive field experience" in this region, in addition to the usual scrutiny of herbarium specimens. In the *Introduction* itself, there is a computer-generated map of the known occurrences of the two species, part of the legend for which is the following:

> Arrows indicate invasion routes along forest islands for conifers (Wells, 1983), mycophagous rodents, and hypogeous fungi around the Pleistocene Lake Bonneville Basin (S) into the Central Basin from the East. Dispersal from the Sierra Nevada to the east is blocked by a low elevation trough (t) of the Pleistocene Lake Lahontan Basin (L). (Fogel, 1994, p. 796)

These data "suggest two hypotheses for their evolution" (p. 796). Thus, for Bob, a *flora* is much more explicative than a regional inventory, which in Bill's words essentially "shows you what you've got, so that you can decide what you should try to save." For Bob Fogel, however, the distribution data are means to ends, not ends in themselves. Doubtless in his case, as in those of Bill, Tony, and Ed, the full assemblage of all the materials needed for a flora may be a long time coming, but for Bob in particular progress toward such a long-term goal is more likely to be dependent or contingent on advances and changes in the biological, ecological, and evolutionary sciences themselves.

Consolidations

Bob is probably the most-cited of the nonemeritus academics in the North University Building, especially since Larry Selinker left the ELI for a chair in London, taking with him the 250 or so citations to his famous 1972 *Interlanguage* paper. But, as we have come to expect, the pattern of citations to Bob's work is weirdly distributed. There are only a few scattered citations to the systematics work, in part because—as we saw with Tony—most references to prior work in this discipline are hidden away in the species descriptions and not consolidated under *Literature Cited*. Like Tony, Bob finds this a bit strange, especially because "it makes us look bad." Although there is a small but growing number of references to the biotron papers, the vast bulk of the citations belong to ecology, perhaps especially to those papers that offer interesting methodologies, for, as Bob says, "Methods papers tend to be cited more." So, as of summer 1995, the Science Citation Index tallies around 185 references to a 1977 paper entitled "Effect of habitat and substrate quality on Douglas-fir litter decomposition in Western Oregon," and six others, including *The Letter to Nature* and Fogel and Trappe (1978), fall into the 30–60 range.

But, as we saw at the outset, Bob is "starting to shed some kinds of research." Although he is still interested in the Soil Biotron, he feels that in the future he will likely in those experiments only be a collaborator and not a Principal Investigator. Today he has had to take on much more serious curatorial responsibilities; moreover, he now sees the root research as not having "a direct feedback into my interests in mycology and truffles." Indeed, these interests now once again take center stage as he moves beyond somewhat occasional papers such as *"Materials for* a hypogeous mycoflora of the Great Basin" (emphasis added) toward constructing and composing the main work itself. He estimated that there will need to be *treatments* of some 35 to 40 genera and around 100 species, for most of which at least preliminary studies have been done. (At this point in our discussion, Bob waved toward a "mini-tower" standing next to one of his monitors, which currently houses those studies.) But, as we have seen, Bob's flora is going to be more than "a regional inventory":

> Well, the way I envision the book, it will have chapters on what are the hypogeous fungi, something about their biology and character, it will have discussion on the Great Basin and its history, and some discussion of the biogeography of the truffles and their relation to their hosts, so what you see in the papers that have been published are some preliminary attempts to grapple with some of those issues.

Bob has focused on the Great Basin for two reasons. First, it has never been properly collected. Secondly, following extensive analysis of pack-rat middens, the region's vegetative paleo-history over the last 10,000 years has become sufficiently well known to set the general background for asking interesting questions "about where the truffles are and how they got there and whether they are actually evolving or just going extinct." But I suspect there is a third, if lesser, reason. Bob, after all, is an "ideas" person, and it is in evolutionary biology that ideas and theories seem particularly forefronted (e.g., Selzer, 1993). When he was speaking earlier about "grappling with issues" in preliminaries for the mycoflora, he added, in what was for him a very guarded and neutral tone, this after-thought: "Some of these [issues] are in conflict with some thinking about the way speciation occurs." Bob later confirmed that the field can antici-pate *some thinking* from him too about speciation in hypogeous fungi.

Although it is obvious that his 1995 promotion has provided Bob with some further reassurance of his place in the world and of his capacity to complete a major project, he still has concerns. One revolves around his writing: "I am below average; I think I write like a German; I have too many dependent clauses." While I do not actually see any of these traits in Bob's writing, it is true that I have only been looking at the final, polished products. Another consistent pressure is the typical-enough aca-demic one of time. So let me end this textography of Bob with one further exchange:

> Bob: The Great Basin project is in its second three-year funding cycle from the National Science Foundation . . . and they're the ones that have told me not to go on and put in for a third grant because they want to see a book.
>
> John: It'll be a book?
>
> Bob: *If* I get it done (laughs) . . .
> It's scary, right now (more laughter)

FINAL REMARKS ON THE QUARTET

In this chapter, I have exposed a quartet of biological scientists to a fair amount of discoursal and paradiscoursal scrutiny. All four have consis-tently responded to these probings with politeness, with tolerance of my misunderstandings, and with good humor. All four are male, but this was close to inevitable as all the curators/professors associated with the Herbarium are male. At least at Michigan then, the world of Plant and Fungal systematics is predominantly masculine (as in much of the sciences here and elsewhere). And yet in the unique and crucial subsystem of genres that forms a principal component of botanical writing (*flora*, *monograph*, and *treatment*), we find an unusually sympathetic and courteous kind of intertextuality that is typically more often associated with scholarly groups wherein, ironically, female voices are frequent and strong (Belcher, 1997). But here collegiality has a multigenerational origin—a family of known lineage and with a full sense of its past.

All four members have curatorial responsibilities and systematic inter-ests, but thereafter they diverge somewhat. Bill and, especially, Ed have been for certain periods seriously involved with nomenclature; Tony with the general public and official bodies of various sorts, and Ed with the latter; Bob with technology and with soil ecology—indeed, he confessed that his Biotron adventures were deemed by some to be marginal to the Herbarium's mission. They also differ in their focus of geographic interest. Bill's is directed at Mexico and countries to the south; Bob's toward the Great Basin area in the west of the United States; Ed is strictly local; and Tony is mostly local, but with an interest in Mexico. They also differ in age, at this time of writing, with Bob and Tony in their 40s, Bill in his 50s, and Ed in his 60s.

All, however, have spent all or a great part of their careers at the University of Michigan. Further, their writing in systematics is broadly similar and, as far as I have been able to observe, broadly similar to that of other systematists elsewhere. Despite Bill's demurrals, they are all part of a major Herbarium, at least in university terms, as most palpably represented by its extensive collections and series of publications. As we have seen, they each have very separate projects that require immense amounts of time and effort. The third volume of Ed's flora was eventually published in December 1996, some four months after his official retirement; Bill is halfway through the 17 volumes that have dominated and will continue to dominate his scholarly life; Bob's monograph is underway but remains for him a "scary" prospect; meanwhile, Tony's comprehensive study on those diabolically difficult sedges remains for a still further future, even though, as a result of his software innovations, when it eventually appears it may cause the "plant taxonomist" community to rethink the nature of a *monograph*.

As textographer of the second floor I have tried to do justice to a number of themes that have emerged over a three-year involvement with its practices, rhythms, texts, and personalities. One is the sense of locale, a sense of autonomous *place*—a sense at least equally apparent on the floor above, but more equivocal on the first floor. Juxtaposed to that, I have tried to capture a feeling of the academic personalities, and especially the scriptural personalities, of those I have chosen for inclusion. There are no towering geniuses here, just as there aren't any elsewhere in the building. But if the NUB second floor by and large offers "normal science," it is one that is distinguished by its taxonomic traditions: lifetime *oeuvres*, limited co-authorship, terminological philosophy and exactitude, and a level of dedicated archival intertextuality usually associated with very traditional humanities' scholarship. And juxtaposed to the partial accounts of careers that a textography engenders, the use of close, but nontechnical, analysis of particular stretches of text, illumined on occasion by text-based interview data, shows how the language of normal science can be subtly imbricated with elements that, often with some persuasive effort on the part of the analyst, can reveal the individual humanities of the authors. All of these themes are doubtless obvious enough to my main protagonists, but it has not been quite so obvious as to how to make them visible to others. There are complex situationalities here, personal, curatorial, institutional, and disciplinary, that coalesce and clash. A full ethnography by an expert ethnographer would doubtless have captured the full social and cultural complexity; a lighter textography, at least as I have envisioned it, can however focus on relating context and textual surface and thus communicate something to those communities that are particularly interested in academic writing as a cultural phenomenon in its own right.

Although my direct evidence comes from just one institution, I feel fairly confident in claiming that Herbarium curators form a distinctive community (whether they are a discourse community, in a sense to be further defined, is a matter for the final chapter). In making such a claim, I am aware of my reconstructive authorial role. As Cintron put it, "the patterned lifeways of a people are not self-evident, but the constructions of a text-maker" (1993, p. 382). Certainly, the regularly patterned *textways* of the quartet have been emphasized in this account. What has not been emphasized, although I trust it has leaked through, is—to echo Ed's closing prefatorial sentence to "his" Code—my sense of privilege in studying and getting to know such a quirkily driven but remarkable group of folks.

4

Textways in the English Language Institute

SOME FURTHER CONTEXT

This chapter is given over to the text-biographies of three individuals who work on the top floor of the building. The first section belongs to Joan who (like Ed) has spent 25 years or more in the North University Building and whose story has some similarities with those of the professors on the floor below. Carolyn is next, and here there are some affinities with Tony, also from the second floor. In both cases I have adopted the procedures outlined previously, except that I asked Margaret to conduct the first round of interviews. I felt that my questioning of two long-standing and close colleagues might be both constrained and compromised by certain prior expectations on my part, and, further, that their responses might be affected by their own expectations of me.

The remaining member of the trio is myself: nosy parker, discourse analyst, and story teller. Because the opening chapter already described how I came to include myself in this volume, and how I came to rely on my old friend, Tony Dudley-Evans, as an *interlinear commentator*, all I need to do here is say a little more about that relationship. Tony and I first met in Tripoli, Libya in the late 1960s and since then our paths, interests, and publications have crossed and recrossed one another on many occasions. We both started in English for Academic Purposes, to which we have both added an interest in discourse and rhetoric (cf. Dudley-Evans, 1987). We have both served as co-editors of *The English for Specific Purposes Journal*, and, for many years, have had comparable jobs, experiences, and professional interests.

English Language Institutes (also known as American Language Institutes) have proliferated across U.S. campuses in recent decades. Most offer "Intensive English Programs" (IEPs), whereby pre-matriculated non-native speakers study English full-time in order to upgrade their English sufficiently to gain admission to degree programs. These IEPs often have close relationships with MA programs in ESL, so that Masters students can gain training, experience, and tuition dollars by teaching in them. In addition to this activity, ELIs may offer courses and services to enrolled students, help international students prepare to be teaching assistants, offer courses to non-native speakers of English in the local community, and undertake contract work with local companies.

Although the University of Michigan was a pioneer in the IEP arena, in the late 1980s it phased out its Intensive Program. There were a number of reasons for this decision, but prominent among them was the fact that very few students in its IEP could actually meet the *academic* admission requirements of the university. Michigan's IEP was, in effect, a preparatory college for some other institution. The ELI was subsequently re-missioned to focus on providing English for Academic Purposes for the NNS graduate students and, to a lesser extent, for the undergraduates. Concomitantly, the MA in Linguistics (ESL) was phased out, and a staff of (mostly) full-time and highly dedicated lecturers and professors consolidated. Ten years later, the ELI's curriculum is as complex and as comprehensive as any in the United States, particularly at the graduate level. This activity is basically orchestrated through seven front-line lecturers and two professors. The three people chosen for this chapter are the two professors (Joan and John) and Carolyn (Lecturer and Associate Director for Curriculum), primarily because this trio has had the most "writerly" careers. In both the ELI and the Herbarium, some selectivity has been inevitable in order to create adequate profiles of a smaller number of individuals. The curators of ferns (Herb), mosses and lichens (Howard), and algae (Mike), and the recently retired other curator of fungi (Bob) have had to be left aside. In a comparable way, in the ELI, there are six lecturers who I have not been able to consider, even though they too have their special areas of expertise: Elizabeth in spoken academic discourse; Maria in business communications; Sue in legal English; Chris in academic writing; Brenda in applied phonetics and oral communication; and Debbie in computer-aided language learning. The preceding summary of areas of expertise does, however, confirm the specialized EAP focus of Michigan's current ELI—just as chapter 2 has clarified its unusual role in providing international testing services.

As in the previous chapter, a number of themes are explored. In each case, there is a dual focus on writing as a career activity and on the character of a particular text or texts. The situated particularities of the writing of each individual are then reviewed at the chapter's close in an assessment of particularity and communality. Again, as before, I try to say something about the configuration of the floor's genre set, and about how minor genres aggregate into major ones. Once more, within this configuration, negotiating the differing claims of "theory" and "practice" emerge as a powerful motive for writing. However, unlike in the Herbarium, in the Institute this relationship is primarily played out in pedagogic terms, such as in the evolution and evaluation of teaching materials, rather than in terms of curatorial roles and their consequences.

JOAN

My introductions are where my little soul pours out. (Joan, in interview)

Joan was promoted to the rank of Professor (of Linguistics) in 1995, and the background to that event is as good a place as any to begin her story. Joan was promoted from Lecturer to Associate Professor with tenure in 1983, but when the directors of the two programs in which she works suggested at the end of the 1980s that it might be time for her to be considered for further promotion, she demurred. She stated that she was not sure how the College of Literature, Science, and Arts would react to "her kind of work." These demurrals continued until 1994 when the Dean and the Associate Dean for Faculty Appointments themselves observed to the two directors, "How come you are always singing Joan's praises in annual reports and merit raise recommendations when she remains an Associate Professor?" When Joan learned that the suggestion had come from the college itself, she agreed to allow her case to go forward—and to a successful conclusion in 1995. I mention this episode because I believe it well reveals Joan's unassuming personality and her continuing modesty about her accomplishments.

Although Joan teaches one course a year for the Program in Linguistics, she spends three quarters of her time in the English Language Institute, where she has worked for more than 25 years. She is in her 60s, a respected national figure in her field of English as a Second language (ESL), and something of an Ambassador at Large for her profession. Among many such duties, she has served as a member of the USIA Advisory Panel, regularly offers advice to federal language-teaching operations including the Foreign Service Institute and the Defense Language Institute, and makes USIA Worldnet Satellite Video broadcasts from time to time. She has also operated as a language consultant for several groups within the Canadian Armed Forces.

Joan is a poised and experienced public speaker; clear, organized, professionally correct, and exceptionally good at the kind of address that both educates and motivates the rank-and-file. In consequence, she is greatly in demand as a plenary speaker at state, regional, and national conventions. Since being promoted to Associate Professor in 1983, she has delivered more than 50 such "plenary," "keynote," or "invited" presentations, plus an equal number of more "ordinary" ones. She has appeared on the program at the International TESOL Convention every year since 1973, and worked long and hard on TESOL committees for more than a decade, eventually becoming President of the then 20,000-strong Association in 1987. In 1992, TESOL bestowed on her its highest honor— The Alatis Award for Distinguished Service to the Profession. As it happens, I personally have seen Joan on several occasions at the National Convention, and observing her passage across the convention floor surrounded by disciples, admirers, and well-wishers is the closest I have come to experiencing what "a royal progress" must have been like.

Joan has an extensive list of publications, which are centered around her ESL textbooks. Her curriculum vitae breaks these publications down into the following categories (I have tabulated the category totals):

Genre	Number in Category
Books	16
Chapters, articles, papers	38
Reviews	5
Video cassettes	13
Audio cassette albums	7
Reprints	3
Technical reports, manuals	5
Organizational/Institutional Reports	25

This breakdown reveals that although Joan's output extends beyond the traditional print media, it is books, and particularly textbooks, that predominate. Starting in 1972, there have been to date ten textbooks, all dealing in some way with listening, pronunciation or speaking, with one or two more "in the pipeline."

Of the non-textbook volumes, which go alongside her published articles and book chapters, there is a Prentice-Hall book, *Listening and Language Learning* (Morley, 1984), and two edited collections. One of these is called *Current Perspectives on Pronunciation* (Morley, 1987), the other *Pronunciation Pedagogy and Theory* (Morley, 1994). It is this body of work, along with the textbooks, that has been a major cause of a North American revival of interest in speaking and listening among the four major language skill areas, now more frequently seen as important, interactive, and beneficial processes in their own right, rather than as simple performance *exhibits* of acquired levels of grammar, vocabulary, and pronunciation. Here is a paragraph from a review of the 1994 volume:

> There are at least two reasons why Morley is an excellent choice to serve as editor for the present collection and, thereby, as a specialist-guide for both teaching and research in L2 [second language] pronunciation. First, she recently published a set of three ESL classroom textbooks covering major aspects of L2 pronunciation (Morley, 1992a, 1992b, 1992c; see Wennerstrom, 1993, for favorable reviews). Teachers and researchers already familiar with Morley's work will be pleased to find that this earlier set of pedagogical materials serves as a coherent instructional extension to her contributions here. Second, there is her state-of-the-art discussion of the pronunciation component in L2 instruction (Morley, 1991b). Taken together, these contributions bridge the gap between theory and practice in the area of L2 pronunciation. Given this background, many readers will turn to the present collection with high expectations. They will not be disappointed. (Murphy, 1995, p. 346)

In this passage the reviewer neatly captures the complex web of contacts among the genres with which Joan works, and further intimates how this reticulation achieves a synergy between the often polarized activities glossed as either "theory" or "practice." Particularly noteworthy is the reviewer's observation that "this earlier set of pedagogical materials serves as a coherent instructional extension to her contributions here." This strikes me as an unusual move in a review of an academic book published in a theoretical Applied Linguistics journal—this suggestion that the textbooks are not so much intellectual dead-meat, but in fact offer a more elaborate conceptualization and implementation of her position. If we were to "borrow," as it were, the genres of the floor below, we could say that paper and editor's introduction in the 1994 volume are *treatments*, but the three-volume textbook series comprises a *monograph*.

There are two main—if interconnected—avenues that lead to Joan's scholarly production. One comes from the textbook writing (of which more later), while the other comes from public addresses. On the latter, she commented in interview, "At any rate, you can put fledgling ideas out, and then gradually clarify them and hone them and sharpen them, to the point where they're an article." The writings that evolve in this way have a distinctive character that Joan recognizes as follows:

> See, my writing is different from some people's writing, definitely. And it does take on the tone of looking at the field and saying to the field "here's what's been done here, and here's what I think ought to be done and why." Or ... it's just a review of "these were some of the past phases we went through and now we're in this phase." So it's partly a keeper of historical documents I suppose. One of my articles was reprinted with that very comment—that that's what it was.

Although Joan has written a few data-driven research papers, she does not particularly regret that she has not personally done more in this area. As she remarked in interview, "you really have to kind of make your peace with what you're good at." Perhaps another reason why Joan has concentrated on textbooks and review articles—rather than get involved in theoretical debate—is her dislike of professional antagonisms and criticisms. She noted (laughing) that "it isn't worth my time to trash something" and later in interview observed "the thing I'm *not* is a criticizer, and that's probably part of the reason I don't like to do [book] reviews."

Unlike Bill, Joan claims she is not much of a correspondent (apart from writing recommendations and such), although, like him, she is enthusiastic about E-mail. Instead, Joan is a phone person: "I just like to pick up the phone and talk to people." Indeed, she comments that the mixture of the individual and the professional—this "socialization of a profession," as she calls it—is an important part of her personal life. It comes as something of a surprise, therefore, to discover that Joan has done extremely little collaborative writing over her long career, and none at all in the genre of textbooks, where co-authorship in ESL (as in other fields) is so prevalent. Much of the answer to this conundrum seems to lie in Joan's first experiences in the ELI, where she was originally appointed as a lecturer with a special responsibility for materials production in listening. I suspect that this unusual appointment detached her somewhat from her professional and faculty colleagues, but, more importantly, forced her, more than 20 years ago, to become a pioneer in an area of ESL that at that time was seriously underdeveloped. On several occasions in the interviews, she stressed the fact that when she became a regular lecturer in the ELI in the late 1960s there was nobody else around who had any real interest in listening comprehension. Having produced in 1972 a first and highly successful textbook on her own, Joan has ever since apparently adopted that same modus operandi. This phenomenon of an early formation of habitual work-style is, of course, not particularly unusual. As we successfully start, so thereafter we often continue.

This outline-sketch of Joan would not be complete without some reference to her recent work on professional standards. Part of this has been concerned with her efforts to bring ESL Certification to Michigan Public Schools, and part with her efforts to raise the status of ESL as a profession across North America. In interviews, this was Joan's one moment of true passion:

> I'm very much on a bandwagon about this, because I don't think you can get the respect until you deserve the respect. And you don't deserve the respect until the whole field has standards and it can make laws, among educational people at least, to follow through with those standards. That still doesn't guarantee it, but it gives you a better guarantee of it. And this is a field that has moved *very very slowly* in standards.

So, alongside the Ambassador-at-Large, the dedicated servant to the profession, the sought-after public speaker, the successful textbook writer, and the even-handed surveyor of the field, we can add a final facet to Joan's profile. As the impromptu, impassioned eloquence of the preceding extract shows, she is also a determined advocate of professionalization.

It is, I hope, clear from the foregoing that Joan occupies a significant place in the affairs of ESL in North America and in its professional organization, TESOL. Specifically, she has become a leader in the teaching of English pronunciation to non-native speakers and one of the country's main authorities in teaching listening comprehension. She has gained this position not so much through a complex research agenda leading to an extensive series of technical papers, but rather through teaching, reflecting on her teaching materials, talking about her materials, publishing them, and then commenting on and surveying the field as a whole in scholarly papers. This, then, has been a practitioner's route to achievement.

A key turning point in Joan's career can be traced to what now might be described in historical hindsight as the "breakthrough of 1968." Here is Joan's businesslike and extremely formal reply to a memo from the ELI Director, a memo in which he proposed that Joan should get some release time to prepare materials for publication in exchange for the ELI receiving a proportion of the University Press royalties:

November 10, 1968

Dear Dr. Wardhaugh,

Thank you for your letter of November 5, 1968, regarding preparation of materials in aural comprehension.

Please consider this reply notification of my desire to proceed with preparation of teaching materials for publication in the said area of aural comprehension and acceptance of the suggested royalty division on a basis of 50% to author and 50% to the institute.

Director Wardhaugh's scheme was a stroke of genius, and after more than 25 years it is still in effective operation. Inasmuch as this scheme has provided Joan with certain specific opportunities—as well as constituting an unusual tradition in an institute of this kind—it is worth a minor digression. These royalty-sharing agreements have, in fact, achieved several objectives. First, textbooks tend to actually get finished and to get finished more quickly: for instance, one I co-authored appeared in late 1994, and another co-authored by Carolyn was published in spring 1997. Secondly, the institute receives a discretionary additional income of an origin and a substance that is very rare for ESL or Composition operations, and which has traditionally been used, inter alia, to support the activities of part-timers, adjuncts, and visitors who are not traditionally eligible for support funds from the general accounts. This "pot" over the years has thus done something toward creating a more democratic atmosphere in the institute. Another consequence is that the University Press has been able to build an effective ESL list that has made useful contributions over the years to its overall finances; in fact, Michigan is now the sole U.S. university press to have such a list. And it is Joan who has been for the last 20 years the Press's best-selling author, with total sales in excess of 500,000 copies. The last and perhaps most gratifying aspect of the benefits of this scheme is one already mentioned at the outset of this account of Joan: the fact that her publications, as oftentimes assisted by these arrangements, in conjunction with her other activities, were deemed sufficient in both quantity and quality for the University in 1983 to promote her from Lecturer to Associate Professor with tenure, and to promote her again to Full Professor a dozen years later.

An Illustrative Text.   The text that I have chosen to use in an attempt to explore Joan as a writer is entitled *Improving Spoken English: Consonants in Context* (Morley, 1992b). This is an opening section that appears unchanged in all three volumes of the pronunciation and oral speaking series published by the University of Michigan Press in 1992, and is referred to in Murphy's review. It consists of ten large-format pages, the first six of which are text and the last four, a series of charts. In each volume, the text is placed after the Preface and Acknowledgments but before the Contents and Introduction.

The fact that *Improving Spoken English: Consonants in Context* (henceforth *ISE:CIC*) is a content-title without any accompanying genre label (in strict contrast to the rest of the front matter) is, I will argue, an omission of considerable significance, especially when we bear in mind a conversational aside from Joan that stands as epigraph to this commentary: "My introductions are where my little soul pours out." Admittedly, squirreled away within the body of the text, there do exist two (but just two) self-referring glosses: "this introduction" at the bottom of the first page, and "this series introduction" on the seventh page. However, I will try to show that these ascriptions are, at best, only part of what the *ISE:CIC* really is.

But we are getting a little ahead of the story. The main text is divided into eight sections, all but the first having subheads, as follows:

1. (Untitled)
2. Background and Development
3. Focus on Principles
4. Focus on the Learner and Learner Goals

5. Focus on the Teacher

6. Focus on Instructional Objectives and Learner Involvement

7. Focus on Context Concepts in the Instructional Program

8. Focus on the Instructional Program

As elements in a textbook "series introduction" there is nothing particularly unexpected in the headings per se, even if the phrase "Context Concepts" in the penultimate section might be considered by many practitioners to be veering toward the cerebral. Overall, though, the headings follow natural and expected developmental paths: for instance, from principles to instructional details, and from background to implementation.

Indeed, there are aspects of the *ISE:CIC* that we can expect to find in any textbook introduction. Considerable space and attention, for example, is given to describing the characteristics of the series as a whole, its component volumes, and their principal parts. Of the 94 sentences in the main text, as many as one third have grammatical subjects that refer to the *ISE* or its components. All of the verbs that follow these "textual" subjects are in the present tense, and all but one are active in voice. Lexical verb choices (and their comparative frequencies) capture well the flavor of this aspect of the *ISE*; numbers refer to the number of occurrences:

ISE:CIC (or variants) . . .

provides . . .	7
focuses on . . .	5
features . . .	3
includes . . .	3
presents . . .	3
encompasses . . .	2
is . . .	2
blends . . .	1
contains . . .	1
are described . . .	1
gives attention to . . .	1
seeks . . .	1

As can be seen, some of these verbs are descriptive (*includes*), some (*focuses on, features*) operate to highlight specific features of the series, and others (such as *provide*) could play either or both of these roles. So far, so good; however, one of genre analysis' most consistent lessons is the importance of noting elements that are unexpectedly missing from a text or discourse. What is strange here—at least at first sight—is that the *ISE:CIC* is totally silent on two topics (or tropes) that are very often found in textbook introductions. First, there are no comparisons, either explicit or implicit, with any of the pre-existing and potentially rival textbooks; there are no statements of the form "Unlike other textbooks in this field, this volume offers . . . ." Second, there is no direct reference to innovations of any kind. There are no statements that have the form or function of "This text contains a number of novel features." The reasons for this are probably several. First, as we shall see, these absences can be related to Joan's communicative purposes as we struggle to tease them out. Second, they can be related to both Joan's position in the field and her consequent ability to resist any temptation (either from herself or from her publisher) to "hype" her volumes. As she said in interview, "The one thing about working with the University of Michigan Press is, you can do your own thing and you can hang on to it; there's very little intervention in the base of the book." Finally, this reticence can also be seen as reflecting Joan's muted stance to criticism of colleagues and her long-standing refusal "to trash the opposition."

Here is the opening paragraph:

> *Improving Spoken English: Consonants in Context (ISE:CIC)* is an intermediate/advanced program in ESL speech-pronunciation, one that is structured to foster active learner involvement in small groups and self-tutorials as well as in regular class use. Contextualized practice formats range across imitative, rehearsed, and extemporaneous speech performance opportunities, and feature a microfocus on pronunciation and a macrofocus on oral communication. While the central focus of the series is on consonants and consonant combinations, both within and across word boundaries, the program also includes an emphasis on syllable structure and stress, rhythm and intonation patterns, and attention to vowels and vowel reduction.

This opening paragraph immediately establishes the tone and style that will be maintained over the coming six pages. As we can see, the focus is strongly on the series, and not at all on the author. Indeed, Joan makes no reference to herself in the body of the entire *ISE:CIC*, passing up doubtless numerous opportunities to refer to her 25 years of experience in the field, to her previous textbooks (by the same publisher), to the way her thoughts have evolved through the years, or to her personal hopes for the series. Somewhat unusually for the genre, there is no personal professional history here. Indeed, the single first-person pronoun in the whole sample text is not authorial, but refers to the field as a whole: "In particular, the following groups of adults and teenagers have challenged *our* expertise as facilitators of learning in the study of pronunciation" (emphasis added). In Geertz's (1988) distinction, this is another example of "author-evacuated" rather than "author-saturated" text, and neither by accident nor from publisher pressure. Indeed, the only signs of the author occur in the two brief footnotes, both of which refer to Joan's previous work. In sum, all the recounting of personal experiences and personal relations is rigorously confined to the Preface and Acknowledgment sections.

Instead, the text presents itself as a piece of formal and technical writing. As we can see, the sentences tend to be quite long and, from the outset, they incorporate fairly abstract and elaborate conceptualizations of what we might otherwise have thought to be the rather ordinary business of teaching pronunciation to non-native speakers. Consider, for instance, these three phrases from the opening paragraph:

- structured to foster active learner involvement
- contextualized practice formats
- extemporaneous speech performance opportunities

Further, this opening paragraph makes several assumptions about background technical knowledge, as signaled by its swift and immediate use of such compound nouns as:

- syllable structure
- intonation patterns
- vowel reduction

The second section, entitled *Background and Development*, is also somewhat unexpected—at least for a textbook introduction—but this time as much for content as for style. I think that most readers would expect from such a section heading some account of the *local* circumstances that led up to the completion of the series, such as some contributing account of her teaching and materials development experiences. However, what we actually get is a brief history of the development of the *field*:

Background and Development

A small groundswell of renewed interest in the learning and teaching of pronunciation in ESL/EFL began in the early 1980s. By the late 1980s, the modest groundswell turned into a clear and serious concern for—and excitement about—the pronunciation component of oral communication in second language learning theory and pedagogy. And today many programs are developing new directions in the speech-pronunciation programs, a "new look" that reflects revised concepts about *goals* for learners and *roles* for teachers and learners. A basic premise underlying these developments is that intelligible pronunciation is an essential component of communicative competence.

A moving force behind the development of new programs has been the specific and urgent needs of several large groups of ESL/EFL learners. In particular, the following groups of adults and teenagers have challenged our expertise as facilitators of learning in the study of pronunciation . . .

In some ways, the preceding text has the appearance of a standard "scene-setting" introduction designed to capture and celebrate the emergence of a new "research front." However, in other ways it is definitely nonstandard. Unlike nearly all academic introductions, the passage is unsupported by citations (even if there is a note at the bottom of the page stating that the section was adapted from the volume edited by Joan and published in 1987). In other words, the text is markedly non-intertextual. A second unusual feature is that the research front has, at least in the author's estimation, already arrived. *ISE:CIC* seems, therefore, to be positioning itself as an ex post facto consolidation. Third and most interesting is Joan's account of causative mechanisms:

> A *moving force* behind the development of new programs has been the specific and urgent needs of several large groups of ESL/EFL learners. (emphasis added)

Admittedly, Joan only talks about "a moving force" rather than "the moving force"; even so, this strong ascription to external agency both diminishes her own role (and that of her close colleagues) by de-centering it to the outside. Yet at the same time it also somehow consolidates that role by presenting it as a direct and inevitable response to need. Strikingly, there is also no mention of any of the constraining "curricular" or "academic" variables that must have intervened. In fact, this absence of individual academic agency becomes even more striking when, as we have already seen, a reading of the relevant literature and knowledge of the field confirm that Joan herself has been one of those responsible for "the new look." And yet the text is curiously devoid of designer labels attachable to individual protagonists, Joan or otherwise.

As we go further into the *ISE:CIC*, a number of its characteristic features emerge, many of which are typical of Joan's writing in general. One—which, I suspect, is also common in textbook introductions as a whole—is heavy use of those paratactic structures that accumulate features and attributes. Here are the first two sentences from the *Focus on Principles* section:

> *ISE:CIC* is one part of an instructional program designed to meet the pronunciation needs of ESL students within those frameworks of today's perspectives on second language learning and teaching that feature communication and language function, even as it emphasizes aspects of spoken language form. The program development has drawn insights from English phonetics and phonology, and focuses on active learner involvement and the affective domain.

Such sentences serve to underscore the integration of potentially disparate components. The first "... meets ... needs ... even as it emphasizes." The second "draws insights from ... phonetics" but yet "focuses on ... the affective domain." These sentential accumulations are, I suspect, closely connected to perhaps the most distinctive rhetorical and stylistic cluster of elements in Joan's writing: her uses of elaborations, lists, and charts.

Joan often re-works her concepts several times as she proceeds through her text. Unlike many others in applied linguistics, she does not do this to "problematize" them in some way, but rather to give them intellectual and operational solidity. The way she handles "learner role" well illustrates her manner of proceeding. She deals with this topic on three occasions: First, as part of the opening sentence:

> ... structured to foster active learner involvement ...

Second, in a complete sentence, one third of the way through the text:

> A focus on intense learner involvement in the learning/teaching (and self-teaching) process including speech awareness, self-monitoring, and self-modification of speech-pronunciation features.

Finally, in two long sentences at the two-thirds stage:

> Through lesson design and activity expectations, *ISE:CIC* focuses on helping learners establish positive affective involvement including: a) assuming self-responsibility, b) developing speech monitoring skills, c) developing speech modification (i.e., self-correction) skills, and d) recognizing self-accomplishment. It is important to note that both cultural background and personal learning styles and learning preferences profoundly influence the learner's development of learning strategies and that each individual will have variations in this component of the program.

This sense of level-by-level development fits well with what Joan herself says about her expository writing: "I am very careful about leading the reader, with no gaps: I like the sequence to go very smoothly, which probably involves some redundancy; I do built-in redundancy in order to achieve that."

Joan also attempts to impose clarity and order on her material by the use of numbered lists. For example, in this text she designatedly identifies and labels:

- *Seven* "high priority" principles
- *Five* groups of learners that have had an influence on developments
- *Four* "more readily attainable" learner goals
- *Three* types of involvement

• *Three* types of instructional context

Joan is, in fact, very well aware of this trait in her work:

> If you look at some of my papers you can see that instantly, that I start out with "we're going to look at 7 things, and we are going to look at this and that about them, and here we go number 1 ..." ... It's the laying out of things in very careful order.

A further element in the multilayered and evolutionary arrangement of the *ISE:CIC* is its concluding set of five charts. The first two provide a further summatory reprise of the main points embedded in the previous text. Chart 3 offers a complex six-level diagnostic "Speech Intelligibility Index," which has a student placement function somewhat akin to the Identification Keys in plant taxonomy. The last two consist of imperative-format checklists for student use and teacher reference.

After this discoursal commentary, we are now in a position to return to the initial puzzle of how best to "read" the chosen sample of Joan's writing. It has, I hope, become clear that the *ISE:CIC* is not a rhetorically transparent, promotional introduction designed to "sell" a series. Nor is its function to demonstrate in practical detail *how* the textbooks are to be used. There are, for instance, no worked examples of how instructors might go about specimen classroom activities. That function is kept for the sections actually labeled *Introduction*, which follow the Contents page in each volume. Nor is it a personal narrative—as some textbook introductions are—of how the books came to be written. Rather, its impersonal stance and academic phraseology indicate a formal statement of some kind.

We can, I believe, make some further progress in understanding Joan's text by taking up the tricky issue of its intended audience. At one level, there is no clear indication of this audience (or audiences); in fact, its univocal tenor prevents us from saying that this particular section is written for student readers, this one is designed to help the instructor, or that one is aimed at encouraging institutional adoptions. Beyond that, everything we have so far learned about the *ISE:CIC* would suggest that it is addressed to the professional community at large, which, in the case of these advanced textbooks, also includes the non-native speaker graduate students she deals with. Certainly in the text itself she makes several references to her students' analytical skills, their capacity to cope with technical metalanguage, and their need for involvement and awareness. Equally certainly, there is nothing in the text to indicate that learners should restrict their attention to the two closing charts specifically targeted for them.

The *ISE:CIC* therefore turns out to be a contribution to professional development, not only for instructors actually using the program, but also for ESL teachers in general, as well as for incipient NNS professionals. Referring to textbooks more generally at one point in our interviews, Joan made the highly pertinent observation that with a textbook "you're training teachers about a *field*" (emphasis added). So, as we suspected, the *ISE:CIC* is not simply or only a "series introduction"—which is why there is no genre heading to that effect. Rather, it is a statement of Joan's current position as conveniently embodied through and by this particular three-volume series—a role clearly recognized in at least one review:

> As a final note, we highly recommend Morley's outstanding introduction, included in all three volumes, and suggest that it should be required reading for all teachers interested in improving the communicative performance of their students. (Thompson, Linney, Fleming, 1994, p. 36)

Further evidence of this role comes from reflecting once again on Joan's career, particularly about how she started with textbooks and later became involved in scholarly papers. In fact, the introduction to her first textbook in 1972 turned out to be an opportunity for her to publish a first statement outlining her particular beliefs and principles. We are again reminded of the earlier comment, "my introductions are where my little soul pours out." It is also important to note that Joan managed to arrange for the *ISE:CIC* to be printed *unchanged* in all three volumes, a strategy that apparently gave rise to considerable concern and misgiving at the Press, and was perhaps only achievable by the editorial control that she has, over many years and many volumes, managed to establish for herself. The "threepeat" of the text, its unwavering tone, its elaborated repetitions, its multiple sections, and its discrete lists, however, all work to shift it away from being a philosophical rationale of some kind to one that is more action-oriented and more field-committed. It thus turns out that the text we have been looking at is a *manifesto*.

Post-Text. After 25 years of teaching oral skills, Joan remains as enthusiastic as ever. Here she is, in interview (in 1994) one last time:

> You can teach a very ordinary pronunciation class and you can teach a very ordinary speech class, but when you begin to look at discourse and look at meaning and look at voice and all the body language as well, how all these things are used, it makes a very exciting way to look at teaching oral communication. And perhaps people could benefit from our experiences here.

The last remark with its hedged advocacy ("perhaps people could benefit") also re-affirms her continuing modesty.

As a writer, Joan has few pretensions to high literary style. This is partly due to the origins of her professional writing in either textbooks or in speeches, and partly to her stress on organization and structure. On the other hand, her style is quite technical and, in fact, can involve the full terminology of phonetics and its concomitant phonetic symbols (which I have not illustrated). Although a much newer field than Systematic Botany, Applied Linguistics/ESL has also evolved a complex verbal apparatus to describe the phenomena in which it is interested. Joan's adoption of this style in her writing, a style we can associate with educational *science*, is keyed to her long-standing concerns about the slow development of professional standards in her field, and her concern to establish a professional rhetoric.

CAROLYN

> Discourse analysis is for people who don't want to have a lot of strings attached and a lot of strong frameworks. And you know that's *not* me . . . and I'm sort of learning and enjoying the learning process of being involved in something that doesn't have all those, you know, well-defined parameters, but . . . certainly there's an uneasiness about it. (Carolyn, in interview)

Carolyn is a New Yorker and, like many people brought up in that city, she is orally gifted; witty, quick, and sure in discussion and conversation. She has been a lecturer in the ELI since 1980, and gained the extra title of Associate Director for Curriculum in 1989. In this latter role, she is primarily responsible, in consultation with the Director, for making teaching arrangements—which courses to offer, how many sections to aim for, who will teach them, and so forth. Rather more independently, she is Chair of the Curriculum Committee, which has overall responsibility for adjusting and developing the institute's extensive menu of courses for non-native speakers of English. Her direct counterpart is Sarah, who has the equivalent administrative position of Associate Director for Testing. In addition to her ELI work, in more recent years she has offered a course for the program in Linguistics (like Joan and John), usually a course for concentrators and a few graduate students on "Principles of Second Language Learning and Instruction." It is obvious to all that this additional teaching role has given her considerable professional and personal satisfaction.

Carolyn's career, at least as far as writing is concerned, can be divided into two main periods: her early work in the 1970s at the Graduate Center at CUNY, where she participated in some influential experimental work on second language acquisition, and her more recent writing in Ann Arbor involving International Teaching Assistants and the teaching of academic oral skills. This latter work is more qualitative and discourse-oriented, and something of Carolyn's ambivalent attitude to these features can already be gleaned from the epigraph to this section. Her career thus both reflects and contributes to some of the major trends in Applied Linguistics and Foreign Language Teaching that have occurred over the last three decades. Although her colleagues, Joan and John, have also shifted their positions somewhat to encompass new developments and new institutional challenges, both have largely remained within the original paradigms they chose for themselves. Not so with Carolyn, who has switched from quantitative research to qualitative applications, and from early to late stages in language learning. And she alone of the study group, at least to my knowledge, has had a career in which family influences and concerns have played a significant role.

In response to these two kinds of phenomena, I have taken two steps. In terms of discourse analysis, I have concentrated on two texts: an influential co-authored article published in 1974, and another co-authored chapter published 20 years later. Secondly, interwoven among and between them is some small account of the personal and professional circumstances that have contributed to the sharp polarity between the two pieces.

In The Beginning. Curricula vitae often show straighter and more certain career paths than is actually the case, because retrospective efforts to tidy up our personal histories allow us to make our lives appear more coherent to others. Carolyn is no exception. From her c.v. it would seem that she has been interested in aspects of ESL right from the beginning; she has a BA in Linguistics (with minors in English as a Second Language and Education), followed by graduate school in her chosen field and then a series of teaching jobs leading up to her present position. However, in interview she corrected this impression, characterizing herself as someone not originally attuned to academia, and who had fallen into ESL quite by accident. In fact, her career had already taken a number of turns before her official c.v. begins. Her 1972 BA hides the fact that she had earlier dropped out of college and worked for a year in a Catholic school that did not require certification. When she decided to go back to school, it was with this positive teaching experience behind her. Although she still had no firm idea of what she wanted to study, she gravitated toward linguistics because the department was small and intimate, and thus seemed more comfortable to her as a slightly older student.

Likewise, it had never occurred to her to go to graduate school, and she applied only because of strong encouragement from faculty in her undergraduate program. In interview, she observed:

> I really never considered that I was going to go for post-graduate work. I asked my mother, I said, "So did you ever think I would go to college?"

and she said "No, I never really thought of that." That just tells you the kind of family background I came from. And for me to go to *college* was extraordinary, no less to think of going on to anything else.

The graduate program she entered in 1972 was strongly theoretical—in her words "Chomsky Chomsky Chomsky." However, one faculty member (Stephen Krashen) was working in the more "useful and practical" sub-field of applied linguistics, doing experimental work in second language acquisition. Because of this and because, according to Carolyn, Krashen treated his graduate students in a highly egalitarian manner and encouraged them to become involved in cutting-edge research, she and a number of other female students began to work with him. Thus, under his mentorship, Carolyn became involved in research work leading to six co-authored papers (five published while she was still a student at CUNY), among them the much-cited Bailey, Madden, and Krashen (1974), "Is There a 'Natural Sequence' in Adult Second Language Learning?"

This article was published in *Language Learning* (at that time the most important scholarly journal in the field) in 1974, and has been reprinted in edited volumes published in 1978 and 1983. Because only a small handful of journals in Applied Linguistics are screened by the Social Sciences Citation Index for citations, the fact that the paper was cited therein 46 times in the six years following publication, and at least 39 times in subsequent years, attests to its lasting significance. Indeed, it has almost certainly been cited at least as often again in books and in non-SSCI journals. It resurfaced in a review article published in 1994:

THE MORPHEME STUDIES

In the progress of science it is not uncommon for interesting and potentially significant findings to be put aside for want of a theoretically motivated explanation. This has certainly been the fate of the morpheme research carried out in the 1970s, which has existed in limbo since then pending such a theoretically motivated explanation.

Criticism of the morpheme studies crystallized around two points. The first charge—that the commonalities reported in the literature (e.g. Anderson 1978; Bailey, Madden & Krashen 1974; Krashen 1977; Larsen-Freeman 1976) are spurious—is now rejected. . . . Yet another objection concerned the linguistic heterogeneity of the morphemes, consisting as they did of free and bound, NP and VP morphemes.

(Zobl & Liceras, 1994, p. 161)

As the reader may anticipate, Zobl and Liceras then argued (in a nutshell) that today's more powerful syntactic theories allow for a more insightful explanation for why it is that certain grammatical morphemes (past tense endings, possessive "s," etc.) tend to be acquired by certain populations of non-native speakers of English in certain orders. The valuable empirical data, they thus suggested, was at the time of original publication too far ahead of a theory that could plausibly interpret it.

In interview, however, Carolyn offered a more "contingent" account (Gilbert & Mulkay, 1984). She joked that one reason the article has been cited so extensively was that other people disagreed with it so strongly, even though she took pains to stress that this had been disagreement "in a healthy academic sense," and did not derive from academic jealousy or rival-theory hostility or whatever:

> It was cited because it was so timely and because we were saying something pretty interesting—that adults were learning language the same way as children. And the psychologists couldn't believe it, you know, they couldn't see adults learning anything in a developmental kind of way.

Bailey, Madden, and Krashen (1974). The text is quite short: nine pages in its original incarnation, including tables and graphs. It begins with an abstract, as do all papers in *Language Learning*. The body of the paper is divided into four parts, including an untitled introduction and three sections with standard experimental titles: Procedure, Results, and Discussion.

The introduction section contains a brief, to-the-point discussion of the problem to be explored, identifying it as a direct progession from previous research, particularly a study conducted by Dulay and Burt (1973), which had appeared the previous year in the same journal. An additional seven articles are cited, and a table is included that summarizes the results from the Dulay and Burt paper and from another relevant study. The use of such a table in an introduction section shows how the authors identify themselves early as members of a group collecting data about the stages of acquiring grammatical elements. Just as notable is the introduction's close where two hypotheses are presented, a clear sign that the paper will offer an experimental rather than descriptive piece of research:

> In this study, the following two hypotheses will be tested:
>
> 1. adults learning English as a second language will show agreement with each other in the relative difficulty of functors in English.
>
> 2. the adult rankings will be similar to that of the child learning English as a second language, rather than that of children learning English as a first language.

The Procedure section consists of four paragraphs. The first gives detailed information about the subjects in the study (e.g., number and age of subjects tested, description of the language programs they were enrolled in, and native language), and the second expounds the instrument used to elicit data, and stresses that it is the same as that used in the Dulay and Burt study. The third paragraph goes on to describe the exact testing procedure, including information about who did the testing:

> Each subject was tested individually by a team of two undergraduate students from the Queens College Linguistics Department. One *E* showed a picture to the *S*, asked the pertinent preliminary questions, then proceeded to the test questions. The second *E* recorded the *S*'s answers to the test questions on the BSM answer sheet.

Within its broadly "social science" stance (past passive, use of *subject*, etc.), the extract is particularly telling for the way the authors have chosen to refer to parties involved with italicized capital letters. A first observation would be that this usage is not glossed earlier, and thus is presented as being standard verbal practice. Second, this decision not only categorizes the participants into the roles they play in the research process, but further reduces their personality and humanity with the initializing convention—as if the students and their interlocutors were mere pieces being moved about on the experimenters' chessboard.

The Results section is also quite short, consisting of four paragraphs of text, two graphs, and two tables. Throughout, the reader is referred to the nonverbal material for details, which are expressed not in terms of raw scores, nor in the form of usage examples, but rather emerge as correlations and degrees of significance. Here, for instance, is the one-sentence first paragraph: "Pearson product–movement correlations were performed on the relative accuracy of use of the eight grammatical morphemes between Spanish and non-Spanish speakers and among the eight instruction levels." "Relative accuracy of use" is thus presented as having a bedrock, fact-like status on which certain statistical maneuvers "were performed," rather than being an end-product of a possibly uncertain process (ambiguities, miscodings, use of undergraduates as testers, etc.). This impression is consolidated by the results appearing in the form of a graph, and here we might note that graphs were identified by Bazerman (1988) as occurring late in a field's progress toward more abstract formulations. The remaining three paragraphs also deal with correlations of various kinds: within the study data and between the study data and other results (including Dulay & Burt).

The Discussion section is slightly longer (six paragraphs) than the others, and contains no graphs, tables, or examples. In part it offers a more discursive explanation of the highly technical previous section. The first two paragraphs note the support in the results for Hypotheses 1 and 2, respectively, while paragraph three carries this a little further. Thus, the first half of the Discussion deals with interpretation and underscores the contrast between intuition and experimental evidence. For a clear instance of this, note the use of "casual" in the closing sentence to paragraph three: "While *casual* observation affirms that errors due to mother tongue interference do occur in second language learning in adults, our data imply that a major source of errors is intra- rather than inter-lingual, and are [*sic*] due to the use of universal language processing strategies" (emphasis added).

The fourth paragraph brings in the results of earlier studies to support or extend the claims of this study, and closes with, "It remains to be determined what combinations of factors account for this apparent uniformity in adult processing ..."—a clear enough indication, I would suggest, of where the research agenda of the group is likely to go next. The final two paragraphs assess what the research might mean for language teaching and discuss possible directions for that research. The paper closes with this paragraph:

> We are thus faced with an *interesting* conclusion: adults seem to profit from instruction, an instruction that often presents the grammatical morphemes in an order different from that implied here. An *interesting* and testable hypothesis is that the most effective instruction is that which follows the observed order of difficulty, one with a "natural syllabus." We will be prepared for such an experiment when we confirm the implied sequence longitudinally, and discover which aspects of language follow a universal sequence, and understand what factors determine such a sequence. (emphasis added)

Two observations seem to be in order here. The first concerns the occurrences of the evaluative adjective "interesting" at the very close of the article, occurrences that stand out from the firmly descriptive and objective stance established in all other paragraphs of the paper. The second concerns the history of the piece, and the apparent fact that the world had to wait 20 years for Zobl and Liceras to explain "what factors determine such a sequence."

Overall, the paper belongs to "the empiricist repertoire" (Gilbert & Mulkay, 1984) and is "rhetorically machined" (Swales, 1990a) to fit into the social science experimental paper format. Hypothesis driven, and methodologically designed "to protect the researcher's results" (Bazerman, 1988, p. 272), it deals with data in an abstract way (we can note the complete lack of examples) by focusing on statistical treatments. Paragraphs are short and clip along; both past tense and passive are common. Overall, the paper presents itself as a "neat" study, positioned firmly within the bounds of then-current SLA research. As the closing sentence implies, the paper also positions itself as one chapter in an interlocking series of experiments by the research group to which Carolyn belonged, one that conscientiously rotated the order of its small band of authors for different publications.

Transitions. Bailey, Madden, and Krashen (1974) was the sort of text that Carolyn co-authored during the graduate-student phase of her professional career. She continued to work in CUNY's stimulating environment for a number of years, receiving her MA in 1976 and becoming a PhD candidate in 1979. However, her progress had already been slowed by family responsibilities, since she had taken 6 months off for the birth of her second child and had accompanied her husband (at that time a teacher in the New York City public schools) on two "sabbaticals," one for 3 months to Mexico in 1973 and the other for 10 months to the Azores in 1977–1978, where, with her usual dynamic interest in educational affairs, she was also able to create for herself additional teaching experiences. When it became clear that her husband's teaching situation in New York was not likely to improve radically, they agreed that Carolyn should take a job at the ELI in Ann Arbor, Michigan, a small city that they both liked and where they had close friends. Because Carolyn was enthusiastic about working at the English Language Institute, the move away from her "academic home" did not distress her unduly. She planned to finish her dissertation on her own, but she never did.

Actually, Carolyn could have continued to do her research in SLA at the ELI, since at the time she arrived (although no longer) there were people working there in that area, including important figures in the field such as Susan Gass and Larry Selinker. But, as she said in interview:

> I was doing my dissertation when I first came here and ... it was OK getting into other aspects: second language teaching, for example, and the training. But ... she [Susan Gass] would have taken me down maybe a slightly different road, since she wasn't looking at the same kinds of second language acquisition. So I could have felt like that would have been too much of a pull.

Close to 15 years later, Carolyn's dual position as Lecturer and Associate Director involves her in a range of tasks, which she identifies as administration, teaching, mentoring, writing, and committee work. In interview, she mentioned enjoying aspects of all of these, with perhaps a little less enthusiasm for the last. She likes the administrative side of the job "more than you might think!" Evidence of this can be seen in the satisfactions she finds in the paperwork itself (not, of course, a universal faculty trait), such as planning time-schedules for future semesters, budgeting, and producing teaching rosters. In addition, she is actively involved in the day-to-day interactional management of the institute and works with the director on possible longer term developments. Further, like Joan and John, she still very much enjoys teaching and puts considerable time and energy into it; and here she particularly relishes her role as an encourager of younger and less experienced ELI staff, helping them develop their strengths in course design and materials writing. Although, in the current ELI ethos, lecturers are encouraged to be visible and productive beyond their local milieu, writing and publishing for Carolyn today is something that has to be fitted in around the edges. Unlike the other members of NUB who form the seven case studies, she, ostensibly at least, has no firm goals for setting aside time for writing, nor for how much she gets written in any one year: as she observed in interview, "if it happens, it happens." In this, she differs most strikingly from her nearest counterpart—Tony in the Herbarium.

In contrast to Joan, Carolyn as author is a collaborator; in fact, all of her publications are co-authored except for one shortish book review. In interview, Carolyn asserted that all this co-authorship (and co-editorship) has been her choice and that she enjoys the process thoroughly. She personally finds it an excellent way to work and holds firmly to the belief that discussing ideas with collaborators always makes the eventual written product stronger. In addition, she claims that her personality is well suited to collaborative work because she likes to talk to and negotiate with people; indeed, she relishes—up to a limit—disagreement and open discussion.

Carolyn's writing projects since coming to the ELI fall roughly into four groups. First she teamed up with other ELI lecturers to produce an article, a textbook, and a number of presentations all having to do with task-based learning (TBL), a rather sophisticated version of the "communicative approach" to ESL that has generally dominated the field for the last 20 years. A second area has been editing conference proceedings on various aspects of SLA, particularly with Susan Gass, but also with other faculty such as Dennis Preston and Larry Selinker. If one of Joan's routes to publication is through public addresses, Carolyn's has been through conference organization—an activity, she noted in interview, very well suited to her personality:

> It's tiring, especially when you're doing other things, and it does drain you, but I really enjoy it. I like problem-solving, and I like that problem-solving part of things . . . You want a successful conference, you have to think of everything, and you've got to think of it before it's going to happen . . . sort of like a good politician.

In the volumes that were produced in the 1986–1990 period, she played a full and largely equal role throughout the editorial process, from invitations through to final textual emendations, even though she was a lecturer and her co-editors were all professors. The style and substance of these volumes is the closest (of the four areas) to the kind of writing she was doing in graduate school; however, she was now required to take the wider, more detached view of an editor, rather than the narrower, more localized one of a primary SLA researcher.

More recently, she has been involved in two other kinds of collaboration. First, at the time of writing, she and Theresa (whose diary we used in chapter 2) were reviewing the proofs of a short textbook they had written for the University of Michigan Press entitled *Discussion and Interaction in the Academic Community* (Madden & Rohlck, 1997). Commenting on the processes of writing, piloting, and revising the book, Carolyn again stressed how partnership and collaboration could easily co-exist with mentoring and being the senior member of the team. At least in ESL, textbook writing (as revealed in Byrd's 1995 collection) is something of a guild-craft and perhaps has connections with the training on the floor below, as witnessed by Bill's comment, "You learn by doing it with somebody watching over your shoulder."

Although the textbook manuscript itself received favorable and encouraging outside reviews, Carolyn has remained somewhat uneasy about its final shape. She worries that it seems a little vague, with its goals and directions not as clear as she might like. As we have seen, she started out in the most "scientific" corner of the field of Applied Linguistics, and the gradual transition to a more "discoursal" approach for more advanced students has, in some ways, increased her uncertainty:

> I love working with discourse analysis now, too. But I think the textbook is . . . an unknown to me . . . and that always makes me a little, you know, whatever, uncomfortable. (in interview, 1995)

A similar combination of excitement and unease is evident in her fourth and final area of authorial collaboration—her work on training programs for International Teaching Assistants, which has produced to date two co-authored articles, five presentations, and a co-edited book published in 1994. Like much of Joan's and John's work, these are explorations of reflective pedagogy, buttressed by several strands of research and scholarship all designed, in their various ways, to try to account for the nature of academic communication. But, especially for Carolyn, this is a fuzzy and opportunistic world of heuristics and strategies—a world of subjective and contextual appropriacies above and beyond the certainties of grammatical correctness and error, or of successful or unsuccessful phonemic discrimination.

Axelson and Madden (1994). The second main text, "Discourse Strategies for ITAs Across Instructional Contexts," is a chapter from Carolyn's co-edited book on International Teaching Assistants published by the TESOL organization (Madden & Myers, 1994). The "ITA problem," as it is sometimes known, is the employment by research universities of non-native speaker graduate students who may variously lack one or more of the following: accuracy and fluency in English pronunciation, prior teaching experience, understanding of American classroom cultures, and knowledge of the likely strengths and weaknesses of students within those classrooms. ESL units within those research universities have, for the last decade or so, often been called upon to do something "about the problem," and their efforts have often been funded by various central administrative bodies, since it is the Presidents and Deans who have to deal with complaints made by undergraduate students, their parents, or their elected state representatives. In consequence, a sizeable literature has developed in this specialized subfield, part of it, including a good number of PhD dissertations, dealing with applied descriptive research on what actually happens discoursally in university classrooms and during office hours. Michigan's ELI, like a number of comparable units elsewhere, has been able to use this concern as a "locomotive" for a train of English for Academic Purposes courses and services for matriculated students on campus. Carolyn's chapter and book constitute further contributions to this newly forged tradition.

One obvious difference between this 1994 chapter (hereafter AM) and Bailey, Madden, and Krashen, 1974 (hereafter BMK) is its length: 33 pages, not including references (which are gathered together at the back of the book) as opposed to nine pages. The length of the later paper can be ascribed to a number of causes. First, about 12 of its pages are given over to extensive transcriptions of oral data, and another eight pages taken up with charts or lists of discourse categories. The contrast with the abstract numerical data of BMK is striking. A second reason for its length is the attempt to move slowly and carefully from research findings to detailed pedagogical outcomes; indeed, about five pages are devoted to this last (again in contrast to BMK). Finally, the authors in their book chapter have tried to carry forward with them a readership that includes people just starting in the ITA subfield, as well as having something to say to its most experienced and "seasoned" practitioners and investigators.

These features can be seen in the following extract from the end of the introduction:

> This chapter addresses the issue of appropriateness and context of the language of ITAs in laboratory, office-hour, and classroom situations. We continue the efforts of Axelson and Madden (1990) and Young (1989a) in specifying the details of the target language discourse strategies appropriate to those academic contexts as well as to provide an informed and organized syllabus of these categories. We take a closer look at these categories and their manifestations from native and nonnative instructors, emphasizing

the similarities and differences across contexts in content, style, form, and purpose. Finally, we summarize our findings in order to enable trainers to bring the information to the ITAs so as to provide organized and meaningful choices that will enrich the discourse repertoire of ITAs.

We can note here the frequent use of metadiscourse, the moderately paced development of their argument, and their avoidance of a heavily passivized style. Observe, in particular, how the following sentence-initiations carry the reader forward:

1. This chapter addresses . . .
2. We continue the efforts of . . .
3. We take a closer look at . . .
4. Finally, we summarize our findings . . .

The chapter begins not with an abstract but with an epigraph. This is the only use of this rhetorical device in the book, and a fairly unusual way of opening a paper in applied linguistics, and even rarer in theoretical linguistics—although apparently not unknown in volumes of this kind. The quoted material, which argues for the study of classroom discourse, is in fact the beginning of the chapter's argument. However, it is also an invocation of authority, as the epigraph's author, John Sinclair, is one of the few "elder statesmen" in the new field of discourse analysis. In interview Carolyn noted that she and her co-author felt it would be a good "framing" for what they wanted to say, helping to justify why they were relying on discourse analysis. She also went on to observe that by invoking Sinclair, who is British, she could also position herself as now being outside the U.S. tradition of "hard" social science research.

The chapter is organized into six sections, and all but the short "Conclusion" contain either extensive transcripts or verbal charts. The first is an untitled introduction, and thereafter we have the following:

Methodology

Creating the Right Atmosphere

Facilitating Problem Solving

Materials for ITA Training

Conclusion

These headings strongly suggest a hybrid genre of some kind, insofar as the first two sections belong to the IMRD tradition of experimental research, whereas the next three indicate a how-to piece with clear pedagogical uptake.

Because introductions have already figured prominently in several of the earlier text-biographies, I will concentrate here on aspects of the later sections. For example, the Methodology section differs from BMK's *Procedure* in interesting ways. Instead of simply giving a swift list of particulars, this section presents itself as a co-constructed personal narrative of discovery:

> We came to the task of identifying discourse categories from two directions. The first was the observation of what teachers actually do in their classrooms, office hours, and labs. As we watched videotapes of TAs and professors in these settings, we made transcripts, notes and lists, which included direct quotes as well as entries such as *greetings, emphasis, explaining* and *responding to questions.* (original emphasis)

In BMK the methodology is taken for granted ("Despite the fact that the Bilingual Syntax Measure was originally designed for children it was successfully used with adults here."), whereas in AM the methodology takes the form of an emerging "analytic framework," which leads to three lists of "discourse categories" presented in a large table, which the authors go to some lengths to explain:

> We are keenly aware that many other possible kinds of interactions in these settings simply may not have occurred during our observations and are therefore not represented here. . . . This awareness notwithstanding, the global view they provide helps us see where significant similarities and differences may lie.

The next two long sections analyze in considerable detail "two of the most salient objectives of TAs" (*Creating the Right Atmosphere* and *Faciltating Problem Solving*) which the authors have identified in the Methodology section. Arguments in these sections are made by offering generalizations and then backing them up with examples variously taking the form of observations, anecdotes, and transcription samples. Here is an instance of the last:

> Moreover, when the tension mounts and the TA makes no move to break it, the student may offer a tension-breaking aside, as in this dialogue:
>
> 3) S: It's kind of hot in here, huh?
>   TA: Yeah, actually suppose the value . . .
>   S: Fun stuff
>   TA: So actually we just find T value, to contain the T value.

These sections do not have extensive conclusions: Their value is taken to lie in the appositeness of the verbal extract chosen for display and in the acuity of the accompanying commentary, not in some general result abstracted from the data. Because these examples function primarily as perceptive demonstrations of points, we can see their multiple use as engendering a kind of cumulative consciousness-raising in the reader.

The fifth section provides what its heading suggests: "Materials for ITA Training." Despite the heavy "advance-labelling" in the introduction (Tadros, 1985), this section in fact takes the reader somewhat by surprise, because it alone has not been explicitly pre-announced. When asked about this section in interview, Carolyn conceded that it seemed a bit "tacked-on," but likened this to the tradition at the TESOL national convention:

> We probably initially presented this at a conference, where there's an expectation that there might be some practical aspect of it. You know there's a big joke in TESOL presentations: here's your theory, BUT! for the teacher! And so the last paragraph always has this little practical aspect for the teacher. I mean it's sort of a joke, but there's a reality to it, there's sort of a feeling that that's what you do.

The reality, however, is that this section extends over several pages and includes—like its predecessors—some substantial transcription samples, thereby indicating that it is more integrated and motivated than Carolyn's comments would suggest. Certainly, despite its lack of announcement, it fits well with the overall design and purpose of the chapter, and with the place of that chapter within the volume itself. This is confirmed by the *Conclusion*, in reality a short, abstract-like summary, which inter alia modestly reminds the reader of the fact that "... we have *tried* to take the fruit of our analysis into the classroom" (emphasis added).

A Busy and Balanced Life. In this account Carolyn has emerged, in some respects, as having rather different textways to those of the other five cases already presented. She alone, for example, is reactive rather than proactive in her approach to writing. As she says "if it happens, it happens," even though this laconic comment does disguise the fact that over 20 years there has been considerable generic range, and considerable writing accomplishment and achievement. Although the other members (Joan aside) engage in some collaborative writing, they often do so in conjunction with specialists elsewhere and seem primarily motivated by a desire to achieve a professional written product. In Carolyn's case, the collaborative processes themselves—indeed, their very existence—seem much more salient as they variously involve apprenticeship, mentorship, on-task discussion, off-task conversation, impression-sharing, and mutual drafting. Although she has worked with men as well as women, the process-satisfactions of writing for Carolyn are more reminiscent than the others of those found by Anne Ruggles Gere in her studies of women's writing groups (1988).

Another interesting difference lies in her reactions to a draft of this section. Of course, reactions are likely to differ: Tony, for example, wrote that he had learned much from the preliminary account and went on to claim that he found therein some matters to ponder as he wrote in the future; Bob congratulated me on putting together "a good read"; and Joan was pleased too at how much I had been able to bring up to the surface, even if she remains somewhat guarded about my "manifesto" interpretation of her thrice-presented *CIC:ISE* and continued for some time to refer to it as "my" reading. Carolyn, in contrast, was decidedly unexcited by the analysis of two framing texts (BMK 1974 and AM 1994) as a way of illustrating her professional career:

> I mean it's sort of like apples and (pause) elephants (laughs). If I had stayed in the same field, and one was to analyze my earlier writing and later writing, I could understand more and be maybe more interested . . . It seems to me that it's not so very interesting to see how my writing has changed from that first article to now, because it went like *that* (waving gesture); I mean it's like you said, families . . . people . . . collaboration; it's not like my writing development.

In response, I would first suggest that in none of the six cases so far (including Carolyn's) have I attempted a fully *developmental* account, such as a literary scholar might offer of a poet or novelist. Of course it is true that the botanists' and Joan's texts have changed relatively little over the years, whereas in Carolyn's case there are, as we have seen, striking differences between the co-produced texts of her graduate student days and those she co-writes in her present roles as the ELI's Associate Director of Curriculum and as a leader in the ITA field. It therefore struck me, for better or worse, that in order to account for Carolyn's textways, I could best proceed by illustrating the contrast between her significant early and late collaborative writing.

Second, the fact that there is an early "apple" and a later "elephant" is not only reflective of personal and family history, but also both reflective and constitutive of wider professional and intellectual developments. Carolyn is by no means alone in moving from a hard social science paradigm to ones in which the "boundaries between the phenomenon and the context" (Yin, 1984, p. 23) are intriguingly but bafflingly unclear. She is not alone in abandoning a hard science style for one that includes an authorial voice and narrative elements; nor, again, is she alone in becoming more closely involved in pedagogical outcomes as she leaves her doctoral days for positions of increasing educational responsibility. And her constitutive influence is not entirely negligible either, especially in her ITA specialty. She is, for instance, the sole ESL editorial board member on the *Journal for Graduate Teaching Assistant Development*, the main refereed journal for this subfield. As far as I know, the 1994 ITA collection has, at the time of writing, garnered only one extensive review, but that was positive enough:

> The early literature about ITAs related in large measure to program de-
> scription and design, and to the assessment of language and teaching. Al-
> though isolated articles and research reports about ITA discourse have ap-
> peared from time to time, the current volume is noteworthy because it is
> the first book devoted exclusively to ITA discourse and performance issues,
> filling a major void in the literature. (Smith, 1995, p. 92)

Despite all this, Carolyn has eventually emerged as a little discomfited by the intellectual, methodological, and compositional transitions that she has undergone, and this unease, I suspect, partly underlies her interview comments on the draft. In truth, all this concern was very surprising to me; I thought I knew Carolyn well and I had noted, with doubtless a manager's stereotypical satisfaction, how in recent years she had become enthusiastically involved in oral discourse analysis and its relevance for NNS students and ITAs. However, in two remarkable taped interviews, my assistant, Margaret Luebs, was able to elicit how far she remains committed to the aims of Second Language Acquisition research: "the excitement of it, that we're trying to understand the processes of the brain, and trying to understand how things develop and happen." Discourse analysis, for all that she admits its heuristic value, can also seem to her rather self-indulgent and somewhat prone to superficiality and inconse-quentiality. Certainly, potted transcripts of communicative episodes offer, at best, oblique entry to what remain for her the important developmental issues. Indeed, the parallel with my own "episodic" treatment of her own written discourse is clear. If I had made a more concerted effort to chart the actual *development* of her writing—by, for instance, investigating her roles in the first and last of the "Krashen" articles—she might have been more impressed with the worth of the endeavor.

Although Carolyn's transitions set her apart from the other members of my study group, she may, more than they, be a more truly repre-sentative figure of our times. She has neither totally resisted nor fully embraced the full gamut of all possible late-20th-century academic shifts. She has her own social, religious, and political beliefs and involvements which, along with her professional concern about her institute's educa-tional practice, cause her to question some of the fashionable "-isms" and "novelties" in her world.

If Carolyn is less *driven* to writing than the other individuals discussed in chapters 3 and 4, she nevertheless emerges as capable and competent in a range of genres: as editor, as textbook author, and as producer of papers and presentations of various kinds. But these products may not come to Carolyn quite so easily. She may at times question whether publishing is worth the substantial effort that it entails; she may find the writing moments overtaken by shorter term demands; she may semicon-sciously cling to the adamantine certainties of hard, positivistic research that at least *attempted* to answer some fundamental questions of foreign language learning and teaching; and she may indeed find the collaborative process itself peculiarly seductive. But, all this said, it would be wrong to conclude with some facile observation such as, "for Carolyn, collabo-ration provides its own reward." Consider these comments from the co-author of Axelson and Madden, 1994:

> She is a stimulating and helpful partner, reads widely and promotes the same in me, makes essential connections between joint brainstorming and existing theory and findings, moves the process along, appreciates and really engages with her partner's ideas and writing. In short, she is totally rewarding to work with. (Elizabeth, E-mail message)

If the process itself does indeed provide some of its own rewards, those rewards of "joint brainstorming" and other forms of engagement remain nested within the rewards of "moving the process along." It is Elizabeth's allusion to the dynamic interplay between the personal and professional that leads me to conclude, as I would for Tony, her nearest counterpart on the floor below, that this is *a busy and balanced life*.

JOHN

> And this brings me to a fourth recurrence in my ESP work; pre-emptive strikes against myself, of the kind where I make a habit of saying I got it wrong in the past, but now I have got it right (or righter). This is not just a way of disarming the opposition, but equally a way of keeping things moving along—proof that there is life in the old dog yet. (in presentation, 1995)

A Career After All. My induction into ESL was, as it happens, even more adventitious than Carolyn's. After a BA in philosophy and psychology at Cambridge, I resisted parental advice to "do something in the city" and found a job teaching ESL (which I did with a not unknown combination—even today—of considerable ignorance and youthful en-thusiasm) in a commmercial high school and the local university in southern Italy for a couple of years (1960–1962). While there I did give my first public talk, but on a topic never to be publicly touched by me again—"Modern American Poetry." I went to Sweden the next year, at the beginning of which I received a decent three-week ESL training course, and where I taught intensively for nine months in dark, chilly, and rural surroundings. The next move was to Benghazi, Libya, as a lecturer in English at the university, and into my first experience of English for Specific Purposes (ESP) at the Faculty of Commerce and Economics. Here I had useful learning experiences with an American, Bill Frazier, who would subsequently teach for a spell at the Michigan ELI, and with David Wilkins, the young British Council ESL expert in Tripoli, who would a decade later be a major factor in the European shift away from grammatical syllabi to ones based on "notional-functional" categories.

Then followed my one year of post-graduate study on the "A" Diploma—the following year re-classified as an MA—in Linguistics and ESL at the University of Leeds. There I worked hard and learned much. After this, I went back to Libya, but this time to the Faculty of Engineering at the Tripoli campus. Almost immediately on arrival, the Head of the small English Section was dismissed for allegedly mismanaging the faculty bookstore, and the Dean asked me to take over because I was "the only one with recent training." I had two lucky breaks in my final months in Libya (late 1969 and the first half of 1970). First, an ESL publisher's representative came to Tripoli, saw the teaching materials I had been working on for the preceding four years, and offered to publish a revised version of them as a textbook—to be eventually entitled *Writing Scientific English* (Swales, 1971). I doubt that I would have thought of taking any such initiative by myself. (More details of this episode are given in Byrd, 1995.) Second, at the end of the year, the monarchy was overthrown, and Moammer Ghaddafi came to power; the university was closed for several weeks, a curfew imposed, and alcohol banned. The last two events in particular had their expected impact on social life, and I had absolutely no excuse for not getting down to this textbook writing business. First the manuscript, and then the published book, certainly helped me to obtain my next two positions.

I returned to England in 1970 for a lecturership in the Institute of Education at the University of Leeds. After a couple of years, however, I became convinced that full-time teacher-training was not for me. So, in 1973, it was back to Africa, this time as Professor and as Director of the newly formed English Language Servicing Unit at the University of Khartoum, Sudan, at that time a vibrant and interesting institution. By this time I had gotten into the habit of trying to write one paper a year. My family and I returned to England in 1978, when I was appointed Senior Lecturer in the Modern Languages Department at the University of Aston in Birmingham and Head of the English Studies section, and then in 1982, *Reader in English for Specific Purposes*. During the Birmingham period and thereafter, I have managed to produce (or co-produce) an average of four to five papers per year, and every 5 years or so, a larger work of some kind. However, by the middle of the 1980s, Thatcherite rigidities were dismembering my excellent unit, and in 1985 I came to Michigan's English Language Institute, where I have been ever since, initially on a visiting appointment, but since 1987 as a tenured Professor of Linguistics and Director of the ELI.

Sources of Writing. The explanation of why I have had "a career after all," and this despite limited graduate education, lack of mentoring, and (prior to Michigan) a penchant for working in fairly remote and unfashionable locations, can most obviously be found in a modest string of publications, or perhaps even an immodest one. Anyway, for the record, there are four textbooks (three co-authored), 70 or so journal articles and book chapters, a few reviews, a couple of encyclopedia entries, a *samizdat* 100-page 1981 monograph, a hybrid 1985 book (either an over-edited anthology or an over-illustrated history, but still one that is, according to Tony, "an excellent and fascinating summary of ESP(EST) of the time"), and the 1990 *Genre Analysis* volume from Cambridge University Press. This last was my own attempt at the botanists' "crowning monograph," and has been successful and influential beyond my hopes.

As we know, a fair proportion of the world's academic publications leave no citational trace and even perhaps leave no imprint on anybody's mind except those of their disappointed authors. Although this has certainly happened to me, there are a few publications of mine that have penetrated to most of those many far-flung corners of the globe where English for Academic Purposes is taken seriously. My influence would thus seem to be more international than Joan's and Carolyn's. Especially since the publication of *Genre Analysis* in 1990, this influence has also been more interdisciplinary, insofar as in recent years one or two of my publications have also been picked up by some of those who work in rhetoric, composition, or literacy, both in the United States and elsewhere. In contrast, Joan, especially, and Carolyn, to a lesser extent, have had a stronger and more direct impact on ESL itself within North America.

How then can I account for all this surprisingly *textual* biography? As far as I can see, the actual impetus for my writing has come from three main sources: administration, teaching, and reading. The first is, prima facie, somewhat unexpected, but it works in the following way. Even the tamest administrator is cast into some kind of leadership role; and, as it happens, the only kind of leadership I am capable of is leadership by example. Because I also believe, for reasons that do not greatly matter at this point, that post-secondary ESL units are much healthier and happier if they are collectively engaged on some modest research and development programs, it follows that I have long seen myself as leading the way in that direction. After all if I, as the boss, cannot demonstrate that publication can be made possible within a busy schedule, how can I expect the others to make that substantial effort? So, in my experience, my written output has been increased much more by being in charge of some small operation than it has been reduced by so-called "administrative load." And if final proof is needed of this, during those three years at Leeds, when I was just a junior member of department, I wrote less than either before or since. On this administrative aspect Tony, the interlinear respondent, wrote:

> I find the comment about having been an administrator an interesting point. My first reaction was surprise, as I have never thought of you running around making sure people got paid as I had to in Tabriz and sorting out the status of lecturers and secretaries as I have tried to do in Birmingham. But indeed in Libya, Khartoum, Aston, and Michigan you have been director and have run departments that always seem to have had an excellent team spirit and which generated lots of good practical research by quite a few people who seemed to reach a kind of peak under your leadership [list of names, not given]. I think that you have it right when you say that you generate this activity by setting an example. What you do not say is that you are an excellent motivator ... I wouldn't necessarily say that you are a good listener, as you can be and usually are obstinate in argument ...

A British approbation then, but like the best of them, with a sting in its tail.

The influences of teaching and reading are more self-evident and can be mentioned albeit briefly. In my own case, my main teaching activities have been typically orchestrated by a wish to help my students communicate effectively in some professional or academic environment. Because gaining a better understanding of that environment, its ways with words and its discoursal perceptions and expectations, is part of that pedagogical enterprise, teaching and research come into much closer alignment for me than they typically do for colleagues who teach basic survey courses and the like. As I like to tell the international graduate students who attend my advanced writing classes, "your experiences, your texts and your stories provide me with an important part of my own research data."

As for reading, recall that I have only one year of official graduate education; perforce, then, I have had to educate myself by reading what I can and what I will. Although there are some well-attested dangers that threaten the largely self-educated, as a group we are often better at crossing disciplinary boundaries precisely because we have not been arduously trained to respect those boundaries in the first place. So, I have been able to bring into my work and into my field, "outsiders" like Wittgenstein, Rosch, Rorty, Becker, and particularly, Geertz. Tony adds:

"I think you could also mention the way in which you introduced Chuck Bazerman and Greg Myers to EAP people; they are now standard references."

First Publication. I have decided to open the textual selection with an extract from my first appearance in print in 1965. I have several reasons for starting at the beginning, a minor one being that what follows can be guaranteed to be a text which no reader of this book will ever have seen before.

Surface finds of coins from the city of Euesperides

R. C. BOND and J. M. SWALES

I.

The first inhabitants of the ancient Greek colony of Euesperides built on rising ground which lies to the east of the present Benghazi ring-road close to its junction with the Tocra road. This site is now occupied by the Sidi Abeid cemetery. The city was later extended in a south-westerly direction as far as the marshes bordering the Sebka El-Selmani. This, the later Euesperides, covers the major part of an area of almost level ground which today is bounded by saltmarsh to the east and south and to the north-west by modern buildings on the landward side of the present coast-road. The later part of the city, at the point of its immediate extension from the earlier hill-site, is approximately 400 metres wide, but by the time it reaches the far perimeter wall it has contracted to less than 200 metres; the length of this extension, along the axis of the central cardo, is a little over 400 metres. (Pl. XXXIX).

The site today has a desolate and devastated aspect as stone-robbers have dug out and removed all but half a dozen of the original stone blocks. This has had the curious result of leaving the streets and the floors of the ancient houses above the general ground level. In recent years the site has been used for the curing of sheep skins and as dump for sundry unwanted articles. Indeed, at the moment of writing it seems that the later part of the old Greek city is about to suffer its final mutilation for work has just begun on the recolmation [sic] of the Sebka el-Selmani and already in a few places the passage of heavy vehicles has started to break up what remains of the ancient streets. (Bond & Swales, 1965, pp. 91–102)

This article was published in Volume II of *Libya Antiqua,* a handsome periodical with many graphic and photographic plates, and printed in Rome for the Libyan Department of Antiquities. Bob Bond, a high school teacher, had found more coins than I had and had done most of the cleaning. So his name came first, even though I did all the background reading, all the analysis, and all the writing. A first lesson then was that if you want to get something done, you may have to do it yourself, and thereafter I have never been much exercised by co-authorship issues and squabbles. It was Richard Goodchild, the Director of Antiquities for Cyrenaica, who originally suggested writing up our finds, liked what he saw, and made only minor editorial emendations.

The opening paragraph was very difficult for me to write, and I must have made 20 or 30 drafts trying to "boil down," in Bill's phrase, all that topographic information into one smooth, clear, and succinct account. Looking back now, I think I largely succeeded, but I have since occasionally wondered whether my extensive later interest in the nature of academic introductions was not in some way subconsciously sparked by my travails with this first venture. The second paragraph strikes me as less successful, and here, alas, we can see some stylistic and rhetorical features that will persist in much of my writing "career." One is the use of double adjective combinations (e.g., "a desolate and devastated aspect") that I experience much trouble in resisting. Another is the use of evaluative epithets for audience effect ("the *curious* result" rather than an unadorned "the result"), a habit that I find to be much less tolerated in America, especially when applied to scholars and their works, than I think it is in Britain. Finally, there is the drama (melodrama?) squeezed out of the situation, as in "the ... city is about to suffer its final mutilation...." Such passages I describe to myself as "perorations" and, although they sometimes work, as I hope is the case with the closing paragraphs to the analysis of Tony's *Revision* of Mexican sedges, they are clearly not without risk, and by no means to everybody's taste. Tony Dudley-Evans commented, "One thing that strikes me about the text is that some of the features, double adjective combinations, a certain parallelism in the text structure and even the 'perorations' are features of Arabic writing style. Perhaps just a coincidence, perhaps not." This may not be entirely a coincidence, I now believe, although I had never considered this possible connection until Tony made his observation. Certainly, at that time, I was trying hard, although not very successfully, to learn to read Arabic prose.

Although the ethos of the 1970s, as shown earlier by Bailey et al., 1974, kept these elements of "heightened color" somewhat subdued, under certain stimuli they are prone to resurface. One such stimulus was my entrancement with the essays collected in Clifford Geertz's *Local Knowledge* (1983). Here are Tony's accurate and perceptive comments on this tendency:

> But, at the time shortly before you left for the U.S., the features you mention about your style and, I suspect, an attempt to match the elegance of Geertz's writing (I may be completely wrong on that one) led to some over-complication in your writing, and some writing almost became a bit of a caricature of itself—perhaps a bit harsh, but I'll leave it.

Completely right, Tony.

As it turned out, the Bond and Swales article continued, to my amaze-
ment, to haunt me for years, because of the following remarks: "The list
from the site has followed the arrangement of the BMC catalogue in all
instances but one. . . . It is, therefore, suggested that BMC 286 really
belongs to the Regal coinage" (p. 94). I have had several questions about
this over the years, and several requests to see the relevant coins (most
of which were left in Libya), or at the least to be provided with rubbings
or "squinches." The one letter I have managed to preserve comes from
the Fitzwilliam Museum in Cambridge and is dated 22 August 1980. Here
is the relevant part: "I don't, however, see the connection you draw
between these and the Ammon/Bowcase issue, BMC 286 (your p. 94, '. . .
therefore . . . BMC 286 really belongs to the Regal coinage'). The obverse
types differ, so too the fabric as far as one can tell; and of course the
legends." Doubtless I was wrong about BMC 286, and doubtless it was
the impudent ignorance of youth that led me to challenge an identification
in that most august and authoritative of numismatic works, *The British
Museum Catalogue*. Even so, I suspect that "revision" in ancient coinages
comes not as easily as it does in Systematic Botany.

Textual Studies. By the time my Khartoum days were coming to an
end, I was writing one reasonably solid paper a year, even though most
did not actually get published until after I left. By the late 1970s, I was
also coming to the conclusion that I had some small talent for taking
unlikely, small bits of textual material of a kind many might assume to
be pretty trivial, and turning them into rather more substantive accounts
than colleagues might have anticipated. Here is a partial list of topics (C
= co-authored):

1971	Linking As-Clauses
1974	"Bare" participles in a Chemistry Text
1981	Definitions in Science and Law
1982	"Marked" references to legal cases in law texts
1983	Examination questions
1983	Complex prepositions in legislative prose (C)
1986	Types of citation in Applied Linguistics
1986	Requests for reprints
1988	Titles
1990	Corporate Mission Statements (C)
1992	Conference abstracts
1995	Species entries in bird field-guides
1996	Submission letters accompanying articles

See what I mean?

The 1974 study was a detailed account of the position of simple passive participles in the university's first year chemistry textbook. The study was published locally in what I have now learned to call "working paper" format, and was officially published in the U.S. in slightly revised form in 1981. In essence, I tried to account for the fact that some participle usages occurred before the noun ("added heat") and some after ("heat added"). The discussion I offered for the most common participle in the corpus ("given") was subsequently referred to by several people, including Henry Widdowson. This was the nearest I ever came to writing a "proper" linguistics paper. Here is the last paragraph of the 1981 version, a paragraph that I recollect undergoing multiple drafts:

> This chapter has attempted to examine a small area of grammar in a particular genre of text, albeit a genre of considerable importance in ESP work. It has not been the purpose here to offer any contribution to syntactic theory, but it may not escape the reader's notice that the findings from the narrow field of pedagogical texts in chemistry support Bolinger's criticism of the facile application of Relative Deletion Transformations, for if we accept that *the stolen jewels* and *the jewels stolen* or *added heat* and *heat added* function differently and, thus, may exhibit differences in meaning, it is difficult to accept a transformational process by which the former is derived from the latter. (Swales, 1981b, p. 50)

Dwight Bolinger was for many years one of the world's most widely respected linguists (he died several years ago), but—nothing ventured, nothing gained—I wrote to him in 1974 in Palo Alto from the banks of the Nile, enclosing a copy of the 23-page mimeographed paper and asking for his reactions. Back came a reply by return mail (or what might pass for such in the Sudanese postal system), in a hastily typed aerogram urging me to carry on, and making a stunning series of observations on my findings. In an hour, or so it seemed to me, Dwight Bolinger had gotten to a position that it had taken me a year's cogitation and endless shuffling of 150 file-cards to eventually reach. I still deeply respect both his kindness and his perspicuity, and, in the case of his first virtue, I try to follow his example with those who now write to *me* from off-the-in-tellectual-map kinds of places, even if I can rarely follow—let alone match—him in the second.

Another recurring feature in this analytical work is my attempt to somehow *use* the analysis to support the interests of non-native speaker academics in "off-network" places—and, as we have seen, I have certainly worked in some of those. Consider the studies on Reprint Requests, whereby scholars ask authors for copies of their publications (see also the "Bob" section in chapter 3). Typically (at least before the recent advent of E-mail), the request is (or was) carried by a card printed by the requester's department with spaces provided for the name of the author, the details of the publication and the name of the requester. My first publication in this area was carried by *Scientometrics*, a European journal of Information Science. Here is the final paragraph:

> Finally, and perhaps most directly, the analysis of the RR has relevance for those concerned with both the connectivity and visibility of Third World Research[12-13]. Evidence from both the *Onuigbo* corpus and the present corpus suggests that the Third World produces few reprint requests. If we further recognize[14] that many non-native speakers with limited English writing abilities find it difficult—often for cultural reasons—to initiate correspondence with potential colleagues in other parts of the world, then we can see the reprint request as an inexpensive and undemanding mechanism for "breaking the ice." Thus, tall oaks from little acorns grow. (Swales, 1988, p. 100)

As a final paragraph, this text is surprisingly replete with references and, in retrospect, I can now see this intertextuality as an attempt to hang the mini-world and the mini-genre of the Reprint Request onto the much broader and more central issues raised in the cited papers. The effect of this advocacy has been muted, although there have been a smattering of Third World letters telling of their authors' (largely) successful attempts to obtain relevant papers via the RR route, but no cross-national growing oaks were reported; and also in retrospect, I wince, doubtless like the reader, at the unfortunate sequence of metaphors in the last two sentences.

In subsequent publications on the Reprint Request topic, I moved into detailed textual analysis of the genre—not, of course, something Information Scientists would likely be interested in. Here is a short passage from *Genre Analysis* that shows, once again, our author trying to squeeze as much significance out of apparently insignificant material as he can:

2. THE REQUEST (IN ENGLISH)

The actual requests varied in length from six to 41 words. The typical opening was the request itself, and in the corpus examined here, there is striking evidence for a *major* structure (107 instances) and a number of *minor* structures (a total of 20 instances). Of the 20 examples of the minor structures, 14 involved the lexical item *send*. The more common variants were:

> (Would you) please send me/us . . . . (6 cases)
> I would be very grateful if you could send me/us . . . (4 cases)

However, the much preferred approach in the RR is not to request that a reprint be *sent*, but rather to express appreciation for a reprint *to be received*. It may not be too fanciful to speculate that the dynamic *send* is thought likely to conjure up images of work in the recipient's mind (finding, ad-

dressing, dispatching, etc.) which the static *receive* seductively and successfully avoids. (Swales, 1990a, pp. 196–197)

This passage can be taken as pretty representative of my discourse analysis
rhetoric. First, the reader is provided with a demonstrated control of the
quantitative data (hey, no stone uncounted or left unturned). Second, a
linguistic-rhetorical generalization then emerges from the numbers, which
is in turn glossed in some way. In this particular case, this takes the form
of a speculative explanation. If the speculation works (i.e., it is, after all,
"not too fanciful"), then it presumably does so only because of the way
the contrast between the two verbs (*receive* versus *send*) has been so
rhetorically and descriptively elaborated.
   At this juncture Tony's commentary takes off from this small textual
ground to make a much larger series of points:

> What has always struck me about what you describe as studies of "small
> bits of textual material" is the way that on the one hand you provide a
> very detailed analysis of the text, but also manage to say something inter-
> esting on a much broader scale about ESP or text analysis. This brings me
> to what perhaps is my main query/point. Your contribution to ESP has
> been extremely significant at a position somewhere between practice (and
> the textual study) and theory. . . . But you haven't written a theoretical
> justification for ESP. Nor do you base *Genre Analysis* on a linguistic or
> sociological theory. I do not say this really as a criticism . . . But many do
> criticise this aspect of your writing.
>   I feel that ESP is at the stage where it does need to produce a theoretical
> justification for its procedures rather than just discuss those procedures.
> Similarly, genre analysis should perhaps try to justify its approach to text
> in either Hallidayan terms or through structuration theory, Bakhtin and the
> other constructs that Berkenkotter and Huckin mention. You are the obvious
> person to do this, but haven't chosen to do so.

There is much that could be said here, but at some risk of straining the
ties of a more general intertextuality by entering into a dialogue with
Tony. As a quick response, I can call first upon Joan's reflection that "you
have to make peace with yourself" and do what you want to do, and can
do. That peace would recognize, I believe, that an interest in apparent
textual minutiae is not likely to go away—as this book itself shows clearly
enough. I find too much challenge and excitement in convincing the reader
that the "mundane" reprint request, garage sale flyer, or brief letter
accompanying a submitted article are more interesting, or more helpful
to the learner (Johns, 1997), than appear at first sight to put all that aside
for constructing some grand and guiding theory for my field (even if I
could). If I am thought to be "the obvious person" for such a task, then
this may be as much a factor of simple longevity in a field that has lost

many of its early leaders to other interests and responsibilities, as it is reflection of the fact that certain opportunities and talents are somehow going to waste. Indeed, further motives for declining a theoretician's role will emerge in the following subsection.

Pre-Emptive Strikes. Aside from these discoursal explorations, there are other kinds of text I produce. Some are textbook materials. Some are of a more conceptual nature, such as those dealing with genre and discourse community, but these latter will not need much of an airing, as this kind of exposition gets it own replay in the final chapter. Others often have the framework of state-of-the-art pieces with some illustrative personal experiences embedded inside. While Joan's comparable texts tend to deal with curricular progress and the like, mine tend to be more admonitory and stress the need for vigilance, persistence, and struggle. In 1980, for instance, I published a paper in one of the British Council's *ELT Documents* series entitled "The Educational Environment and Its Relevance to ESP Programme Design." I was at pains to point out that as new ESP techniques had developed, old educational sensitivities were in danger of being lost. I listed (like Joan might have done) *six difficulties* that ESP programs commonly faced, and then put my Khartoum experience into that perspective. Here is an extract:

> Although ELSU in Khartoum suffered from some of the fragilities mentioned under the six earlier points, it did have reasonable representation, up to Senate. In addition, the more senior members of the Unit served on a number of committees, the support arrangments through the Inter-University Council were enlightened and quite the reverse of patronizing, expatriate staff stayed on average for 3 to 4 years, and programmes were continuously revised in the light of teaching experience. Nevertheless, we failed to achieve external validity. Although we convinced everybody else, we failed to convince the students that we were a serious department. The most striking instances of this occurred at examination time. Our largest teaching commitment was to 750 students doing a preliminary year in Biological Sciences. On evenings before Science exams one could visit the Library and find 150–200 students revising their notes; on the evenings before the English exam one would be fortunate to find 15–20. I now believe that we had failed to live up to the students' expectations of hard work in two important respects. First, our consistently small classes and informal teaching methods had prevented us from becoming academically respectable in our students' eyes; and secondly, our functional materials had deprived the students of an opportunity to utilize their rote-learning skills. (Swales, 1980, pp. 65–66)

This is plain straight-from-the-shoulder talk from a guy who purports to be close to his students' world. Who, after all, is this "one" who wanders around the University Library at night? Here then is a worried "contingent" voice, speaking for a unit generally recognized to have been productive and successful, in an era when managerial-type systems analysis seemed to be the dominating influence in the big ESP projects. More strategically, the pre-emptive strike against *one's* own achievements opens up further areas of necessary sophistication and expertise to be explored and demonstrated—and, of course, to be discussed in their own turn, as the epigraphic opening to this section attests.

However, although this strategy has worked moderately well for me when tackling broader educational issues, it has also badly rebounded in other contexts. As in the next extract:

PREFACE

> This small volume is very much an interim report and I dare say it shows all the signs of being brought to term in unseemly haste: the establishment of categories and the criteria used to underpin them lack the solidity I would like; in terminological matters there is much arch and evasive use of inverted commas; important considerations such as *thematicity* and the choice of *active* or *passive* have merely been trifled with; and often the writing itself falls below even the indifferent standard I usually set for myself. Nevertheless, there are a number of reasons why I have decided to offer the following "quick and dirty" analysis of journal-introductions. First, . . .
> (Swales, 1981a)

An instinct for self-preservation prevents me from re-typing any more of this mealy-mouthed cant, and, alas, the style and substance of it continues for another six sentences. Indeed, the very archness of the language further contributes to its rhetorical downfall. This silly preface to *Aspects of Article Introductions* (1981a) compromises what turned out to be the most sustained analytic effort of my life (my surrogate mini-PhD thesis perhaps), and what has come to be the most-cited mimeographed work in the short history of English for Specific Purposes. I used to variously cringe or curse when colleagues would *inevitably* refer to Swales' "quick and dirty" 1981 analysis, for it was nothing of the sort (at least by the standards of those days), but rather a laborious, finicky, and even perhaps honorable attempt to account for both the wood and nearly every tree in a sizeable chunk of textual data. Although neither Tony nor I can today recollect whether the "quick and dirty" phrase was original to me (I suspect not), and despite Tony's sense that it did communicate an agreeable "hesitation and modesty," he says that it did lay me open to what he thinks of as "the 'applied linguistic morality police,' " as well as to those who "argue quite moderately and sensibly that genre analysis needs to take on board the issue of showing where boundaries between units come." Further, the *Aspects* monograph was an enterprise that I largely conducted ab initio, even though I now know of prior American work in rhetoric that would have helped me if I had known about it and had been able to access it from the English Midlands.

It is interesting that Bhatia's 1997 paper on "Genre-Mixing in Academic Introductions" concentrates primarily on the incorporation of promotional material, and ignores apologia elements in such texts—"a poor thing, but mine own" as in my wimpish 1981 example. After all, there is a long tradition for such demurrals, in English at least going back to John Ray's famous preface to his *The Wisdom of God Manifested in the Works of Creation* (1691), the one which starts "In all Ages wherein Learning hath flourished, complaint hath been made of the Itch of Writing, and the multitude of worthless books, wherein importunate Scribblers have pestered the World . . . ," and which indeed opens William Stearn's *Apologia pro Libro meo* to his *Botanical Latin*. But in the case of my own preface, the apologia turned more into a self-inflicted wound than into a pre-emptive strike.

Just over a decade later, settled in at Michigan, reassured by the success of *Genre Analysis*, and secure in my membership in a loose multidiscipli-nary grouping of scholars interested in nonliterary genres, I could at last produce texts that reflected this section's epigraph with better balance, greater maturity, and maybe even a little panache:

> And so to the last of the four questions. The incorporation of structura-tion theory into many of the recent genre studies that I know (Bazerman: 1992, Miller: 1992, Berkenkotter and Huckin: 1992b, Yates and Orlikowski: 1992) subtly diminishes the value of a social constructionist account of the contemporary world. It was that account that has led me in recent years to spend some effort in trying to use the concept of discourse community as an actual sociorhetorical entity operating as a controlling matrix of genre use. I was, I suspect, rather too easily seduced by the concept of discourse community. Perhaps all too willingly I made common cause with all those who have their own agendas for viewing discourse communities as real, stable groups of consensus holders. Admittedly, there are powerful forces out there including some of the intellecual heavyweights of our time: phi-losophers like Rorty who need a prevailing mindset on which to base a non-representational theory of truth; sociologists like Kuhn who need a paradigm in order to talk about a paradigm shift; and Sociologists of Knowl-edge like Latour and Woolgar who need a social consensus on which to build a social account of scientific facts. (Swales, 1993, p. 694)

The paragraph's start in the (then) super-contemporary literature of my specialty, its ironically confessional middle passage, and then its linked invocation of "intellectual heavyweights of our time" all work well enough, together enough, and swiftly enough to enliven, and perhaps to validate, this small account of a personal intellectual journey. It is, I think, about the best I can do.

The self-questioning evident in the last extract, as in the previous parts of the subsection, shows why a leap to theory-building is not, education-ally or cognitively, a comfortable extension of my work. Further, like Shotter (1993), I am unsure how well social constructionists (a club in which I have at least associate membership) are actually served by theories of either the *system* or even the *tool-kit* kind (Foucault, 1972). Certainly, as an EAP specialist, I am drawn, like Schon's *The Reflective Practitioner* (1983), away from the systematic and system-building aspects of technical rationality and attracted more toward various kinds of acquired practical competence. On many occasions I have seen how conceptual and opera-tional systems that proved successful in some other place collapse and wither when imposed on different ground; indeed, this phenomenon is a major affliction of Third World development projects.

Of course, any countervailing insistence on purely *local knowledge* can itself fall prey to an effete kind of particularism, and ESP has been prone to an unfortunate "we have nothing to learn from anybody else because our situation is a little bit special" frame of mind. What can most sensibly save that knowledge from that kind of fate is the kind of "cases and interpreta-tions" approach that Becker or Geertz have advocated, since it leads to the multivocal rendition of reflected experience as opposed to the narrower and more uncertain triumph of some univocal theory. Which is why Tony . . .

Reprise. On only one previous occasion have I overviewed my textual production in print, and that was in a 1990 short essay for a Japanese ESL/Applied Linguistics journal called *Cross Currents*. The title was "The Teacher-Researcher: Personal Reflections"; and in the extract that follows I begin by asking whether my publications *are* research:

> To what extent and in what number these papers can validly be described as *research* is a question to which there is no easy answer. For now, we can simply call them *stories*. Apart from a number of "where we are now" stories, they are essentially accounts of data. Some are accounts of textual data; some are accounts of success and failure in our own professional affairs; some are accounts of nonnative speaker strategies, attitudes and problems in what has become my main domain of investigation, the world of graduate education and research.
>
> These accounts often involve numbers, but rarely statistics. They often involve analysis of performance, but rarely in the form of the pre- and post-testing of treatment effects. They often involve some discussion of situation, but one more typically characterized by anecdote than by serious ethnographic study. Perhaps in the end they are all versions of "where we are now" stories: where groups of students are; where the English language is; where scholars in particular fields are; where certain genres are; and where our programs are. (Swales, 1990b, p. 93)

When I look back at this in 1996, in one sense this passage strikes me as itself being a reasonable account of 30 years devoted primarily to English for Academic Purposes, ranging from grading papers, to devising teaching materials, to "running the shop," to supervising doctoral dissertations, or to co-editing the main journal in the field. In another, it hints at a surer adjustment to audience in more recent years. Here, as in a number of other pieces, the *tone* of my writing for the profession at large does now seem adequately constructed to encourage others to follow me down the teacher-researcher route, and not just as junior collaborators, but as authors in their own right. Indeed, the contrast between this designedly modest account and the quasi-brazen intellectual reach of the discourse community paragraph discussed earlier will be obvious enough.

Just before the *Conclusions* to the 1990 short essay, there occurs one of those "perorations" on the importance of writing in my "area" (with the usual echoes of T. S. Eliot). The paragraph concludes with this aphoristic statement: "After all, *a good teller of a tale* may in the end become *a teller of a good tale.*" In an early draft of this section, I had in fact chosen this sentence to act as its epigraph. Perhaps fortunately, I came to see that such a bold affirmation might only lead to hubris, such as a rather too obvious invitation for a reviewer or commentator to respond with "All Swales shows us is how '*a poor teller of a tale*' can easily become '*a teller of a poor tale.*' " Maybe, approaching 60, I have, in putting this account together with Tony and with the outside readers, still been learning something about how to construct a more nuanced space for confession and claim.

THE ELI TRIO

The textways of the Herbarium Quartet were remarkable for their employment of a closed Systematics genre-set including monograph, flora, code, and treatment, all situated within a very busy intertextual world. The genre-set of the ELI Trio, if it can be called such, is both more variable and shows much more compatability and overlap with the genre-sets of broadly similar fields. Their papers, as we have seen, cover SLA and genre theory, "straight" discourse analysis and English phonetics, as well as "state of the art" pieces, descriptive evaluations of curricular and pedagogic innovations, and discussions of professionalism in an applied field. Their books are mostly, but by no means exclusively, textbooks. Of course, all established fields have textbooks (indeed this is a well-known criterion for seeing whether an embryonic field *is* established), and ESL is decidedly no exception. But, within the ELI Trio, the place of the textbook in the life's work is rather different. The opening section to this chapter attempted to show how for Joan the textbook provides her with the prime location for the most elaborated exposition of her beliefs and understandings, a position shrewdly detected by John Murphy in his review. Further, this has been both a position she has adhered to throughout a long ELI career and one that she feels comfortable with as a forceful advocate for raising professional expertise in her chosen specialty.

With Carolyn and myself, the textbook role is perhaps more context-sensitive. Whereas the quartet and Joan have spent all or nearly all of their careers at the University of Michigan, Carolyn and I are 1980s imports. Carolyn was brought in early in the decade by Larry Selinker (along with one or two others) to reconceptualize and revitalize what went on in ELI classrooms. I was imported a few years later to do something about the general *mission* of the institute. As the then-Dean expressed it: "I don't see why, Mr. Swales, the ELI spends all its time on strangers [i.e., non-U-M students in its intensive program], when we have so many of our own foreign graduate students who need help." So, Carolyn's two textbooks, both (naturally) co-authored, are, in their slightly different ways, public offerings that demonstrate what might be done in the classroom via imaginative task-based methods. However, as our discussions on my draft revealed, Carolyn is not fully comfortable with the authority intrinsically invested in the textbook genre, and would prefer to spread her ideas by teacher workshops and the like. The third section, entitled "John," briefly describes how my *first* textbook became, in those early days of English for Specific Purposes, a not insignificant event both for myself and my field (it even garners a brief mention in Tony Howatt's *A History of English Language Teaching*, 1984). By the 1990s, however, my aims in Swales and Feak (1994) were rather different and certainly better articulated. First, I wanted to give a practical demonstration of how the approach outlined in *Genre Analysis* could be made to work. Just as importantly, and with Chris Feak's help, I wanted to try to show how a textbook might do better by admitting to under-researched areas of academic English and by admitting to the uncertain disciplinary appropriacy of the kinds of advice being offered.

These rather subtle divergences are one factor that needs some further reflection in the final chapter. Another is the fact that the ELI Trio have, broadly, non-overlapping pedagogical roles within the Institute. Oversimplifying somewhat, Joan is in overall charge of the courses aimed at improving graduate students' pronunciation and oral communication skills, Carolyn oversees course offerings for those international students hoping to become Graduate Student Instructors (often known elsewhere as teaching assistants), while I am responsible for the advanced-level writing courses. As instructors, our immediate collaborators tend to be other members of the ELI and not other members of the Trio. Even so, and despite these curricula disjunctions, all three of us have in recent years consolidated our interests around the merits of *discourse-based* pedagogical materials, and around the advantages of seeking the processes that mediate the implementation of *academic tasks* (Prior, 1994). In response, we have come to share a sense of how important and how enabling it is to develop the rhetorical and linguistic awareness of our (advanced) NNS students as they prepare to take their places in a larger and wider academic world. Thereby, perhaps, at some superordinate level are the ties that bind one particular community nurtured and strengthened.

Reflections

EXCLUSIONS AND INCLUSIONS

> Of course, a discourse analyst's basic methodology consists of little more
> than staring at lots of texts for a very long time, hoping for something to
> happen. (Kirstin Fredrickson, 1996, in presentation)

As I have been at pains to point out, this has been a deliberately circumscribed investigation. Toward the end of the first chapter I raised some
questions about the study's possible scope, in terms of types of written
text, types of contributing oral discourse, and types of participants. Toward the beginning of the final chapter, we can see the limitations. True,
a fair range of texts has been introduced, but they have been very largely
discussed as *textual products*. There is no account of the mental events,
hesitations, and false starts that can congregate around the blinking cursor
on today's computer screen, as discussed by Haas (1996) and others. There
is no investigation, most obviously missing in the CRS, of the online
communications of consultants and relevant user-groups. And one reason
for avoiding this aspect was my sense of the large numbers of discoursal
toilers already at work in those virtual vineyards (see, e.g., several of the
essays in Sullivan & Dautermann, 1996). Nor has there been any serious
attempt to reconstruct the processes whereby those textual products were
drafted, edited, revised and reviewed, even though the insights derivable
from such investigations have been shown to be substantial (e.g., Berkenkotter & Huckin, 1995; Myers, 1990). Further, the fragments of conversation and extracts of oral discourse that (I hope) enliven and inform the

textual analysis are largely of a *secondary* nature, as they principally derive from the text-based interviews. Only comparatively rarely were they caught *en plein air* as part of everyday conversation and discussion.

Finally, I have self-limited the participants, most stringently to the *employees* of the building, and in chapters 3 and 4, to those who occupy more senior positions. Most obviously, this procedure has excluded the perspectives and experiences of the *students*. On one level, these are the students who attend classes on the top floor, who more occasionally make use of the Herbarium collections, and who, at any hour of day or night, use the CRS facilities. On another, I have not investigated the processes of advanced apprenticeship whereby doctoral students attempt to acquire the genres of their chosen field by closer association with the likes of Bill, Bob, Joan, and myself, or elicited their reactions, as informed outsiders, to the ethos and character of their disciplinary floors. And finally, there are one or two things that I had planned to do, but have not now done, such as investigate over a fixed period of time the inflows and outflows of mail on each floor. In effect, *Other Floors, Other Voices* is not a work that can compare with the major ethnographies of modern U.S. academic and research life, such as those by Knorr-Cetina (1981), Latour and Woolgar (1986), or Traweek (1988).

Against this litany of omissions, there are of course some positives. The examined texts—and I too have been "staring at a lot of texts for a very long time, waiting for something to happen"—are fairly comprehensively *situated*. They are situated within the evolution of a building and its occupying units; they are situated within disciplinary matrices, at least insofar as these are represented by evolving genre systems; but, most significantly, they are situated within the textual careers of their authors. In addition, the *accounts* of those texts and their enveloping contexts have themselves been reflected upon, annotated, and discussed by their originators, and these reactions have then been parlayed into the final versions. These negotiations have certainly had their difficult moments. Carolyn's reactions and my reactions to her reactions have already been aired; Joan may yet be unpersuaded that my "manifesto" reading of her "threepeat" introduction is the right one, and Sarah sees my characterization of the Testing Division as "a prisoner of its own success" as less than sympathetic. And in one case, negotiations broke down altogether: the European botanist with the long loan discussed in chapter 2 ultimately refused me permission to publish his correspondence. A final reflection on my way of proceeding concerns the expositions that discuss the chosen texts. On several occasions, perhaps most obviously in the case of Joan, I have adopted the stance of a textual sleuth, examining first one fragmentary clue and then another and then another until my considered rhetorical reading is ultimately revealed. I do not think I need to apologize unduly for these delayed denouements, but neither do I think that they are, in any sense, a necessary or integral part of a textographic approach.

In terms of findings, this inquiry into textual ways of life at the close of the 20th century complicates a number of widely held current perceptions. At least within its own localized context, many simple and stereotyping dichotomies are undone. The detached nature of scholarship and of the scholar is subverted, as is the detached nature of scholarly writing (although this latter has already been well enough documented within the narrower compasses of rhetoric, discourse analysis, and the sociology of knowledge). In addition, the belief that professorial faculty operate in both local and broader arenas—as members of national or international "invisible colleges"—while the staff, especially those in submanagerial positions, are somehow only local and parochial in their concerns and interests—is laid to well-deserved rest. The secretaries and item-writers in the ELI's Testing Division are in regular contact with testing centers around the world, and are often very aware of conditions, beliefs, traditions, and regulations that impinge upon "Michigan tests" in overseas localities. Comparably, the workroom team in the Herbarium is deeply committed to the quality of the material in its outgoing loans to herbaria, wherever in the world they may be situated. Even the consultants in the CRS are now spending some of their "wait time" on tinkering with their individual but internationally accessible homepages.

There is other evidence of the disruptive and unsettling effects of textography. Systematic botany turns out to have extremely deep and highly distinctive patterns of intertextuality that far exceed those prevalent in the humanities. Textbooks in the ELI emerging under the aegis of the University of Michigan Press turn out to be exemplars of a genre that can lead a professional discipline in new directions, rather than being market-savvy pot-boilers retrospectively summarizing the previous decade's insights.

Beyond these floor-level generalities and communalities, there are just a few observations that pertain to the building as whole. As we have seen, one concerns its service role, or rather, the somewhat different service roles of each of its three floors. And connected to this, and again as we have seen, is its partial disarticulation from the academic year "clock" that so dominates life in traditional departments. Meanwhile, behind those floor-level generalities and communalities, tucked away in the interstices of these communal matrixes, are the particularities of the individual textual ways of life that a textography can at least aspire to bring to life. There is much individual color and pattern here: Tung's instructions, Rich's correspondence, Mary's test items, Bill's botanical Latin, Tony's scatter plots, Ed's terminological ratiocinations, Bob's methodological accounts, Joan's introductions, Carolyn's half-willing conversion to discourse analysis, and my own *Other Floors, Other Voices*, as a kaleidoscope of that very color and pattern.

In this particular case, the individual textographies that I have constructed are related to and mediated through the "communities of practice" which engage with and, in one way or another, support them. These accounts are then aligned with more general activities within a particular unit. It could be otherwise. A textographically inclined work might instead examine the processes of institutional acculturation and socialization, as in Dorothy Winsor's (1996) study of the "rhetorical education" of four engineering students. Equally, it could examine the role of texts, and the processes of their creation, as a function of some regulatory enterprise, as in Graham Smart's extensive study of the Federal Bank of Canada (e.g., Smart, 1996). Or it might explore the "intertextuality" of text, image, and built environment, as in John Ackerman and Scott Oakes' study of architectural practice (Ackerman & Oakes, 1995).

In fact, none of these three studies, nor my own, is avowedly "critical" in the sense advocated by the Critical Discourse Analysis movement (e.g., Fairclough, 1992), even though, in her short concluding chapter, Winsor did raise and discuss a number of the issues, as in: "One question we might want to ask in response to the experiences of Al, Chris, Jason and Ted is whether we see their gradual enculturation into engineering as a success story or a story of increased acceptance of a distorted view of the world" (p. 105). As it turns out, I also have had little to say about such questions of "power," "ideology," and "indoctrination," largely because of a belief that contextual description should precede judgment of such matters. Indeed, Norman Fairclough, on some recent occasions such as at the 1996 Congress of the International Association of Applied Linguistics (AILA), has also been reflecting on the fact that Critical Discourse Analysis has rather too easily assumed that instititions, whether in industry, finance, the academy, or the media, are "monolithic." Some of his own most striking work has been on the *commodification* of higher education in the United Kingdom. However, although that commodification can be detected in centrally produced university publicity materials on both sides of the Atlantic, more *locally* this trend may be highly variable. Almost without exception, the curators use the phrase "pay for service" when explaining why they may, if they wish, keep for their herbarium duplicate specimens sent to them for identification. However, even the most aggressive of the new "value-centered" university accounting systems will fail to capture these peculiar exchanges. In fact, the transactions of the Herbarium at Michigan are, at the end of this century, amazingly uncommodified. The Testing operations on the top floor do have a "fee for service" that accountants will immediately recognize, but these fees have been sustained for many years by *product reliability*, both in terms of tests being available on their appointed test days (even if sometimes only just), and in terms of those tests being "new forms" but yet "normed" with older versions so that the test-takers know what they are getting and can have confidence that their English proficiency is being fairly and accurately assessed. As Sarah stressed, test-takers have the *right* to expect such things. Further, the testing operation remains uninterested, for all sorts of reasons, in expanding its services *simply* in order to increase its income. On the other hand, the ITD has been becoming increasingly "business-like" in its presentation of its costs and services to its wholly dependent customers and clients. All in all, commodification seems at best a partial, and perhaps even a reversible, trend.

As a final pass at these difficult issues of appropriate critique, let me briefly reprise the top-down nature of herbaria business. Request letters go from a senior administrator in one institution to his or her counterpart in another. At first, this seemed to me to be just one more instance of the hierarchical character of institutional science—top scientists as barons in their labs, getting their names on research papers they may have had little to do with, and so forth. This certainly would be an external, "monolithic" view of this particular institutional arrangement; however, it transpired that the rationale for this particular convention had less to do with *power* and more to do with the *longevity* of the loans. Such small moments of understanding thus undermine the ground for the most straightforwardly "critical" accounts of the processes of administrative control.

POSSIBLE FURTHER USES OF TEXTOGRAPHY

> The university's good that way; it's got these little pockets of expertise around that you never hear about, unless you happen to have an office next door, or be in the business. Many of them are just sort of sitting there doing their own thing, and, you know, they're perhaps famous elsewhere in the world, but virtually unknown in Ann Arbor. (Mike Alexander, in interview)

In this short section, I would like to briefly indicate a few uses of investigations of the kind I have presented in this book. A first value is intrinsic, as shown in the following quotation from sociologist Anthony Giddens: "To provide an account of the conventions involved in a given cultural milieu, or a given community, allows a grasp of the intentions and reasons the agents have for what they do, which may entirely escape us in the absence of such an account" (1987, p. 6). This account presents Systematic Botany as rhetorically very distinct from the broader area of Biology of which it is traditionally an integral part (although there may be as-yet unexamined similarities with Systematics in other areas, such as Entomology). The Curators in the Herbarium constitute *sub specie rhetoricae* a different genus to those biologists studied by Williamson (1988), Myers (1990), and Stockton (1994), to Darwin in Gross (1990) and to Gould and Lewontin in Selzer (1993), to the conservation biologist in Samraj (1995), or to the environmentalists in Killingsworth and Palmer (1988) and in Herndl and Brown (1996). To those concerned with academic discourse and the teaching of it, the textual map of the biological sciences has therefore gone through another revised edition. The detailed work in any academic textography should always promise that kind of small advance.

The equivalent "surprise" from the English Language Institute, Giddens' "grasp of the intentions and reasons the agents have for what they do," lies in the sheer variety of texts emerging from the four foci examined: Testing, Carolyn, Joan, and John. To the rest of the university, as I know all too well, the ELI is seen as a strictly *pedagogical* place devoted to helping its international students survive and flourish in a competitive environment. Although we do find teaching materials in abundance on the third floor, we also discover specs and stats, discourse analysis, complex phonetics, national advocacy, international presence, even *Other Floors, Other Voices*. Finally, if the climate of change in the Computing (Resource) Site emerges as having been more easily predictable, some of the consequences, such as the terminological twists and turns in the renaming of itself, are perhaps less so.

A second use emerges from the first. At least on the two top floors, we now have a reasonable basis for making interinstitutional comparisons. The *Index Herbariorum* lists approximately 3,000 herbaria across the world. For reasons shortly to be discussed, a colleague or two elsewhere might like to examine their institutional or national herbaria in order to tease out similarities and differences, or, better, discover things about systematic botany that I have failed to find. The kind of English for Academic Purposes program housed in the ELI is equally widespread around the world. Indeed, especially overseas, a good number of these programs are considerably larger than the one at Michigan, employing up to 100 staff and faculty. Although few, if any, of these programs will have a fee-funded test-making operation, many have constructed "communities of practice" to carry out the task of producing an evolving stream of ESL teaching and testing materials. Again, comparisons would be enlightening.

A particularly strong incentive for suggesting such comparative work derives from the largely monolingual character of the North University Building. Although international students can be heard conversing with co-nationals in their native tongues, and the ELI Administrative Assistant, Gemma, can sometimes be heard speaking on the telephone in one of her Philippine languages, and Bill can be found E-mailing in Portuguese or, along with his colleagues, constructing diagnostic paragraphs in Botanical Latin, verbal events and activities in the building are prevailingly anglophone. Meanwhile, outside English-speaking countries, academic buildings in most parts of the world are becoming increasingly multilingual as English strengthens its role as the academics' *lingua franca*. Site studies of units that are, on the one hand, multilingual in language practice, but, on the other, univocal in disciplinary focus would be particularly valuable, a development also strongly argued for by Olsen (1993). Meanwhile sociolinguists, with their interests in language choice and code-switching, have largely focused their research on what goes on in families, in classrooms, and among adolescent groups (see Milroy & Muysken, 1995 for a review). It would be my hope that academic-building site-studies might be able to bridge the gap between expertise in academic discourse and expertise in sociolinguistic language choice, perhaps (as Bex, 1996, also suggested) by utilizing and developing some version of the Milroys' "social network" program, especially because this model offers a sophisticated view of community in a period of modernization and urbanization (Milroy & Milroy, 1992).

Likewise, the textual biographies discussed in this book have hardly engaged with the pressing contemporary issues (discussed briefly at the end of the section on Ed) of language of publication, if only because here all seven subjects are native speakers of English. Textual biographies of others in other situations are urgently needed as a way of complementing the strong recent line of work in Contrastive Rhetoric per se (Connor, 1995; Duszak, 1997; Ventola & Mauranen, 1996). We now need to know more about how sociolinguistic and sociorhetorical threats and opportunities play out, to give just a few instances, for a Mexican herbarium curator, an Italian mycologist, a Tunisian expert in EAP, a Finnish applied discourse analyst, a computer site manager in Taiwan, or an expert in testing Japanese for academic purposes in Japan. I certainly have hopes of making, along with others, some small contribution here to our understanding of anglophone pressures, particularly by exploring such pressures within the kinds of individual *textographies* I have offered in this volume.

THE CONCEPT
OF DISCOURSE COMMUNITY REVISITED

> Large thoughts depend more heavily on small thoughts than you might think. (Nicholson Baker, *The Size of Thoughts*, 1996, p. 15)

> Anybody any good at what they do, that's what they *are*, right. (Molly in William Gibson's *Neuromancer*, 1986, p. 66)

Although I did not hear that intriguing compound-noun "discourse community" until early 1986 (and from Lillian Bridwell-Bowles), I suspect it had already been circulating for a year or two. In any case, I adopted it immediately as it captured and crystallized some of my thinking at the time. In the opening chapter, I have already said something about my struggles with this concept; here, I close by addressing the *theory* of discourse community as re-seen by what we have learned about the North University Building. The use of the term is widespread, as are its near cousins "disciplinary community" and (increasingly) "community of practice," but the more significant and extensive discussions I take to be the following. I list them in chronological order of publication, although this—especially in the case of collections—often disguises their earlier walk-throughs as conference presentations:

Porter, 1986
Cooper, 1989
Harris, 1989
Swales, 1990a
Lave & Wenger, 1991
Bizzell, 1992
Lyon, 1992
Killingsworth & Gilbertson, 1992
Porter, 1992
Olsen, 1993
Swales, 1993
Miller, 1994
Van Nostrand, 1994
Berkenkotter & Huckin, 1995
Casanave, 1995
Bex, 1996
Grabe & Kaplan, 1996
Hanks, 1996
Devitt, 1996
Johns, 1997

A first observation about this list is its dominant North American flavor. Although certain European Critical Discourse Analysts, such as Fairclough (1992), have questioned the viability of the "community" concept, the issue of "discourse community" has not attracted the attention of either Australian systemic linguists or of the strong European groups of discourse analysts. Even a cursory reading of this literature also reveals that some of these pieces are intellectually—and perhaps ideologically and pedagogically—bullish about the prospects of *discourse community*

(Berkenkotter & Huckin, 1995; Bex, 1996; Hanks, 1996; Killingsworth & Gilbertson, 1992; Olsen, 1993; Porter, 1992; Swales, 1990; Van Nostrand, 1994); others are bearish (Casanave, 1995; Cooper, 1989; Harris, 1989; Lyon, 1992); and still others are neither particularly one or the other, or perhaps both (Bizzell, 1992; Devitt, 1996; Grabe & Kaplan, 1996; Johns, 1997; Miller, 1994; Swales, 1993). As mentioned in chapter 1, part of the uncertainty is definitional. For example, Herndl, Fennell, and Miller (1991) concluded, "Since the relationships between language use and social structure are various and describable with different analytic methods, the term discourse community becomes either misleadingly vague or intriguingly rich" (p. 304), and Bazerman (1994) observed that "most definitions of discourse community get ragged around the edges rapidly" (p. 128). A third observation about this literature is that the preferred label is revealing. Those who opt for *disciplinary community* can be seen as centering on the "invisible college" idea of a dispersed group of like-minded specialists or enthusiasts, whereas the preference for *discourse community* may focus equally on a local grouping. (I will leave it for others to decide whether this distinction is eroded by the rapid advance of electronic intercommunications.)

Two other issues of contention can also be dealt with fairly quickly. One is the idea that the concept of discourse community is intrinsically and damagingly idealistic and utopian. Harris (1989) was the first to make this observation, inter alia citing with approval Raymond Williams' suggestion that "community" is suspect because it has no opposite. Even if this is correct, it is equally true of "family" (also commonly used as a metaphor to in-fold the members of organizations), but this does not mean that we cannot categorize families, and by extension communities, as "dysfunctional," "broken," or "disintegrated." Of course, if we ourselves use *discourse community* as a rallying cry ("our discourse community"), as Minock did in her description of her own multidisciplinary Writing Across the Curriculum team, it is likely that the "Definitions of discourse community that emerged from time to time seemed always to include a touch of the ideal" (1996, p. 514). However, such direct invocation is rare. Much more typically, explorations of the concept have placed the investigator as an outsider looking in; this is a very different rhetorical exigency and one that permits a "critical" stance.

A second potential contention concerns the charge of circularity—whereby the discourse will be defined by the community and vice versa. In 1990a, I argued that this circularity can be avoided by creating "tight" concepts designed to establish the possibilities of not all communities being discourse communities and not all discourses as being subsumed into discourse communities. The obvious existence of "public" genres, such as general *weather forecasts*, deals with the second kind of potential circularity, while the existence of both sociologically narrow speech communities (Labov's Martha's Vineyard), and diffuse, poorly connected groupings (subscribers to cable television) deals with the first. Even when there might be a presumption of discourse community, as with a shared topic of interest, this presumption can still be logically or empirically denied. Don Bialostosky (personal communication) has told me that *The International Bakhtin Society* (to which he belongs) is not in fact a discourse community because of the wildly different perspectives and purposes of its members.

In my view, the two most important discussions of discourse community in the preceding list are those by Porter (1992) and by Killingsworth and Gilbertson (1992), although neither (again in my view) has received the attention it has deserved, especially overseas or in ESL. Neither, for example, is referenced anywhere in Belcher and Braine's outstanding edited collection entitled *Academic Writing in a Second Language* (1995). Because Killingsworth and Gilbertson premised their discussion on Porter's earlier (1986) version of his argument, let us start with Porter (1992).

James Porter offered us a post-structuralist, indeed Foucaultian, account of discourse community signaled clearly enough—to those in the know—by his book's subtitle: *An Archeological Composition of the Discourse Community.* He made some early arguments that will be familiar to social constructionists and their allies, such as the following:

> The term "discourse community" is useful for describing a space that was unacknowledged before because we did not have a term for it. The term realigns the traditional unities—writer, audience, text—into a new configuration. What was before largely scene, unnoticed background, becomes foreground. (1992, p. 84)

His first really significant move is to adapt Foucault's sense of "discursive formations" and argue against any first-principled sociological account of discourse community, as might be exemplified by a suburb, the humanities, a corporation, WASPS, and so forth. Instead, *for rhetoric*, the discourse community should rather be seen as constituted of and constituting various kinds of principles and practices, linguistic, rhetorical, methodological, and ethical. He claimed four advantages for such a perspective:

> (1) it focuses directly on texts in terms of rhetorical principles of operation (and is, thus, closely allied to rhetoric as discipline); (2) it allows us, because of its rhetorical orientation, to tolerate, even welcome, a high degree of instability and ambiguity; (3) it takes a broad historical view of communities and examines both the changes within and between communities and the relationship of these communities to "general culture"; and, (4) it provides insight into the operation of communities, which are *not* nice neat packages

but which are messy, ill-defined, and unstable. (original emphasis) (Porter, 1992, p. 88)

Note that Porter has offered a nuanced heuristic here. In effect, he argued that the concept of *discourse community* has value for the purposes of discoursal or rhetorical analysis. He did not argue that a historian, a sociologist, a communication expert, or an educationist need see matters in terms of this concept, or indeed need to use the concept at all. A historian remains fully at liberty to argue that such a vision lacks materiality, a sociologist that it neglects structure, or a communication expert or educationist that it downplays individual agency. I would suggest then that Porter's approach mitigates some of the concerns of those who find themselves opposed to the concept for other than investigative reasons.

Porter's agenda does, nevertheless, leave him with a fairly broad, although interesting, definition of the term:

> A discourse community is a local and temporary constraining system, defined by a body of texts (or more generally, practices) that are unified by a common focus. A discourse community is a textual system with stated and unstated conventions, a vital history, mechanisms for wielding power, institutional hierarchies, vested interests, and so on. Thus, a *discourse* community cuts across sociological or institutional boundaries. (original emphasis) (1992, p. 106)

There is doubtless much to say here, but let me first conclude my reading of the arguments of the main protagonists. Porter next discussed the problematic complexities that devolve from such multi-audienced networks, but then offered a neat solution—that of the *forum*. A forum is a "concrete, local manifestation of the operation of a discourse community" (1992, p. 107). For Porter these fora can range from being a defined place of assembly, to being an occupational location, and on to being a vehicle for discourse community connection, such as a conference or a journal. He then suggested that it is these forum-like discourse community "traces" (p. 108) that provide convenient points of entry and research locales for rhetorical studies (see also Schryer, 1994, and Berkenkotter & Huckin, 1995).

From this discussion of fora, and from a wider reading of his book, it is clear that Porter finished up with a concept of discourse community that is highly variable and fluid in its spatial composition, from being site-based (even being family-based) to being focus- or ethos-based, as with the regular attendees at the College Composition and Communication Convention (CCCC) in which he himself participates. Further, it is also a concept that comfortably encompasses in its singularity both "high" genres (conference presentations) and "low" genres (commentaries on students' work) (Johns, personal communication).

This is not so for Killingsworth and Gilbertson (1992). Although they started from comparable discourse community advocacy, particularly stressing the value of the concept for more refined studies of technical communication, their major contribution lies in their distinction between what they have called the "local" and "global":

> *Local discourse communities* are groups of readers and writers who habitually work together in companies, colleges, departments, neighborhoods, government agencies, or other groups defined by specific demographic features.
> *Global discourse communities*, by contrast, are groups of writers and readers defined exclusively by a commitment to particular kinds of action and discourse, regardless of where and with whom they work. (original emphasis) (p. 162)

Somewhat later (in the same book), they offered this expansion:

> While local communities, in addition to prescribing styles of discourse, may monitor membership by physical surveillance (corporate badges, parking stickers, correct dress, and so forth), membership in global communities tends to be regulated exclusively by discourse-governed criteria (writing style, publication in certain journals, presentations at national conventions, professional correspondence, and so forth). (p. 169)

Although we might want to question the possibly ethnocentric adoption of the term "global," the distinction is an important one, because, as Killingsworth and Gilbertson copiously illustrated, the two types of discourse community can often come into *conflict* as they compete for the loyalties of individual members of both. Many (e.g., Johns, 1997), have commented on the tensions in the academic world between "global" publishing and "local" administration and teaching. Indeed, Killingsworth and Gilbertson went so far as to suggest that "In the second half of the twentieth century, global communities have all but totally supplanted local communities in the hearts and minds of Western intellectuals and the educated elite" (1992, p. 169).

At this juncture I propose that we take Killingsworth and Gilbertson's dichotomy as offering a useful clarification in both definitional and procedural terms. Initially, then, we can examine *place* discourse communities and *focus* discourse communities (borrowing Porter's term) differently, since in the former the typical fora offer both more regular and less prestigious, unusual or "apical" structurations than the latter. Following Johns, as well as the earlier parts of this book, we can also see these fora as consisting of either genres (broadly conceived as text–task interactions) or as circumscribed genre sets.

The place discourse community (PDC) obviously has some affinities with the "community of practice," as discussed by Eckert and McConnell-Ginet (1992), Hanks (1996), and Lave and Wenger (1991). It also has affinities with the narrow sense of discourse community as "project site" discussed by Bizzell (1992) and others. Eckert and McConnell-Ginet glossed the concept as follows:

> A community of practice is an aggregate of people who come together around mutual engagement in an endeavor. Ways of doing things, ways of talking, beliefs, values, power relations—in short, practices—emerge in the course of this mutual endeavor. As a social construct, a community of practice is different from the traditional community, primarily because it is defined simultaneously by its membership and by the practice in which that membership engages. (1992, p. 464)

Hanks then put this concept in a broader context:

> This way of defining community is both smaller than the traditional speech community and more dynamic than the social structure posited by correlational sociolinguistics. It also shifts the ground of definition from either language or social structure per se to the engagement of actors in some project ... Because some endeavors last longer than others, communities so defined clearly have different durations and arise under different circumstances. And because we all engage in multiple group endeavors at any time and throughout our social lives, we are members of multiple communities, simultaneously and over time. (1996, p. 221)

We might want, however, to view this particular contextualization with somewhat mixed feelings. On the one hand, the shared endeavor motif accords well with such experiences as, say, being a member of some search committee, or with the co-construction of some plan for future developments, or with the teamwork involved in some investigative project. Additionally, it reinforces our sense that such shared endeavors can be generic learning experiences for the leaders as well as the led. On the other hand, the idea of the "multiple communities" to which Hanks assigned us membership conflicts with Geertz' significative occupational or professional "ways of being in the world" (1983, p. 155). Human beings are not chameleons. I am *officially* a member of a number of groups. For example, I have a monthly meeting with an associate dean and my fellow chairs and directors of "the humanities." However, much of the discussion therein is pretty alien to my "practitioner" principles and beliefs. This is not a community to which I belong in any fundamental or constitutive sense, however much as a "tourist" I may relish, and even occasionally contribute to, its exchanges.

As it happens, the current level of scholarly interest in communities of practice has arisen as much (or more) from what they may contribute to our understanding of situated learning and apprenticeship, as in terms of getting a handle on sociorhetorical fora. Lave and Wenger opened their influential book with this account:

> Learning viewed as situated activity has as its central defining characteristic a process that we call *legitimate peripheral participation*. By this we mean to draw attention to the point that learners inevitably participate in communities of practitioners and that the mastery of knowledge and skill requires newcomers to move toward full participation in the sociocultural practice of a community. "Legitimate peripheral participation" provides a way to speak about the relations between newcomers and old-timers, and about activities, identities, artifacts, and communities of knowledge and practice. (1991, p. 29)

Although Lave and Wenger did later discuss some problems that can arise in such "communities of practice," such as the tension between the continuity of old-timers and their eventual displacement of newcomers, their committed stance is for me rather idealistic. Most of the case studies deal with solid and traditional apprenticeship arrangements, and much of the discussion has the rather hortatory character of the preceding extract. When they said that "learners inevitably participate in communities of practitioners," we do not quite know whether this is anything more than a self-defining truism; if they do not so participate they cannot be counted as "learners"? Nor do we have a clear sense of what level of engagement might constitute "participation," especially as we know that in many communities "full participation in the sociocultural practice" may in fact be restricted to the members of some kind of inner circle who have survived various rites of passage. After all, assistant professors, hardly newcomers to their fields, are usually excluded from certain important departmental fora, such as those set up to deal with issues of promotion and tenure. It thus seems that the work of Lave and Wenger can be best seen as making a useful contribution to what an *ideal* PDC might look like.

Similarly, if discourse community is not to remain a vague "term of art," it needs, I suggest, to be sufficiently criterial to separate those various human aggregations we come across in our worldly travels into those that have community status and those that do not. We need something that is more than Porter's "messy, ill-defined and unstable" groupings (1992, p. 88), but somewhat less than the rather perfectionist descriptions of Lave and Wenger. I offer the following working definition of a place discourse community (the other kind I leave, as it has not been central to this book's orientation, although there will be both similarities and differences with the ensuing depiction):

> A place discourse community (PDC) is a group of people who regularly work together (if not always or all the time in the same place). This group typically has a name. Members of the group (or most of them) have a settled (if evolving) sense of their aggregation's roles and purposes, whether these be group decision making, group projects, routine business, or individual enterprises endorsed (tacitly or otherwise) by most of the other members.
>
> During its existence, the PDC has evolved a range of spoken, spoken–written, and written genres to channel, develop, and monitor those roles and purposes; either at least one of these genres will be tailor-made, and/or there will be something distinctive about the relationships among them. To "old-timers" and perhaps others, these genres have self-evident discoursal and rhetorical characteristics; further, to such people, these genres are seen as an interactive system or network that additionally validates the PDC's activities outside its own sphere.
>
> A PDC has reached some degree of consensus regarding such things as rhythms of work, levels of productivity, horizons of expectation, and the roles of and relationships between "theory" (however conceived) and practice. In the furtherance of its communicative practices, a PDC has developed some specific lexis, such as abbreviations and other shorthands, and has evolved a specific set of values for what it considers to be good and less good work (cf. Becher, 1989). It will also have evolved a sense of what does *not* need to be discussed—a sense of its "silential relations" (Becker, 1995).
>
> Last but not least, a place discourse community has a sense of its history, and tries to communicate its traditions and *modi operandi* to its newcomers just as it tries, by legitimate peripheral participation, to inculcate them into "appropriate" discoursal practices.

Thus, this is a definition for a *functioning* PDC, and also one that is, for its members—at least when operating within the community—"a way of being in the world." However, such a PDC does not have to be "congenial" or "supportive" or "democratic" or "close-knit" (Bex, 1996), or "egalitarian" or "consensual" (Eckert & McConnell-Ginet, 1992), or even particularly successful, or free of gender, racial, and other kinds of prejudice. However, if fissures fester, the ensuing dysfunctionality will preclude PDC status.

Against such a definitional platform, it is clear that neither the North University Building, nor indeed the greater umbrella of the University of Michigan, comprises a discourse community. As the foregoing chapters have been at pains to describe, differences of all kinds divide the three floors. There are indeed three different "voices" that we can detect here: ambience, aspirations, return on activity, type of scholarly profile and public genre-set (including their absence on the first floor) all make their contributions to such divisions. The live remaining issue is whether we find a PDC on each floor.

The first floor Computing Site is one of several such centers operated by one limb of the octopus-like Information Technology Division, itself a "business-like" operation nested within the University's infrastructure. Although the CRS is generally reckoned to have something of a distinctive "ethos" among the sites, this distinction today is upheld more by its customers (a greater proportion of graduate students and staff) than by its services or personnel. The rapid pace of technical development consistently impacts job classifications and occupational roles. Staff turnover is high and increased by the fact that young computer specialists are prone to accept offers from local software companies. Among the consultants, at least, there is little sense of the unit's history. Informant comments do suggest that a viable working relationship between *theory* (aka technical expertise) and *practice* (aka customer service) has emerged. On the other hand, the CRS would seem to be, as the botanists would say, "depauperate" of texts. The limited internal documentation produced on site, only abutted by Tung's written responses to FAQs, reinforces the "outpost" nature of the CRS. Although Liz and her various site-managers (her "eyes and ears") look like a working group, the CRS itself fails to qualify for PDC status.

In the Herbarium we find, despite a certain parsimony in personal relations among and across the various classes of personnel, a coherent vision that sustains remarkably unchanged—despite some technological innovation—a set of activities that are deeply rooted into the past and are long projected into the future. Recall that the *Flora Novo-Galiciana* project is due for completion for some time in the 2020s. This seems an operation, viewed from the slightly different perspectives of professor, curator, collections manager, and mounter, as a coherent whole, even though the last in particular may not indeed enter into the full "sociocultural practice" of the community. Even so, chapter 2 demonstrates clearly enough the mounters' achieved sense of their contributions to the overall enterprise. All the descriptive criteria for the existence of a local discourse community seem to be met, most exceptionally in its use of a highly original genre-set. Especially now that Bob is less "distracted" by his Soil Biotron research, the Herbarium easily qualifies for PDC status.

This is also a PDC that totally belies the many perceptions that in research universities especially (as iterated by Killingsworth & Gilbertson, 1992; Johns, 1997, etc.) "global" interests, such as journal publication, are in direct competition with "local" activities. Again and again we have seen, perhaps most especially with the vascular plant curators, that their daily curatorial and identificatory activities *add to* rather than subtract from their floristic, monographic, and treatmental agendas. Indeed, we see a very similar phenomenon with the chosen trio of ELI authors, for again there is a synergistic relationship between their teaching activities, their reflections on and modifications of them, and much of their published *oeuvre*. In both units, the theory-practice genres sustain community life and avoid the dichotomies that tend to afflict more purely "academic" units. There are wider lessons here, I suspect.

The question of PDC status for the English Language Institute is more uncertain. Although most of the criteria fit well, there is one potentially constraining issue: the relationship between the Testing Division and the rest of the ELI. ESL testers, perhaps for very good reasons, have a markedly conservative attitude toward change, whereas EAP teachers are often in search of the experimental and the novel. However, this potential clash of cultures is mitigated by a number of factors. First, at least three members of the Testing Division also regularly teach in the ELI. Second, all three of the research associates spend a fair proportion of their time on testing, and developing tests for, the international student population, and thus perforce have to liaise closely with the lecturers. Third, perhaps mostly by good historical fortune, the ELI has managed to avoid a situation common enough elsewhere whereby one part of the operation "earns" money from fees, while another part "spends" that money on research and allied activities. Both the Testing and Teaching Divisions are partly supported by General Funds and partly by "soft-money" earnings. Although the call is closer than on the floor below, PDC status remains intact.

However, if the Herbarium and ELI discourse communities are for "real," part of that reality is constructed by external pressure. Both units have, over the last decade, experienced much difficulty in securing "replacement positions" for retiring professors. Among the scientists in the college, there is a perceptible decline in the educational value assigned to the kind of fieldwork championed by the Herbarium and to the scholarly value of taxonomic curatorial work, doubtless caused by the rise of molecular biology. As one of the university's most senior biologists said to me, "Those guys are OK as long as what they do doesn't degenerate into a kind of postage stamp collecting." In a different but comparable manner, the ELI experiences "a chilly climate" toward applied endeavors in the liberal arts and science college of a prestigious U.S. university. The college Executive Committee continues to question the ELI's "level of scholarship" and continues to suggest that the Institute does not really need (more expensive) researchers and professors. Recall how hesitant Joan was at putting her life's work under the scrutiny of that committee—and for good reason. History, of course, is littered with instances of the binding and centripetal force of this "us versus them" condition. An interesting, if ironic, research hypothesis thus emerges: Will it turn out to be the case that most (or even all) "true" discourse communities are defensive—that internal coherence is created, reinforced, and ratified by external opposition, disregard, or disdain?

The site-study textography additionally has an empirical contribution to make to the vexed connection between *discourse community* and *genre*. Perhaps the prevailing position (e.g., Berkenkotter & Huckin, 1995; Swales, 1990a) is that discourse communities somehow "own" their genres. One of Berkenkotter and Huckin's five principles states, "Genre conventions signal a discourse community's norms, epistemology, ideology, and social ontology" (1995, p. 21). Mauranen (1993), however, argued for the opposite; that it is the genres that "own" the discourse communities. Others perhaps look for some more reciprocal relationship. Devitt, in a recent review article, made the following observation: "One of the most important current assumptions needing questioning is the dependence of genre theory on the concept of discourse community—which is, like context, another conceptual link that genre theorists need to examine" (1996, p. 612). In fact, the North University Building can provide a perspective on this issue of ownership or direction. The immensely far-reaching and dense intertextuality of Systematic Botany, its hallowed genres, and the typical length of its major projects all suggest that the dominating genres were there before the present incumbents got to them and will remain in existence after they leave or retire. Here then is evidence for Mauranen's position. In contrast, in English for Academic Purposes, only now moving into its third decade, leading practitioners in the field have had certain opportunities to adapt, develop, and experiment with genres and part-genres as they attempt to establish their theory-practice subdiscipline. As witness to such community fashioning, we could point to Joan's "threepeat" introduction, the close to Axelson and Madden, perhaps even my self-critical ruminations. Here then is support for a proactive role for the discourse community itself. Finally, in the Computing Site, genres are basically imported from other and textually more productive units in the organization, and so fall outside of the ownership issue. Thus, one response to Devitt's call for reconceptualization is to undertake more investigative studies *on the ground* (see Charney, 1996, for a strong recent defense of empirical work in rhetorical and composition studies).

The very last issue concerns what this textographic study might mean for our understanding of academic literacy and for our teaching of academic writing. Frankly, when I started the study, I thought there would be no relevance. However, I find within the building a range of genres with greater similarities to those produced by upper-division undergraduates and junior graduates than I had imagined. Many of these students have to produce technical projects, evaluative reports, specimen documentations, prototype analytic descriptions, and treatments of data in various formats, all designed (at least in theory) to ease the passage across Cheryl Geisler's "great divide" toward their disciplinary-specific expertise (Geisler, 1994). Indeed, Samraj (1994, 1995), in her study of first-year graduate student writing in Michigan's *School of Natural Resources and the Environment*, shows the para-academic nature of these assignments very clearly. My previous concern with the "high" genre of the research article now looks a little narrow, even a touch quaint. So, the textual distributions found in the study have forced me to expand my sense of academic discourse; and, during this long process, I have found myself again challenged and reinvigorated as an EAP writing instructor.

References

Ackerman, J., & Oates, S. (1995). Image, text, and power in architectural design and workplace writing. In A. Duin & C. Hansen (Eds.), *Multidisciplinary research in workplace writing settings: Challenging the boundaries* (pp. 81–121). Mahwah, NJ: Lawrence Erlbaum Associates.

Anderson, W. R., & McVaugh, R. (Eds.) (Various volumes and dates) *Flora Novo-Galiciana*. Ann Arbor, MI: The University of Michigan Press (to 1987); The University of Michigan Herbarium (from 1989).

Anderson, W. R. (1993). Notes on neotropical Malpighiaceae IV. *Contributions from the University of Michigan Herbarium, 19*, 355–392.

Anon. (1930). The department store of the university. *The Alumnus, 36*, 364.

Arden, B. C. (1963). The computing center. *The Michigan Technic, February, 25*, 46–51.

Ashmore, M. (1989). *The reflexive thesis: Wrighting sociology of scientific knowledge.* Chicago: University of Chicago Press.

Atkinson, D. (1993). *A historical discourse analysis of scientific research writing from 1675 to 1975: The case of the "Philosophical Transactions of the Royal Society of London."* Unpublished doctoral dissertation, University of Southern California.

Axelson, E., & Madden, C. (1994). Discourse strategies for ITAs across instructional contexts. In C. Madden & C. Myers (Eds.), *Discourse and performance of international teaching assistants* (pp. 153–185). Alexandria, VA: TESOL Publications.

Bailey, N., Madden, C., & Krashen, S. (1974). Is there a "natural sequence" in adult second language learning? *Language Learning, 24*, 235–243.

Baker, N. (1996). *The size of thoughts: Essays and other lumber.* New York: Random House.

Ballard, B., & Clanchy, J. (1984). *Study abroad: A manual for Asian students.* Kuala Lumpur: Longman.

Bazerman, C. (1988). *Shaping written knowledge: The genre and activity of the experimental article in science.* Madison: The University of Wisconsin Press.

Bazerman, C. (1993). Intertextual self-fashioning: Gould and Lewontin's representations of the literature. In J. Selzer (Ed.), *Understanding scientific prose* (pp. 20–41). Madison: University of Wisconsin Press.

Bazerman, C. (1994). *Constructing experience.* Carbondale: Southern Illinois University Press.

Beadle, S. J. (1996). Herbarium adventures. *LSA Magazine*, Spring, 10–16.

Becher, T. (1989). *Academic tribes and territories: Intellectual enquiry and the cultures of disciplines.* Milton Keynes, UK: The Society for Research into Higher Education and Open University Press.

Becker, A. L. (1995). *Beyond translation: Essays toward a modern philology.* Ann Arbor, MI: The University of Michigan Press.

Belcher, D. (1997). An argument for nonadversarial argumentation: On the relevance of the feminist critique of academic discourse to L2 writing pedagogy. *Journal of Second Language Writing, 6,* 1–21.

Belcher, D., & Braine, G. (Eds.). (1995). *Academic writing in a second language: Essays on research and pedagogy.* Norwood, NJ: Ablex.

Berkenkotter, C., & Huckin, T. N. (1995). *Genre knowledge in disciplinary communication: Cognition/culture/power.* Hillsdale, NJ: Lawrence Erlbaum Associates.

Bex, T. (1996). *Variety in written English: Texts in society—Societies in texts.* London: Routledge.

Bhatia, V. K. (1997). Genre-mixing in academic introductions. *English for Specific Purposes, 16,* 181–197.

Bizzell, P. (1992). *Academic discourse and critical consciousness.* Pittsburgh: University of Pittsburgh Press.

Bloor, M. (1996). Academic writing in computer science: A comparison of genres. In E. Ventola & A. Mauranen (Eds.), *Academic writing: Intercultural and textual issues* (pp. 59–88). Amsterdam: John Benjamins.

Bond, R. C., & Swales, J. M. (1965). Surface finds of coins from the city of Euesperides. *Libya Antiqua, 2,* 91–102.

Briggs, S., & Dobson, B. (1994). *MELAB technical manual.* Ann Arbor: English Language Institute Testing and Certification Division (The University of Michigan).

Byrd, P. (Ed.). (1995). *Material writer's guide.* New York: Heinle & Heinle.

Casanave, P. C. (1995). Local interactions: Constructing contexts for composing in a graduate sociology program. In D. Belcher & G. Braine (Eds.), *Academic writing in a second language: Essays on research and pedagogy* (pp. 83–110). Norwood, NJ: Ablex.

Chang, Y-Y. (1996). *The emergence of discourse communities in Usenet.* Unpublished manuscript.

Charney, D. (1996). Empiricism is not a four-letter word. *College Communication and Composition, 47,* 567–593.

Cintron, R. (1993). Wearing a pith helmet at a sly angle: Or, can writing researchers do ethnography in a postmodern era? *Written Communication, 10,* 371–412.

Cohen, M. D., & Bacdayan, P. (1994). Organizational routines are stored in procedural memory: Evidence from laboratory study. *Organization Science, 5,* 554–568.

Connor, U. (1995). *Contrastive rhetoric.* Cambridge: Cambridge University Press.

Cooper, M. (1989). Why are we talking about discourse communities? Or foundationalism rears its ugly head once more. In M. Cooper & M.Holzman (Eds.), *Writing in social practice* (pp. 202–220). Portsmouth, NH: Boynton/Cook.

de Candolle, A. (1880). *La phytographie, ou l'art de décrire les vegetaux.* Paris: G. Masson.

Devitt, A. J. (1996). Genre, genres, and the teaching of genre. *College, Composition and Communication, 47,* 605–616.

Donnelly, W. A., Shaw, W. B., & Gjelsness, R. W. (Eds). (1958). *The University of Michigan: An encyclopedic survey.* Ann Arbor: The University of Michigan Press.

Douglas, D., & Selinker, L. (1994). Native and nonnative teaching assistants: A case study of discourse domains and genres. In C. A. Madden & C. L. Myers (Eds.), *Discourse and performance of international teaching assistants* (pp. 221–230). Alexandria, VA: TESOL publications.

Dudley-Evans, T. (Ed.). (1987). *Genre analysis and E.S.P.* Birmingham, UK: University of Birmingham, English Language Research.

Dulay, H., & Burt, M. (1973). Should we teach children syntax? *Language Learning, 23,* 245–58.

Duszak, A. (Ed.). (1997). *Intellectual styles and cross-cultural communication.* Berlin: Mouton de Gruyter.

Eckert, P., & McConnell-Ginet, S. (1992). Think practically and look locally: Language and gender as community-based practice. *Annual Review of Anthropology, 21,* 461–490.

Fairclough, N. (1992). *Discourse and social change.* Cambridge: Polity Press.

Fitzpatrick, J. W., Willard, J. E., & Terborgh, J. W. (1979). A new species of hummingbird from Peru. *Wilson Bulletin, 91,* 177–186.

Fogel, R. (1976). Ecological studies of hypogeous fungi: II. Sporocarp phenology in a western Oregon Douglas-fir stand. *Canadian Journal of Botany, 54,* 1152–1162.

Fogel, R. (1983). Root turnover and productivity of coniferous forests. *Plant and Soil, 71,* 75–85.

Fogel, R. (1985). Studies of *Hymenogaster* (Basidiomycotina): A re-evaluation of the subgenus *Dentrogaster. Mycologia, 77,* 72–82.

Fogel, R. (1994). Materials for a hypogeous mycoflora of the Great Basin and adjacent cordilleras of the Western United States. II: Two subemergent species: *Cortinarius saxamontanous* sp. nov. and *C. magnivellatus,* plus comments on their evolution. *Mycologia, 86,* 795–801.

Fogel, R., & Trappe, J. M. (1978). Fungus consumption (mycophagy) by small animals. *Northwest Science, 52,* 1–31.

Fogel, R., & Trappe, J. M. (1985). Studies of *Hymenogaster* (Basidiomycotina): *Destuntzia,* a new genus in the Hymenogastraceae (Basidiomycotina). *Mycologia, 77,* 72–82.

Foucault, M. (1972). *The archaeology of knowledge.* New York: Pantheon Books.

Foucault, M. (1984). *The Foucault reader.* New York: Pantheon Books.

Geertz, C. (1983). *Local knowledge: Further essays in interpretive anthropology.* New York: Basic Books.

Geertz, C. (1988). *Works and lives: The anthropologist as author.* Stanford, CA: Stanford University Press.

Geertz, C. (1995). *After the fact: Two countries, four decades, one anthropologist.* Cambridge, MA: Harvard University Press.

Geisler, C. (1994). Literacy and expertise in the academy. *Language and Learning Across the Disciplines, 1,* 35–57.

Gere, A. R. (1988). *Writing groups: History, theory and implications.* Carbondale, IL: Southern Illinois University Press.

Gibson, W. (1986). *Neuromancer.* London: Grafton Books.

Giddens, A. (1979). *Central problems in social theory.* London: Macmillan.

Giddens, A. (1984). *The constitution of society: Outline of the theory of structuration.* Cambridge: Polity Press.

Giddens, A. (1987). *Social theory and modern sociology.* Stanford: Stanford University Press.

Gilbert, G. N., & Mulkay, M. (1984). *Opening Pandora's box: A sociological analysis of scientific discourse.* Cambridge: Cambridge University Press.

Grabe, W., & Kaplan, R. B. (1996). *Theory and practice of writing.* London: Longman.

Grafton, A. (1994). The footnote from de Thon to Ranke. In S. Marchand & A. Grafton (Eds.), *Proof and persuasion in history* (pp. 53–76). Germany: Beiheft.

Greuter, W., et al. (1988). *International code of botanical nomenclature: Adopted by the Fourteenth International Botanical Congress, Berlin, July–August 1987.* Konigstein: Koeltz Scientific Books.

Gross, A. G. (1990). *The rhetoric of science.* Cambridge, MA: Harvard University Press.

Gunnarsson, B-L., Bäcklund, I., & Andersson, B. (1995). Texts in European writing communities. In B-L. Gunnarsson & I. Bäcklund (Eds.), *Writing in academic contexts* (pp. 30–53). Uppsala: FUMS.

Gusfield, J. (1976). The literary rhetoric of science: Comedy and pathos in drinking driver research. *American Sociological Review, 41,* 16–34.

Haas, C. (1996). *Writing technology: Studies on the materiality of literacy*. Mahwah, NJ: Lawrence Erlbaum Associates.

Hanks, W. F. (1996). *Language and communicative practices*. Boulder, CO: Westview Press.

Harris, J. (1989). The idea of community in the study of writing. *College Composition and Communication, 40*, 11–22.

Hartley, J. (1994). Three ways to improve the clarity of journal abstracts. *British Journal of Educational Psychology, 64*, 331–343.

Herndl, C. G, Fennell, B. A., & Miller, C. R. (1991). In C. Bazerman & J. Paradis (Eds), *Textual dynamics of the professions* (pp. 279–305). Madison: University of Wisconsin Press.

Herndl, C. G., & Brown, S. C. (Eds.). (1996). *Green culture: Environmental rhetoric in contemporary America*. Madison: University of Wisconsin Press.

Howatt, A. P. R. (1984). *A history of English language teaching*. Oxford: Oxford University Press.

International Association for Plant Taxonomy. (1990). *Index Herbariorum* (8th ed.). Bronx, NY: New York Botanical Gardens.

Johns, A. (1997). *Text, role and context: Developing academic literacies*. New York: Cambridge University Press.

Killingsworth, M. J., & Gilbertson, M. K. (1992). *Signs, genres, and communities in technical communication*. Amityville, NJ: Baywood.

Killingsworth, K. J., & Palmer, J. S. (1988). *Ecospeak: Rhetoric and environmental politics in America*. Carbondale: Southern Illinois University Press.

Knorr-Cetina, K. (1981). *The manufacture of knowledge*. Oxford: Pergamon Press.

Labov, W. (1963). The social motivation of a sound change. *Word, 19*, 273–309.

Latour, B., & Woolgar, S. (1986). *Laboratory life: The social construction of scientific facts*. Princeton, NJ: Princeton University Press.

Lave, J., & Wenger, E. (1991). *Situated learning: Legitimate peripheral participation*. Cambridge: Cambridge University Press.

Luebs, M. A. (1996). *Frozen speech: The rhetoric of transciption*. Unpublished PhD dissertation, University of Michigan.

Luebs, M. A., & Coon, H. (1997, March). Teaching research psychologists to write: The APA vs. reality. Paper presented at the meeting of the American Association of Applied Linguistics, Orlando, FL.

Lussenhop, J., Fogel, R., & Pregitzer, K. (1991). A new dawn for soil biology: Video analysis of root-soil-microbial-faunal interactions. *Agriculture, Ecosystems and the Environment, 34*, 235–249.

Lutz, G. T. (1935). *Data on campus development and reminiscences*. (Manuscript in the Bentley Historical Library, Ann Arbor)

Lyon, A. (1992). Re-presenting communities: Teaching turbulence. *Rhetoric Review, 10*, 279–290.

MacInnes, M., & Stevens, W. (1978). *A guide to the campus of the University of Michigan*. Ann Arbor, MI: University of Michigan Press.

Madden, C. A., & Myers, C. L. (Eds.). (1994). *Discourse and performance of international teaching assistants*. Alexandria, VA: TESOL publications.

Madden, C. A., & Rohlck, T. (1997). *Discussion and interaction in the academic community*. Ann Arbor, MI: University of Michigan Press.

Maher, J. (1986). The development of English as the international language of medicine. *Applied Linguistics, 7*, 206–218.

Mauranen, A. (1993). *Cultural differences in academic rhetoric*. Frankfurt: Peter Lang.

McCloskey, D. N. (1994). *Knowledge and persuasion in economics*. New York: Cambridge University Press.

McVaugh, R., & Anderson, R. A. (1993). Eriocaulaceae. In *Flora Novo-Galiciana: A descriptive account of the vascular plants of Western Mexico* (Vol. 13, pp. 202–207). Ann Arbor, MI: University of Michigan Herbarium.

Miller, C. R. (1994). Rhetorical community: The cultural basis of genre. In A. Freedman & P. Medway (Eds.), *Genre and the new rhetoric* (pp. 67–78). London: Taylor & Francis.

Miller, C. R., & Halloran, S. M. (1993). Reading Darwin, reading nature: Or, on the ethos of historical science. In J. Selzer (Ed.), *Understanding scientific prose* (pp. 106–126). Madison: University of Wisconsin Press.

Milroy, L., & Milroy, J. (1992). Social network and social class: Towards an integrated sociolinguistic model. *Language in Society, 21*, 1–26.

Milroy, L., & Muysken, P. (1995). *One speaker, two languages: Cross-disciplinary perspectives on code-switching.* Cambridge: Cambridge University Press.

Minock, M. (1996). A(n) (Un)certain synergy: Rhetoric, hermeneutics, and transdisciplinary conversations about writing. *College Composition and Communication, 47*, 502–522.

Montgomery, S. L. (1996). *The scientific voice.* New York: Guilford.

Morley, J. (1984). *Listening and language learning: Developing self-study activities for listening comprehension practice.* Washington, DC: Prentice Hall Regents.

Morley, J. (Ed.). (1987). *Current perspectives on pronunciation: Practices anchored in theory.* Washington, DC: TESOL.

Morley, J. (1992a). *Extempore speaking practice.* Ann Arbor: University of Michigan Press.

Morley, J. (1992b). *Intensive consonant pronunciation practice.* Ann Arbor: University of Michigan Press.

Morley, J. (1992c). *Rapid review of vowel and prosodic contexts.* Ann Arbor: University of Michigan Press.

Morley, J. (Ed.). (1994). *Pronunciation pedagogy and theory: New views, new directions.* Alexandra, VA: TESOL Publications.

Murphy, J. M. (1995). Review of "Pronunciation pedagogy and theory: New views, new directions. Joan Morley, (Ed.)." *Language Learning, 45*, 345–353.

Myers, G. (1990). *Writing biology: Texts in the social construction of scientific knowledge.* Madison: University of Wisconsin Press.

Niedenzu, F. J. (1928). *Malpighiaceae—Pars I–III.* Leipzig: H. R. Engelmann.

Ochs, E. (1979). Transcription as theory. In E. Ochs & B. B. Schiefflin (Eds.), *Developmental pragmatics* (pp. 43–72). New York: Academic Press.

Olsen, L. (1993). Research on discourse communities: An overview. In R. Spilka (Ed.), *Writing in the workplace* (pp. 181–194). Carbondale: Southern Illinois University Press.

Patthey-Chavez, G. G. (1994). Producing the authoritative voice in a computer lab. *Text, 14,* 77–111.

Paul, D., & Charney, D. (1995). Introducing chaos (theory) into science and engineering: Effects of rhetorical strategies on scientific readers. *Written Communication, 12*, 396–438.

Perelman, C., & Olbrechts-Tyteca, L. (1971). *The new rhetoric: A treatise on argumentation.* Notre Dame, IN: Notre Dame University Press.

Porter, J. E. (1986). Intertextuality and the discourse community. *Rhetoric Review, 5*, 34–47.

Porter, J. E. (1992). *Audience and rhetoric: An archaelogical composition of the discourse community.* Englewood Cliffs, NJ: Prentice-Hall.

Prior, P. (1994). Girl talk tales, causal models and the dissertation: Exploring the topical contours of context in sociology talk and text. *Language and Learning Across the Disciplines, 1*, 5–34.

Ray, J. (1691). *The wisdom of God manifested in the works of creation.* London: Printed for Samuel Smith.

Reznicek, A. A. (1993). Revision of Carex section ovales (Cyperaceae) in Mexico. *Contributions from the University of Michigan Herbarium, 19*, 97–136.

Samraj, B. (1994). Coping with a complex environment: Writing in a school of natural resources. In R. Khoo (Ed.), *Problems and prospects* (pp. 127–143). Singapore: Singapore University Press.

Samraj, B. (1995). *The nature of academic writing in an interdisciplinary field.* Unpublished doctoral dissertation, University of Michigan.

Schon, D. A. (1983). *The reflective practitioner: How professionals think in action.* New York: Basic Books.

Schryer, C. F. (1994). The lab vs. the clinic: Sites of competing genres. In A. Freedman & P. Medway (Eds.), *Genre and the new rhetoric* (pp. 105–124). London: Taylor & Francis.

Scollon, R., & Scollon, S. W. (1995). *Intercultural communication: A discourse approach.* Cambridge, MA: Blackwell.

Selinker, L. (1972). Interlanguage. *International Review of Applied Linguistics, 10,* 209–230.

Selzer, J. (Ed.). (1993). *Understanding scientific prose.* Madison: University of Wisconsin Press.

Shotter, J. (1993). *Conversational realities: Constructing life through language.* Thousand Oaks, CA: Sage Publications.

Smart, G. (1996, August). *Issues of interpretive inquiry into professional genres.* Paper presented at the Applied Linguistics Congress, Finland.

Smith, R. (1995). Review of "Discourse and performance of international teaching assistants." *English for Specific Purposes, 14,* 92–94.

Spolsky, B. (1995). *Measured words.* Oxford: Oxford University Press.

Stafleu, F. A. (1971). *Linnaeus and the Linnaeans.* Utrecht: A. Oosthoek's Uitgeversmaatschappij.

Stearn, W. T. (1992). *Botanical Latin* (4th ed.). New York: Hafner Publishing Company.

Stockton, S. (1994). Students and professionals writing biology: Disciplinary work and apprentice storytelling. *Language and Learning across the Disciplines, 1,* 79–104.

Sullivan, P., & Dautermann, J. (Eds). (1996). *Electronic literacies in the workplace: Technologies of writing.* Urbana, IL: NCTE.

Swales, J. M. (1971). *Writing scientific English.* London: Thomas Nelson.

Swales, J. M. (1980). The educational environment and its relevance to ESP programme design. *ELT Documents Special,* 61–70.

Swales, J. M. (1981a). *Aspects of article introductions.* Birmingham, UK: Language Studies Unit, Aston University.

Swales, J. M. (1981b). The function of one type of participle in a chemistry text. In L. Selinker, E. Tarone, & V. Hanzeli (Eds.), *English for academic and technical purposes* (pp. 40–52). Rowley, MA: Newbury House.

Swales, J. M. (1988). Language and scientific communication: The case of reprint requests. *Scientometrics, 13,* 93–101.

Swales, J. M. (1990a). *Genre analysis: English in academic and research settings.* Cambridge: Cambridge University Press.

Swales, J. M. (1990b). The teacher-researcher: Personal reflections. *Cross-Currents, 17,* 93–95.

Swales, J. M. (1993). Genre and engagement. *Revue Belge de Philologie et d'Histoire, 71,* 687–698.

Swales, J. M. (1997). English as Tyrannosaurus Rex. *World-wide Englishes, 16,* 373–382.

Swales, J. M., & Feak, C. B. (1994). *Academic writing for graduate students: Essential tasks and skills.* Ann Arbor: University of Michigan Press.

Swales, J. M., & Luebs, M. (1995). Toward textography. In B-L. Gunnarson & I. Bäcklund (Eds.), *Writing in academic contexts* (pp. 12–29). Uppsala: FUMS.

Tadros, A. A. (1985). *Prediction in text.* Birmingham: University of Birmingham, English Language Research.

Teeri, J. A. (1992). The Soil Biotron: An underground research laboratory. In R. J. Weber & D. N. Perkins (Eds.), *Inventive minds: Creativity in technology* (pp. 142–153). New York: Oxford University Press.

Thompson, D. K. (1993). Arguing for experimental "facts" in science. *Written Communication*, *8*, 106–128.

Thompson, D. K., Linney, L., & Fleming, N. (1994). Review of "Rapid review of vowels and prosodic contexts, Intensive consonant pronunciation practice, and extempore speaking practice (all H. J. Morley, University of Michigan Press)." *TESOL Journal*, *3*, 35–36.

Thompson, E. P. (1967). Time, work-discipline and industrial capitalism. *Past and Present*, *38*, 56–97.

Traweek, S. (1988). *Beamtimes and lifetimes: The world of high energy physicists*. Cambridge, MA: Harvard University Press.

Van Maanen, J. (1995). *Representation in ethnography*. Thousand Oaks, CA: Sage.

Van Nostrand, A. D. (1994). A genre map of R & D knowledge production for the U.S. Department of Defense. In A. Freedman & P. Medway (Eds.), *Genre and the new rhetoric* (pp. 133–145). London: Taylor & Francis.

Ventola, E., & Mauranen, A. (1996). *Academic writing: Intercultural and textual issues*. Amsterdam: John Benjamins.

Voss, E. G. (1966). Nomenclatural notes on monocots. *Rhodera 68*, 435–463.

Voss, E. G. (1972). *Michigan Flora: Part I. Gymnosperms and monocots*. Cranbrook, MI: Cranbrook Institute of Science and University of Michigan Herbarium.

Voss, E. G., et al. (Eds.). (1983). *International code of botanical nomenclature: Adopted by the thirteenth International Botanical Congress, Sydney, August 1981*. Utrecht/Antwerp: Bohn, Scheltema & Holkema.

Voss, E. G. (1991). Moths of the Douglas Lake region (Emmet and Cheboygan Counties), Michigan: IV Geometridae (Lepitoptera). *Great Lakes Entomologist*, *24*, 187–201.

Williamson, M. M. (1988). A model for investigating the functions of written language in different disciplines. In D. Jolliffe (Ed.), *Advances in writing. Vol. 2* (pp. 89–132). Norwood, NJ: Ablex.

Winsor, D. A. (1996). *Writing like an engineer: A rhetorical education*. Mahwah, NJ: Lawrence Erlbaum Associates.

Yin, R. E. (1984). *Case study research: Design and methods*. Beverly Hills, CA: Sage Publications.

Zak, D. R., Pregitzer, K. S., Curtis, P. S., Teeri, J. A., Fogel, R., & Randler, D. L. (1993). Elevated atmospheric CO_2 and feedback between carbon and nitrogen cycles. *Plant Soil*, *151*, 105–117.

Zobl, H., & Liceras, J. (1994). Functional categories and acquisition orders. *Language Learning*, *44*, 159–179.

Author Index

Subject Index

A

Academic calendar, *see* Time
Academic discourse, *see also* Science
   writing, Writing in the disciplines
   approaches to studying, 2
   at the ELI, 3, 166
   how it is "situated," 1
   relation to textography, 207-208
   social science format, 163
Agriculture, Ecosystems and Environment,
   132
AILA, *see* International Association of
   Applied Linguistics
Alexander, Michael, 9, 194
American Psychological Association
   Publication Manual, 120
American Rock Garden Society, 95
American Society of Plant Taxonomists,
   81
Anderson, William R., "Bill"
   (Herbarium director), 81-94
   see also Flora Novo-Galiciana
   as curator, 45, 55-56, 81
   as linguist, 85-86, 89, 94, 192
   Bunchosia itacarensis (plant species),
      85-89, 91-92, 100, 112
   compared to Bob, 131, 138
   compared to Ed, 114, 122
   compared to Joan, 148
   compared to others, 140-141
   compared to Tony, 96-98, 100-101,
      106-107
   correspondence, 46-47, 77
   Eriocaulon L. (plant genus), 83
   introduction, 80
   Malpighiaceae (tropical plant
      family), 90, 92, 112
   mounting preferences, 57
   naming plants, 90-91
   revisionist stance, 92-93
Ann Arbor, Michigan, 2-3, 9, 164
Apprenticeship
   approach to study of academic
      discourse, 2, 191

and discourse community, 20
   in the ELI, 165-166, 170, 191
   in the Herbarium, 51-52, 94, 191
L'Aquila University, 126
Audience design, 22
Author Abbreviations
   Working Party on, 117
Axelson, Elizabeth (ELI lecturer), 144,
   166-170, 173

B

Barbara (ELI research associate), 63-67,
   69-70
Bartels, R. C. F., 5
Bazerman, Charles, 177
Becker, Alton, 176
Bentley Historical Library, 5, 7
Betty (Herbarium Mounter) *see* Mounters
Bev (vascular plant technician in
   Herbarium), 41, 49, 55
"Big Ten" consortium, 65
Bill, *see* Anderson, William R.
Biological Research Station, 30, 114, 132,
   135
Biotron, *see* Soil biotron
Blue Heron, 95
Bob, *see* Fogel, Robert
Bob (retired fungi curator at Herbarium),
   144
Bolinger, Dwight, 180
Bond, Robert C., 177-179
Botany, *see* Systematic Botany
Brenda (ELI lecturer), 144
Bridwell-Bowles, Lillian, 197
British Museum Catalogue, The, 179
Buildings and Grounds department,
   B & G News, 7
   history of, 5-9
   Plant department, 9-10

C

Cambridge First Certificate, 60
Cambridge University, 173